$7.00

(So Brill Reading for you)

Born in Margate, Iain Aitch spent his formative years holidaying in near-identical seaside resorts around the English coast. Emerging relatively unscathed he has gone on to write for the *Guardian*, *London Evening Standard*, *Independent on Sunday* and *Bizarre* magazine. Somewhere between the seaside and the Sunday papers he also found time to invent World Phone in Sick Day and waste several years perfecting his card-playing skills while working in a dole office. He lives in London.

March 13 '05

Happy Birthday Mum !
And Happy Reading !!!
Love Jean

☺

A FÊTE WORSE THAN DEATH

A Journey Through an
English Summer

IAIN AITCH

review

First published in the UK in 2003
by REVIEW

An imprint of Headline Book Publishing

First published in paperback in 2004
by REVIEW

10 9 8 7 6 5 4 3 2 1

ISBN 0 7553 1191 4

Typeset in Zapf-Elliptical by Palimpsest Book Production Limited,
Polmont, Stirlingshire
Printed and bound in Great Britain by
Mackays of Chatham plc, Chatham, Kent

Papers and cover board used by Headline are natural recyclable
products made from wood grown in sustainable forests.
The manufacturing processes conform to the environmental
regulations of the country of origin.

HEADLINE BOOK PUBLISHING
A division of Hodder Headline
338 Euston Road
London NW1 3BH

www.reviewbooks.co.uk
www.hodderheadline.com

CONTENTS

PROLOGUE

As for many English people, the summer of 1976 was my most memorable. The sun beat down for weeks on end, severe drought meant that many got their water from standpipes on street corners and you didn't dare stand near the tinder-dry trees for fear of them bursting spontaneously into flames. It was how the English summer was supposed to be, just like the ones Enid Blyton described and, of course, it gave everyone the chance to complain about how it was too hot, they couldn't have a bath and – if they were landed gentry – how their forest had burned down.

For me, 1976 was the beginning of my love–hate relationship with the English summer. I remember the warm sun beating down on my back, but I also recall how much it hurt as the soft skin burned and blistered (though my sister Karen seemed to enjoy pulling the dead skin off afterwards, screaming with delight when she got a three-inch by one-inch strip off in one piece). It was the year that I first went to Pontin's at Camber Sands, but I contracted mumps when I was there. It was also the year that I was stung by a bee on the beach and run over by a car as, in a scene reminiscent of a Tufty road safety film, I ran out from behind an ice-cream van.

As I lay there, dazed and bruised, Karen ate my Captain Rainbow ice lolly. Thankfully the onset of my pollen allergy waited until the next year.

Living in Margate, I became all too aware of the demise of the English holiday as I grew up. In 1976 the beaches were bursting to capacity with holidaymakers, daytrippers and rival youth cults battling for territory, but by the time I left in 1987 there were empty stretches of sand and the town had become a run-down dole-on-sea – a victim of the English working classes' discovery that Spanish Tummy was just a vicious rumour and you didn't need jabs to visit Lanzarote or Greece.

My family stuck to what they knew, though, holidaying exclusively at holiday camps on the east and south coasts in towns that looked almost identical to the one we came from. After all, who needed water you couldn't drink, sombreros and straw donkeys when you could have Ribena, a kiss-me-quick hat and a ride on a real donkey? It meant that the years when my parents couldn't afford a holiday weren't so bad, as we could get all the essential accoutrements of an English summer break by just walking down the road to our own seafront.

Anyway, we had heard that you could only get those

horrible thin chips in Spain. And that's just not right. They probably only had malt vinegar too, rather than the industrial-strength 'non-brewed condiment' that real chip shops should have. Chips are a very important part of any English holiday and I have not been able to stomach malt vinegar near mine since the girlfriend I had as a teenager spent one summer doused in the stuff, convinced that it would give her a better tan.

After leaving home, waving goodbye to Margate and the Sarson's-soaked girlfriend, I kept up the family's summer tradition, though I did at least venture inland a little. For my first holiday as an adult, I visited Leeds and then took in a ride on the wonderfully scenic Settle to Carlisle railway. I couldn't resist rounding off the five-day rail rover journey with a trip to Blackpool. There I ended up staying at a B&B which had an unfeasibly large number of stone garden ornament animals embedded in its fascia and landlords who were even stranger than the decor. A taste for the more bizarre side of England was born, and soon I was visiting seaside towns well-known and obscure, before branching out into trips to phoney Tudor fantasy resorts and villages themed around Siamese twins.

The more summers I spent engaged in seeking out strange festivals, talking to oddballs at the snug in country pubs and revisiting hotels that were so bad they were good, the more my love of English oddity began to outweigh the risk of sunburn and sneezing fits I had inherited from my more pallid and wheezy ancestors. I was hooked.

After all, why would I want to go and 'find myself' in India when instead I could find some demented-looking knitted toys at a school fête or watch grown men throwing themselves down hills after dairy products? It was true that nine out of ten trips would be tinged with disappointment, dampness or the creeping feeling that the locals may not actually be a hundred per cent human, but then perhaps that's half the fun – an adventure through England is the only undiscovered trail left. It's so close that no one bothers to take a closer look. The dearth of recent travel writing about my country certainly seems to reflect that, with the two most notable exceptions both written by American citizens.

Mapping my progress on a ... well, on a map as I went, I noticed a distinct geographical trend. As I searched for the real English summer, not one drawing pin fell inside the M25. This was not a deliberate attempt to avoid the territory of fellow two 'i'-ed Iain, the pyschogeographer Sinclair – despite the threatening letters in cut up newsprint warning me to 'stay off my turf' – it's just that London, my current home, can't do English summer. There may be attempts to turn part of East London into a beach once a year and the odd game of cricket here and there, but the English summer can't cope with the capital's breakneck speed of life, cultural diversity or occasionally reliable transport system. Perhaps London is no longer a part of England at all, but a semi-autonomous land-locked state all by itself. After all, it has more in common with New York or Paris than it does with either Devon or Derbyshire.

With this route map on my office wall and a schedule largely dictated by the timing of annual events I set out to discover just what it is that makes an English summer so unique. Was our reputation as the only race stupid enough to share the midday sun with crazed canines deserved, and would we all be a little saner if we stayed indoors until tea time or wore big, floppy hats to protect our brains from frying? Could a pagan ritual be as much fun as a church tombola? And what really drove people to waste their time on what seem to be the most ridiculous of pastimes when they could be just putting their feet up and enjoying a pot of tea? I was determined to find out.

Despite how it may read at times, I really did enjoy my journey through the English summer, from the warm beer and wet weekends to the surprise of sun-drenched sands and idyllic views. Some of it was awful, the public transport seldom worked at all and I encountered far too many jugglers for my liking, but that is part of the deal you make when you decide to spend June, July and August chasing bunting, bus-spotters and outsized pastry products.

You really should try it some time.

1. BRUISED SHINS, WEBBED HANDS AND TANGLED TOES

Summer, for me at least, began with a bang. And then a whimper.

The bang, actually more of a crack, was a boot hitting my shinbone and the whimper was the sound of me realising that I hadn't really thought this whole shin-kicking thing out too well. Perhaps I should have realised that allowing someone to take a good swing at what is, perhaps, your boniest of bones was actually going to be painful.

The reason behind the fact that I was voluntarily allowing another man to kick me in the shins was my infatuation with the strange pursuits that pepper the English countryside in summer in much the same way that buckshot peppers the backsides of young burglars who stray a little too close to the outbuildings of rural landowners. Robert Dover's Olimpick Games, of which shin-kicking is a part, is one of the larger fixtures in the calendar of such events and seemed the perfect way to start my journey. And as it spilled over into 1 June it just made it into my definition of the summer, which I believe starts on that day and ends on 31 August. Anyone who tries to tell you that British Summer Time begins on 21 March or any other similar date is suffering from either a grand bout of wishful thinking or senile dementia, possibly both.

Robert Dover's Olimpick Games, or The Cotswold Olimpicks as they are more commonly known, began life in 1612 shortly after Dover, a barrister and low-ranking member of the gentry, set up home in Saintbury, near to the hill just outside Chipping Campden where the games are held. The games have come and gone over the years, ending first in 1652 after Dover's death and then running from 1660 to 1852, when they were closed due to the local clergy's concern at the amount of gambling, disorder, drunken behaviour and any number of similarly enjoyable pastimes they attracted.

The games were revived in 1951 as part of the celebrations for the Festival of Britain. Once again, locals could climb a greased pole for a leg of mutton, bowl for a pig and, more importantly, belt each other in the shins. Which is where I come in.

Even as I was stuffing straw up my trouser leg – the traditional and only legal form of shin protection allowed – I was blissfully unaware of how much being kicked in the shins actually hurt. My brain was telling me that this was a jolly English summer pursuit with a family audience. Even the C-list celebrity shouting 'Are you mad?' at me, while her colleague stuck a TV camera in my face, didn't seem to ram the message home. I simply replied 'Yes, I am' and continued to stuff the primitive shin-padding into my socks and trousers.

At this stage it had really not registered with me that the countryside is the kind of place where men regularly rip their arms off in combine harvesters just to get in the local newspaper, packing the severed limb in ice and happily hiking for two days to the nearest casualty department. In fact, nineteenth-century locals are said to have hardened their shins by hitting them with planks or hammers and forgone the straw, even though they used to compete in steel-toed boots.

The celebrity jabbering in my ear was Michaela Strachan, or 'that one off that animal programme, I think' as the woman in front of me in the crowd described the television presenter as she took part in the sack race earlier in the evening. I prefer to remember her as the one from the bizarre *Hit Man and Her* myself. A stroke of genius late-1980s programming where she played 'Her' to Pete Waterman's 'Hit Man' and provided live post-pub reportage from Preston nightclubs for people who were too poor or lazy to go clubbing themselves. It was almost as horrible as being there, though obviously you missed out on the chance of being glassed or contracting a sexually transmitted disease.

The woman in front of me was, amid disparaging remarks about Strachan's teeth, berating her for not pulling the sack up to her neck with her arms inside, as is the tradition in the Olimpicks.

3

'Get your arms in!' she shouted. 'It's a body bag!'

Strachan was there to film a segment on the games for BBC's *Country File* but seemed to be drawing the ire of the locals by insisting that certain races be run again for the cameras, generally getting in the way and having teeth that you could see from the top of the hill down into the dip where the action was taking place.

A good deal of the spectators just wandered off to look round the funfair, win goldfish in a plastic bag and wonder who on earth had decided that it was in keeping with the event to bring an armoured car up the hill to show off. But then, I suppose the same could be said of the Utterly Butterly stunt plane and wing-walking display that had opened the games. They didn't really make it clear what the connection between butter-like products and aerial derring-do was, but I do like to think that the wing-walkers are greased up with a good tub's worth of the yellow spread to protect themselves from the wind, in much the same way that cross-channel swimmers slaver themselves with goose fat before setting out.

Although this was the Olimpicks, I didn't have to take part in any qualifying heats, prove my prowess or even appear before the Olimpick committee to state my commitment to the Olimpick ideals, these apparently being ale swilling, gambling and riotous behaviour – all of which I was more than willing to embrace should I be so asked. Or even if I wasn't. All I had to do in the end was to answer a call on the night from the master of ceremonies for 'any shin-kickers, can you make your way down to the front'.

At first, and for a good three minutes, it was just me. 'Hurray,' I thought, 'I'm going to win by default.' But then Martin turned up.

Martin was about the same build as me, a little taller, a little heavier perhaps and definitely with a pointier nose, but I reckoned if it came to it I could beat him in a straight fight, even though I hadn't had one since leaving school. A man just knows these things.

But I was thinking in London terms, where Martin would be a web designer, a coffee shop manager or an advertising sales executive rather than someone who did Manual Labour. He probably even had muscles that weren't produced while wearing Nike and watching Kylie on MTV.

Before we squared up and started kicking, the referee handed us each a white coat. I assume that this was supposed to give us the appearance of the farm lads of old, but it actually made me feel more like a member of one of the 1970s football hooligan 'firms' who used to don butcher's coats, which they decorated with their gang names or blood-curdling threats to rival teams' fans. In fact, it is highly likely that we looked like a couple of lab technicians.

We were instructed to grab each other by the shoulders and then the referee gave us the order to start kicking. We both looked at each other for a moment as if struck by the ridiculousness of the situation we found ourselves in. I then gave Martin a hefty kick to the shin, my toes connecting with bone satisfyingly. This served to remind my opponent why he was there, though he looked a little taken aback, as if I shouldn't have actually kicked him. But he soon got the hang of the game and started to lash out at me.

I managed to parry a good few blows with the side of my foot and the sole of my trainers but eventually a quick right followed a blocked left and I received a full-on whack on the shin. 'Ow,' I said under my breath. Martin then flipped into wrestling mode and managed to throw me on to my back for the first fall. I felt a bit cheated, I thought we had to stand there kicking until one fell over, I hadn't considered trying to throw my opponent. I'd assumed it would just carry on until our shins were bleeding and one of us would need major physiotherapy to walk again. Given the amount of pain that would have entailed, I'm glad he took the initiative.

The next fall came much sooner, as I managed to get one half-decent hack at Martin's shin before attempting to replicate his throwing technique. He tried to throw me at the same time and we both fell to the ground. My back hit the ground first though, making Martin the winner. My disappointment lasted about half a second, until my brain caught up and registered the fact that Martin had to go into the next round and fight again, thus putting his shins through more trauma.

I stood and watched the next bout and found myself amazed at the brutality. If this had been taking place in the back room of a pub rather than on the side of a hill in Gloucestershire then someone would probably have called the police, or at least Donal MacIntyre. It was like bareknuckle boxing, except with feet – which weren't bare. But the sound of boot on bone had the crowd moaning 'Ooh' and 'Aagh' in sympathy with the combatants in much the same way as people do while watching those endless television shows that revolve around videos of young children being hit in the face by swings or men water-skiing into concrete posts.

As the rounds went on, so the fights became more and more violent. Watching was almost worse than taking part, especially as my shin was, by then, beginning to ache from the bruise that was coming up and I knew that those who had got through a couple of rounds must have received at least four or five hard kicks to the shins each. Between bouts the victors winced a lot and rubbed their black-and-blue shins through their pathetically flimsy straw padding. This being a family-oriented bout of unfettered brutality the use of bad language when kicked was frowned upon, so each bone-cracking blow was met with cries of 'F . . . lipping 'eck!' and 'Sh . . . ugar!' Swearing: bad, violence: family entertainment – such is the moral code of Chipping Campden.

Seeing Martin taking his place for the final made me feel a bit better about being beaten by him so easily. At least I could say I lost to the champ if he won. And I could always exaggerate his size a bit too.

The final was easily the most vicious fight of the evening. Both kickers had proved that they were able combatants and they were also tired and a little blasé about further shin pain since the adrenaline was pumping and their legs were numb all over.

The close-matched abilities of the competitors meant that the contest lasted so long that it looked as if either one of them might expire from exhaustion or heart failure before a conclusion could be drawn. Even some of the experienced shin-kickers had to watch the blur of brutality through their fingers as the rapid exchange of mostly undefended kicks finally resulted in defeat for Martin.

There was no outward sign of splintered bone or loss of blood, but then the straw padding would at least be useful for keeping that kind of thing from our view. I imagine that the local casualty department has become most adept at picking pieces of shattered fibula out of cattle fodder for use in reconstructive surgery.

As both the finalists limped away to sympathetic girl-friends, I hobbled up the hill in the direction of the gigantic bonfire, which was due to be lit to bring the evening to a close.

I also bumped into Dave.

I had met Dave earlier, in the Dover's bar of the Noel Arms in the High Street, where I was staying. He had come down for the games from Birmingham before heading off to take part in an English Civil War re-enactment in Stratford after the weekend, but he had just found out that he couldn't get there because it was the day of the Queen's Golden Jubilee and there was no public transport. This seemed a bit out of order, especially as, technically, he was to be fighting on the Queen's side during the re-enactment.

Dave seemed to spend a good deal of his time and money travelling to strange events and historical re-enactments around the country, and the events that he enthused about most all had one thing in common. And that one thing was fire.

Lewes, Wicker Man, Marsden, Dave wanted to know if I had been to any of them and could provide encyclopaedic knowledge on when to go, where to stay and how to get there, ending each explanation with something along the lines of '. . . and then they have a big fire'.

His favourite event is undoubtedly the Bonfire Night chaos of Lewes in Sussex, with its effigy burning and fireworks in the street, in the fields and possibly in your pocket if you don't watch the local kids too carefully. And then they have a big fire.

Dave even let me in on the secrets of the innocent-looking carpet shop from where much of this incendiary mayhem is planned. Perhaps more than any other Guy Fawkes' Night celebrations around the country, the event in Lewes lives up to the original reason we have fires and fireworks on 5 November. And it isn't particularly pretty or politically correct, with the Pope still being one of the most popular effigies burned.

So it was no surprise to find Dave hanging around the fire at the Olimpicks, waiting for it to be lit. By then he was wearing his English Civil War peasant's outfit, but he was still easily recognisable. He had armed himself with a small fire in the shape of one of the flaming torches that were on sale at £2 a piece to those who wanted to take part in a torchlit procession back to the town square. Amazingly, he had resisted the temptation to light it and was saving it for the parade.

9

The fire, once lit, was certainly big and it felt as if standing too close was definitely a bad idea. As Dave moved towards the flames, I backed away from the increasing heat, losing him in the crowd. I imagined him emerging from the throng with singed eyebrows and his blazing torch held aloft, but somehow I missed him.

Once the fire was burning ferociously, crowds of torch-bearing locals began to gather at the gate to the hill in a manner that suggested well-worn ritual. It also suggested a lynch mob.

There is something about being right in the middle of a group of several thousand people holding burning torches aloft and walking purposefully in the same direction that just makes you ache for the mob to grab someone, anyone, and string them up from the tallest tree or the town square gallows. If tabloid editors really had their wits about them they would be printing 'free flaming torch for all our readers' coupons alongside pictures of particularly loathsome paedophiles whom they wished to see given some community justice.

Sadly, no one found anyone objectionable enough to hang or burn, though a couple of local policemen did look decidedly worried when faced with a mob coming towards them brandishing fire. But they swiftly remembered that we were in the genteel, picturesque Cotswolds and not London, Bristol or Burnley and regained their composure. Some children did try to set fire to some bushes on the way down the hill, but they were obviously a little damp and the kind of conflagration that Dave might have enjoyed did not ensue.

We were clapped back into the town by a roadside welcoming committee of old ladies wearing slippers, which was a little unnerving. Where had they all come from? Perhaps they were responsible for the huge amount of red, white and blue bunting and Union flags that swamped the small town. In my time in Chipping Campden, I saw more red, white and blue and special Golden Jubilee flags than in all the other places I visited in England put together.

On our arrival in the town square, the crowd was treated to a brief display by the pipe and drum bands that had played us down the hill. Most people took this as a cue to hit the pubs before some fool decided that it was last orders and called time on our potential to turn into a lawless band and burn down the vicarage while our torches still had a bit of life in them. Rather disappointingly, the publicans seemed to think that allowing large groups of people with naked flames into their hostelries was a bit of a no-no, so most ended up being extinguished on the pavement outside the bars, one thing, along with hotels, of which Chipping Campden has an abundance.

The only other thing, apart from bored teenagers, that the town has in excess is antiques shops. One in particular had used the Golden Jubilee celebrations to dig out any royal-related tat they had in the cellar and put it in pride of place, along with the inevitable bunting, in the front window. Among the Silver Jubilee teapots, busts of Queen Victoria and black-and-white framed photographs of various royals, was a small figurine of Adolf Hitler – peeking out from behind a Charles and Diana mug. Did the proprietors of this establishment know something that we haven't been told? Perhaps they were just big fans of Edward VIII.

Emerging from the packed Dover's Bar with a pint of Guinness, I witnessed the kind of wild dancing in the street you usually only see on old news footage about The Beatles. But instead of John, Paul, George and Ringo, Chipping Campden was grooving to the sounds of Ford Zephyr and the Dansettes, who seemed to specialise in covering all the songs from the 1980s and early 1990s that reached number thirty-four in the charts. The sort of tracks that have you asking yourself: is this Mike and the Mechanics or Hue and Cry? Whoever it was, I got the impression that this was the first time that the citizens of Chipping Campden had ever heard live amplified music and, sadly, they liked what they heard. I just hope for all their sakes' that Cliff Richard doesn't decide to play an impromptu gig in the town square at any time in the near future. There could well be hysteria, trampling and, ultimately, deaths.

When I had booked my hotel, the receptionist went to great lengths to warn me about the late-night, riotous revelry that occurred around the games and subsequent festivities in the square, even going so far as to post me a leaflet outlining road closures and the potential for noise. On the night, however, the bars were all shut by midnight and the crowds began to disperse, leaving me to retire to bed shortly after twelve.

On removing my T-shirt, I was somewhat alarmed to discover a hand-shaped bruise on both shoulders, where my shin-kicking opponent had been gripping me. There was no visible bruising on my legs by that point but, as I soon discovered, I had the next six weeks to enjoy the dull ache that emanated from my left shin on a daily basis.

One of the main problems of getting to obscure village events when you don't drive – as I don't – is that the bus service to them only runs once a day or even, if the village is particularly in the wilds, once a week. Wetton in Staffordshire, just over the border with Derbyshire, is one such village. It consists of one very nice pub, a handful of holiday homes in converted barns, a few scattered cottages and a tiny shop. It is also home to the World Toe Wrestling Championships, which seemed the only sensible contest to enter after allowing another man to wreak havoc upon my shins in the name of entertainment.

My friend Chris has lived in rural Derbyshire all of his life and fortuitously had recently passed his driving test and bought a car, which made him an ideal candidate to be the person from whom I could blag a lift to Wetton. He seemed keen to oblige, but pointed out that the twenty-one miles to Wetton was further than he had ever driven before. This did make me wonder where exactly it was that he drove his ageing VW Polo to, but he was willing to embrace the spirit of adventure and who was I to complain?

Chris spent the day before our journey calling friends and consulting maps to prepare for our brave trek across Derbyshire from his home on the outskirts of Belper. I arrived

13

the afternoon before our journey so that I could catch Chris playing his acoustic guitar and singing at a pub by Derby railway station and so that we could get a reasonably early start the following day.

When I woke the next morning, Chris was already out washing the car in preparation for our momentous journey. After grooming the Polo to a shine that we could both be proud of, he came in and made me a cup of tea and some beans on toast to fortify me for my combat later in the day. He seemed more than a little concerned about our drive, but put on a brave face nonetheless.

We left Belper at 11 a.m., which gave us ninety minutes to get to Wetton in time for the toe-urnament. Actually, that was perhaps the one toe-related pun that the organisers didn't use in relation to the contest. The rules for toe wrestling, which I had read prior to my entry into the championships, pointed out that the wrestling area was known as the toedium, contestants who were in too much pain could cry out 'Toe much!' and that male and female competitors were not allowed to wrestle each other because of the risk of *myxoma-toe-sis*.

Bad puns aside, Chris's main concern for the safety of my toes was that the local competitors might well have an unfair advantage.

'It's like Royston Vasey up there,' he said shortly after we left Belper, doing impressions of the various inbred freaks from the comedy show *The League of Gentlemen* that call the fictional village of that name home. 'Make sure you count how many toes they have.'

After all the effort with preparation that Chris had made the day before, the one elementary mistake he made was not to bring a road atlas with him in the car. He did have a set of 'left here, right there' instructions that he had printed off from a website, but these weren't all that useful when we didn't actually know where we were. He did think he knew where an ex-Derby County footballer used to live on the country road on which we were travelling, and possibly where Roy Wood's house was, but unfortunately he didn't seem to know where we had to turn off, leaving us entirely at the mercy of road signs.

Anyone who has ever driven around the English countryside trying to navigate using road signs alone will know what a fruitless exercise that is. They only seem to exist at about every third major junction and then only point to villages you have never heard of or large towns that you know you are nowhere near and have no intention of visiting. I think some villagers still believe that World War II is continuing and tear down any new signs erected by the council lest Hitler's henchmen find their way to the local Women's Institute, steal the jam recipes and forcibly employ the leading lights of the whist drive as comfort women.

Amazingly, a combination of Chris's memory, the vague instructions from the print-outs and some lucky guesswork on my part got us to Ye Olde Royal Oak Inn in Wetton at bang on 12.30 p.m., just in time for me to register for the contest, pay my £2.50 entrance fee and have my toes inspected for verrucas and fungal infections by the official competition toe doctor.

After passing the requisite-number-of-toes-on-each-foot and hygiene tests I was handed an antiseptic swab with which to wipe my feet down, a small bar towel to dry them off and a T-shirt emblazoned with the sponsor's logo. The ice-cream company that sponsors the event provide a year's supply of ice-cream for the winner. I always wonder exactly how they gauge such measurements. Is it simply 52 or 104 tubs of ice-cream? Is it based on weight? Or can you really just call them up at any time day or night and say: 'Hey Icey, bring me over some mint chocolate chip and some wafers, oh, and can you pick me up some cigarettes, a four-pack of Stella and a pint of milk on the way? I'll give you the cash for those when you get here.' And if it is just the one-off bulk supply, where the hell do you keep it all?

Any thoughts of where to store vast quantities of ice-cream went out of my head after the organiser pointed out my opponent for the first round. He looked to me like a 208- or maybe even a 365-tubs-a-year kind of a guy and had at least a four-stone weight advantage over me. Somewhat disturbingly, he was attired only in a shorts and open waistcoat combination that was fashioned entirely from bar towels. His natty outfit bore the name of all the major UK breweries and beers, with a few foreign brands thrown in for good measure. And judging by the ample gut he had on show, he had sampled all of them on more than one occasion. The beer monster also wore mirrored wraparound shades and had his hair shaved into a kind of triple mohican which, when combined with his towelling outfit, gave him a kind of Hell's Angel at a beach party look.

The suit looked pretty comfy, though, and I imagine that, had the marketing people from Marks & Spencer been present, you would soon be seeing a range of towelling shorts and waistcoat combinations aimed at the more rotund of our senior citizens to wear on holiday in Malta. I imagine that sales to ex-pats in Gibraltar and on the Costa del Sol alone would have been worth the initial investment.

My opponent wasn't the only one in strange attire. As with the wrestling that brightened up Saturday afternoon television during the 1970s, or WWF today, a good deal of the contestants had adopted a character or outlandish outfit to mark them out from the crowd. There was a Mexican bandit, a thin man in a dinner jacket and Lycra cycling shorts and a muscular baddie who the crowd loved to hate. It turned out that the baddie was four-times champion Alan 'Nasty' Nash, who was favourite to walk away with the ice-cream. He strutted around the arena – well, marquee in the pub garden – waving his Union Jack cape and sneering at small children in the way that all baddies worth their salt should. Nash's main worry was Ian 'The Destroyer' Davies, who had won and been a defeated finalist several times since the World Toe Wrestling Championship was unleashed upon the world in 1994. The Destroyer's glamorous wife, Karen 'Kamikaze' Davies, had won the women's competition on the previous three occasions. Not

17

a pair you would care to go toe-to-toe with down a dark alley, if indeed that sort of thing happens.

Chris returned from the bar with some drinks. He was still muttering something about inbreeding and webbed hands, but I tried to blank him out and concentrate on the toe wrestling demonstration that was taking place. I had thought that it might be a bit like a variation on arm-wrestling that was dependent upon strength in the legs rather than the arms. I felt I might have a chance if that were the case. But the 'toe down', as it is called, is actually achieved by making the side of your opponent's foot touch a vertical piece of wood that is adjacent to his foot. Two toe downs or two incidents of your opponent crying 'Toe much' and you win. The secret is to push sideways rather than down and, despite the fact that you have to keep your non-wrestling foot in the air and one buttock on the ground, this means that overall body strength is more important than flexible toes or a well-toned calf muscle.

After watching the demonstration, I figured that gamesmanship was my only hope of avoiding total humiliation and possibly getting beyond the first round. I decided to seek out my opponent and see if I could perceive any psychological flaws or at least any ticklish spots that might help me to overcome him.

I wandered over to Bar Towel Man outside the marquee, where he was standing with his mate enjoying a pint of lager.

'Hi, I'm Iain,' I said. 'I'm up against you in the first round.'

'Mick,' he replied, wrapping his hand around mine and looking me up and down.

'That's not fair,' he said.

'What isn't?'

'That,' he replied, pointing to the red England football shirt I was wearing. 'I can't beat you if you're wearing that.'

Ah, so I had at least found some kind of weakness. I made small talk with him for a few moments more, before heading back to the marquee to watch the first bout and work out how I could possibly exploit his respect for the England shirt.

Toe wrestling is nowhere near as brutal or unfettered as shin-kicking but the looks on the faces of the competitors in the first couple of bouts, as they strained to lock their legs and to negate the effect of their adversary's sideways pushing, made it look every bit as painful. Eventually one wrestler would make a swift, sharp push and score a toe down, but no matter how much pain they were in, even if cramp was beginning to set in, no one cried out 'Toe much'. It would have been far too embarrassing.

'And the next bout will be Iain Aitch versus Mick Grimmett,' came the announcement over the public address system.

I puffed up my chest and tried to push my way through the crowd. No one seemed to be paying too much attention to me. 'Excuse me,' I offered weakly, as I tried to squeeze past an elderly woman and her becardiganed husband. I couldn't see Mick but imagined that he was swiping the crowd aside with the back of his hand and growling, 'Get out of the effin' way.'

Once I had reached the toedium, everything went incredibly quickly. Mick and I made a couple of obligatory growls at each other for the benefit of the crowd and then, just as we were about to sit down and assume our wrestling positions on the toesrack, I went for my match-winning psycheout. I grabbed the breast of my football shirt and, in the manner of a player who has just scored the match-winning goal, pressed the three-lioned England badge to my lips. I expected the crowd to cheer me on, or at least burst into applause at this gesture, but instead was greeted with near silence. Mick bowed his head slightly to get a kiss at the badge too, but as his lips met the man-made fibres I span round and pointed at my backside in a 'kiss this' motion. No one seemed that impressed, especially the referee who tutted a bit. So, with my only hope of victory embarrassingly blown out of the water, we sat down and prepared to wrestle.

The first toe down came in under ten seconds. I simply forgot everything I had learned from watching the demonstration and the other bouts and tried to push Mick's foot over using an imitation of arm-wrestling style, which was useless. After taking the pressure for about three seconds, Mick simply slammed my right foot across the toesrack and it hit the side for the first toe down.

We both stood up to stretch our legs and prepare to switch feet, as toe wrestling rules demand the combatants wrestle with right then left then right toes again should a decider be required. I had a feeling that it wouldn't be. I suspect that the audience felt the same. After all, in Saturday afternoon wrestling terms, this was the wiry weed Catweazle up against the impressive girth and strength of Big Daddy. No prizes for guessing which one I was.

The referee squished our big toes together so that they interlocked and then pushed our legs around a bit until we were both in the legal fighting position. On the shout of 'Toes away!' I braced my leg and ankle into a holding position, negating Mick's strong sideways pushes. I could probably have held him like that for a good thirty seconds or more, but foolishly I went for glory just as I thought that his strength was draining. As I attempted to swipe Mick's foot to the right, I had to release my holding lock and he easily slid my foot into the board again for his second and winning toe down. It was not total humiliation, but it was pretty close to it.

I stayed in the marquee and watched a few more bouts, but I must say that toe wrestling becomes pretty dull when you are not actually participating. A lot of grimacing, a lot of re-starts for technical reasons and not much in the way of exciting action.

Given the close proximity of the referees to the toes, toe wrestling doesn't actually lend itself that well to gamesmanship but there must be some crafty moves that could be executed by the likes of Nasty Nash in order to gain some legitimate notoriety. Growing your nails long and filing them down until they are razor-sharp could be one way of livening things up. It would make the event a lot more like the ever-popular sport that is cock-fighting and no doubt bring in a lot more illegal gambling too.

In the absence of any gratuitous bloodletting, I retired to the bar with Chris to sample some of the real ale for which the pub was well known. I plumped for the Ankle Kracker as it seemed appropriate. Fortunately it didn't taste of anything remotely pertaining to feet and was very pleasant. After I had drained my second pint, I was convinced that if only I had the chance again I could have beaten Mick Grimmett by tactical genius alone, once and for all settling the brains versus brawn debate.

Luckily for me, there was no question of a re-match. As I returned to the marquee, Mick was polishing off his second-round opponent to the cheers of his mates, one of whom had a near-identical madman's buzz cut, though he had forgone the towelling leisure suit in favour of an outfit that looked less like something a toddler might wear.

The women's contest started up with much the same lack of lustre as the men's did, though the grimacing and grunting was not quite as bad. However, it was enlivened by the presence of toe wrestling's very own Anna Kournikova, Karen 'Kamikaze' Davies. Much to the disappointment of some of the crowd, she also avoided the open waistcoat and beer towel shorts look in favour of something red and close-fitting.

The contest went on in a fairly unremarkable fashion for what seemed like days. Some people won, some lost, there was quite a bit of shouting and grimacing, Nasty Nash tried somewhat half-heartedly to play the baddie and people drank a lot, though to their credit no one fell over. Toe wrestling is definitely a sport to compete in rather than one to watch, as

Chris would no doubt testify to. He was looking more and more likely to slip into an ennui-induced coma as the day dragged on.

To break up the monotony of the long grind towards the finals, and once everyone was suitably inebriated, there was a charity auction of the kind of items that you usually see lying around at the end of a car boot sale. Bidding was surprisingly fierce for the complimentary T-shirts and polo shirts bearing the names of various breweries, and even the items of outmoded electronic equipment raised a few pounds.

The auction was made all the more exciting by the auctioneer being deaf in one ear. This meant that although he was still receiving bids from one side of the room, he would sell the item for somewhat less to a buyer on the side of the marquee that he could actually hear. Despite this he was pretty good at his job; he even managed to shift a knitting machine for £5. I suspect that this item had been doing the rounds at charity auctions for some years and may by now have been auctioned several times over for a sum total that surpasses what its original owner paid for it. From the box it appeared to date from the 1970s, but it did look as if it had never been opened. Some of the crowd may well have been a little backward on the technological front, but even they must have known that no one has ever actually finished making a whole jumper on a home knitting machine and that they are merely domestic space fillers to be filed alongside the similarly redundant breadmaking machine.

Once the useless tat had been cleared away and the combatants had returned to the toedium, Mick Grimmett easily gurned and grunted his way to a place in the final against the favourite, Nasty Nash. Just as at the shin-kicking contest, this left me in the potentially face-saving position of being able to say that although I was beaten easily in the first round, it was by the eventual winner. After all, who knows what would have happened had I been up against the slightly disturbing looking skinny man in the dinner jacket and the cycling shorts?

The women's final was easily won for the fourth year running by grappling glamour-puss Karen 'Kamikaze' Davies, but the men's final was a far closer affair. The bout began, surprisingly, and annoyingly for me, with Mick blatantly stealing the last-ditch psyche-out trick that I had used on him. As the two opponents went to sit down, Mick made a move to shake hands with Nasty Nash, but as Nash stretched out his meaty paw, Mick swivelled round and presented him with his towelling-clad backside. When I did this you could have heard a pin drop but at the sight of bar towels emblazoned with 'Skol' and 'Carlsberg' straining to contain Mick's voluminous arse the crowd cheered as if the Chancellor of the Exchequer had just abolished income tax and introduced 'Free Beer Week' in the same budget speech.

The bout itself was a real stop-start affair with an endless succession of technical infringements, warnings about technique and lengthy huddles between the judges over whether toe downs should be allowed or disallowed. At one toe down each the deciding grapple was a tense affair, with the crowd swinging from roaring encouragement to hushed reverence at moments when it looked as if one competitor was about to give way to the pain in their hamstrings and those muscles you never really notice at the centre of each buttock.

Finally Nasty Nash won it with a controversial toe down, nudging Mick's foot against the side of the toesrack. Mick was not happy with the call, and come to think of it neither was I, as it blew my story of being beaten by the eventual winner. But there was no point in either of us arguing. After all, as the rules clearly stated, 'The referee's decision is toetally final in all cases.'

Mick looked devastated by his defeat, though he seemed buoyed by the news that he would be receiving six months' worth of ice-cream for being the beaten finalist. I tried to make out whether the sponsor's representative was explaining the bit about not being able to ring them up for ice-cream at any time of day or night for the next twenty-six weeks, but my view was obscured by Nasty Nash parading around the tent, beating his chest.

As the presentation was made to both the winners, Nash attempted to live up to his Nasty label by spraying the crowd with a bottle of champagne in the style preferred by Formula One drivers. To me this seemed more likely to earn him the title 'Mildly Irritating' Nash.

His comeuppance came when he went to spray his vanquished opponent with the cheap French bubbles. I mean, what kind of problem is being sprayed with booze to a guy who is wearing an outfit made entirely of small rectangles of towelling made specifically for absorbing alcoholic beverages?

Mick may not have taken the trophy but he did stay dry and have the last laugh. I imagine that he also enjoyed a good glass or two of champagne, freshly wrung from his outfit, once he got home that night.

2. STONES, COLD, SOBER

Champagne was the last thing on the mind of my two travelling companions as we wandered through the doors of the Safeway situated next to an anonymous stretch of dual carriageway somewhere outside Basingstoke. We were there to stock up on water and snacks for our trip to Stonehenge for the summer solstice, and most importantly to grab a healthy supply of the extra-strength lager that Fisheye assured John and me was the only accepted currency at the stones. And anyway, bringing champagne would mark us out as members of the Ascot-and-Henley brigade out slumming it for the night and undoubtedly lead to more requests for 'spare change' than the average wedding DJ gets for 'Hi-Ho Silver Lining' in a lifetime.

'Where's the Brew?' asked Fisheye – who, as a veteran of many a solstice festival was our man on the inside – scouring the area close to the entrance where the sandwiches and the individual orange juice servings are displayed.

While John and I perused the bananas and discussed what food was most likely to keep us awake until the sun came up, Fisheye skipped the food aisles and headed straight for the furthest flung shelves of the barn-like superstore. We later found him there, carrying out complex calculations involving the price, alcohol content and liquid volume of various beers, even sidling off to consider everything from Pimms to cheap vodka. But, still a member of the New Age travelling community at heart, Fisheye finally plumped for the four-pack of Carlsberg Special Brew, the Cristal champagne of crusty-punk beverages.

John grabbed some horse tranquilliser-strength cider but I decided against joining him, as from years of experience I know that strong booze either sends me to sleep or – on the odd occasion – makes me long for some kind of post-pub altercation by about 11 p.m. As I was hoping to stay awake to witness events at the stones and still sported a severely bruised shin, I figured it would be best to stick to coffee and water for the duration. Anyway, I really couldn't think of anything that I would need to exchange Special Brew for once we had reached Stonehenge. The image I had conjured up of ageing patchouli oil-doused hippies trading sexual favours for luke-warm industrial-strength lager was enough to put me off the stuff for life.

I did buy some shortcake biscuits, though, as they looked a little like the large stones that make up the ancient monument we were travelling to and, well, just because a trip to the big outdoors always seems to me a good excuse to eat a whole packet of biscuits in one go. I was also beginning to feel pretty hungry again after the far from filling meal I had eaten when the three of us met up in Reading two hours previously.

The café where we had arranged to rendezvous specialised in slooowwww food. They really weren't joking either. I think they actually grew the vegetables for my bruschetta, marinated them overnight and then, finally, grilled them, all while I waited. They also seemed to think that it was a good idea to chill the beer to order. 'Oh, a nice cold one, sir? I'll just go and pop it in the fridge and you come back tonight. We'll have it waiting for you.'

To make things worse, they were playing what we all agreed must have been *Now That's What I Call Summer Solstice Chill Out Volume 3*. This had the dual effect of making the whole thing seem much more like an endurance test to me and making the staff more and more lethargic as the CD went on. That kind of music may be fine when you are coming down from a cocktail of pills at around 5 a.m., but in a restaurant where the staff had all the get up and go of a sloth on downers it really didn't seem like such a good idea.

After loading our purchases into John's blue Ford Escort, we set off on our way through weather that offered us fleeting glimpses of clear blue skies amid a more constant threat that the solstice would be marked by wind and downpours. That was all I needed. The prospect of spending the night in a field with a few thousand hippies, New Agers and crusties didn't exactly fill me with joy, but the thought of that wet dog smell that dreadlocks give off in the rain multiplied by that number was almost enough to make me gag. And that was without even considering the wet dog smell given off by the numerous wet dogs that were bound to be present at the stones too.

I had never seen Stonehenge close-up and was at least looking forward to that part. I had viewed the stone circle on numerous occasions while being driven past in a car, but had never bothered to stop and visit the site as the stones had been fenced off by English Heritage back in the 1970s and also because there is usually an admission charge. My objection to the admission charge was not on any particular ethical grounds, though there are those who argue that admission should be free to such an important monument, but rather because I could see it from the road, so why should I stump up to see it slightly closer if I couldn't touch? Perhaps if I had got into marijuana, prog rock and Dungeons and Dragons as a teenager I would have felt differently.

If I were of a more spiritual bent, I may have felt a good deal of anger rather than a warming sense of relief when we ran into a police road block near to the Hampshire–Wiltshire border as we drove Henge-wards. But my thoughts of 'Oh well, never mind, we did try' were soon blotted out by Fisheye's increasingly loud reminiscences about the mid-1980s, when the solstice festival had been a ritual game of cat and mouse between travellers and police, regularly punctuated by truncheon blows to the heads and bodies of Fisheye and his friends. Fisheye is a veteran of the notorious Battle of the Beanfield in 1985, when all-out war raged between the police, armed with batons and riot shields, and the travellers, armed only with the babies they were carrying and a really good recipe for veggie burgers.

'Ram 'em,' he cried, only half-jokingly, momentarily forgetting that we were in an Escort and not one of the reinforced battle buses that he had been telling us about. 'Pigs!'

It seems no one had told the Hampshire Constabulary about the new nicey-nicey policy towards visitors to Stonehenge on the eve of the summer solstice and they had decided that the best approach to dealing with the thousands that would be heading there was to block the main direct route. This seemed a peculiar piece of planning, as it offered the potential for them to be faced with large numbers of pissed off hippies, crusties, druids and party-goers driving round and round Hampshire, when they could have just let them drive on through to Wiltshire to become the problem of the local police there. Maybe they like the sport or, at least, the overtime.

Fisheye's roadblock ramming option seemed a little too drastic for John and me, so we opted instead for the relatively minor rebellion of completely ignoring the diversion signs that the police had erected and heading in the opposite direction.

Unfortunately for us, the Hampshire police had obviously pre-empted this kind of anarchist manoeuvre and had set up another roadblock at the next roundabout. Again we drove the opposite way to that which the signs pointed and suddenly found ourselves driving along a road running through the middle of some kind of military establishment. We had absolutely no idea where we were, especially as the road map we had seemed to ignore the need to mark military bases in the area.

After pulling over briefly and staring blankly at the map for a while, we managed to figure out – through the use of logic, guesswork and some vague intuition – that we were somewhere near to East Cholderton. Fisheye used to have a friend who lived there and once we reached the village he issued a few 'I think it's right here' and 'erm . . . left, I think' instructions and we soon found ourselves back on the A303 heading towards Amesbury and the turn off for Stonehenge.

'Oh shit,' said John as we hit the dual carriageway again.

I looked up from the map.

'Oh shit,' I concurred. As did Fisheye.

For as far as the eye could see in both directions, we were the only car on the A303. Four lanes of carriageway and John's Escort was the only vehicle for miles. Our anarchic powers were obviously so strong that we had been the one and only car to work out the way around the roadblock and we were now driving down a supposedly blocked road all by ourselves.

I was beginning to mourn the demise of CB radio. If John had had a rig on board then at least we could have informed others of the way round the police and got us a convoy large enough to blow a hole in the barricade of police cars and dog vans that we knew must be waiting for us at the other end of the road.

We started to discuss the likelihood of being buzzed by police helicopters, so Fisheye suggested that we should at least get our cover story straight.

'We could say we are druids,' he offered.

This seemed like a truly great idea. After all, John is Welsh and that would surely count for something. If we let him do all the talking, and he swore that we came from a silent order of druids, then they'd just have to wave us through, wouldn't they? We didn't really discuss the whole why we weren't wearing robes part of the story, or why a silent order of druids would need so much Special Brew, but we had faith that John's Welsh accent could get us out of any trouble.

On we drove. There was still no sign of any other traffic.

Then Fisheye came up with another great idea. He really should be working for some kind of think tank. The idea was to tell the police that we were just ignorant locals from East Cholderton out for a drive. Fisheye knew the name of the pub should there be some kind of general knowledge quiz about the area to contend with, which made this idea seem even better than the silent druid ruse.

I started to practise a West Country accent in my head, but really can't say whether it was more East Anglia or East Cholderton. 'We bain't be knowing about no stone hedge off-isarrrr.' These rural accents are all pretty confusing. I tried to recall where The Wurzels are from and decided to imitate them should the need arise.

Still no other cars on the road.

I couldn't help but feel smug that we had outfoxed the police, but I was getting increasingly concerned that Fisheye would get his wish and we really would have to end up ramming a roadblock once we reached the Amesbury end of the road. I was guessing that our relative wealth in strong cider and lager would not actually be that helpful in bribing the local constabulary to let us pass without a fuss.

Finally, after a good fifteen minutes driving, we passed a junction and to our great relief some more cars joined the A303 from a small turning. I realised from looking at the map that we had now reached Wiltshire. We had done it! We had crossed the border and evaded capture, just like those Duke boys crossing the state line and frustrating Boss Hogg in *The Dukes of Hazzard*. Sure, we didn't manage to run anyone off the road or leap any rivers or canyons, but it felt good nonetheless. I inwardly shouted 'Yee-haw'. By now I was even quite looking forward to spending a night at the stones.

Drawing closer to Stonehenge, we began to see more and more brightly coloured buses, ramshackle trucks and cars full of revellers on their way to the solstice celebrations. As we turned off to join the queue for the car park, the Wiltshire police appeared to be pulling over anything bigger than a family saloon for a thorough inspection, but this seemed to be fairly good-natured and was ostensibly to stop people bringing large sound systems in with them and turning the solstice into an impromptu rave. There was one armoured car parked near to the entrance gates to the car park, but whether this was stationed there for a reason or merely a broken-down vehicle from a nearby army base was not immediately clear.

Fisheye seemed to get a little hot under the collar about the searches but I for one was glad that this meant that we wouldn't have to suffer one person's god-awful music selection blaring out all night. Especially if it was that same damned whale music relaxation cassette meets *The Sound of The Pan Pipes* mushed through a synthesiser drivel that we had suffered back in Reading. These people may be very concerned about the environment and dedicated in their efforts to save the planet, but if it is a planet where we all have to listen to speeded up lift music channelled by acid casualties then you can sign me up for shares in toxic waste production and fast food chains right now.

As we turned right into the car park Fisheye spotted a few old friends from his travelling days and was soon straining to get out and catch up like a puppy arriving at a park.

'There's Boggo, oh and Grim Boy, and look – Stickleback,' he said, or something similar. Everyone had a nickname, as if upon becoming a member of the travelling community you dropped your boring old name and the baggage that came with it and became born again with a clean slate. I guess that this opportunity for a fresh start is what makes the lifestyle so attractive to some. Fisheye, as you may have guessed, was not given that name at birth but had it thrust upon him by members of a circus skills school he was attending in Hay on Wye, as it rhymed with the name of the famous village of many bookshops. Before that he had been known as Sam and was also, no doubt, unburdened by the need to ride a unicycle, juggle beanbags or any other similarly nasty afflictions.

As we drove into the car park a steward handed us a leaflet about the conditions of our visit to the stones as well as a black bin liner to ensure that we took all our rubbish home with us. The leaflet explained that no dogs were allowed past the gate that allowed access to the field where the stone circle stands, no glass bottles and no tents or sleeping bags. There was also a request for revellers to drink sensibly, not start fires and not to clamber up on to the stones.

To some this was a direct sign that they should challenge authority at all costs by attempting to wrap their dog in a sleeping bag, get it drunk from a glass vodka bottle and then set fire to it in a tent on top of the stones. But most of the 20,000 solstice-goers were willing to put up with a little bit of being told what to do in exchange for access to the stones. I witnessed several arguments at the gate over the 'no dogs' rule, mostly initiated by travellers who had misread this part of the English Heritage leaflet we were all given as 'No dogs, apart from skinny dogs secured on flimsy string or knotted rope'.

Walking up from the car park to the stone circle, I was surprised to see a wide variety of ages and lifestyles represented among those who walked with us. I was expecting more or less just groups of old hippies and younger New Age traveller types, but there were Japanese tourists, middle-aged women in Barbours, young skate punks, well-dressed thirty-something couples and small groups of men wearing football shirts and Reeboks.

Passing through the security checks at the gate to the main field, it felt a bit like entering some kind of adult theme park. There in the near distance was the 'ride' we had all been waiting to see, illuminated by an eerie green glow, and there was also that instant feeling that the rules of the outside world did not quite apply any more. As you reached the stones the air was thick with marijuana smoke and people were already busy ignoring the 'do not climb on the stones' request from English Heritage and the various activist groups which had negotiated the open access to the monument. The stones that lay down were covered with revellers dancing and straining their necks to see the drummers who had taken over the east end of the circle and were providing the rhythm. The occasional daredevil would clamber up on to the giant slabs that balanced upon two uprights and were initially shouted down by the old school with cries of:

'Get down.'

'Don't be so selfish.'

'It's our solstice too.'

But as the night went on and the drink and drugs kicked in, the naysayers were drowned out by those cheering the stone-to-stone bounding of the climbers.

There seemed to be a definite divide between those who had come for some kind of spiritual or religious reason and those who came to party. By the time the sun went down and the green glow of the floodlights had become more prevalent, the centre of the circle was full to capacity and resembled the inside of any nightclub you could care to mention. If your spiritual quest did not involve loud drumming or waving your arms in the air to the beats then you were, as they say, shit out of luck. A few of the older hands waded into the crowd to try to get a feel for the stones, but soon came out looking bedraggled and frowning, much as your grandmother would if you suddenly threw her headfirst through the doors of the Ministry of Sound.

I wandered into the centre of the mêlée myself and it was amazing how the stone circle amplified the sound, not that this was a good thing, you understand. I find it pretty hard to swallow the idea that an authentic Stonehenge summer solstice experience should involve third-rate samba drumming. I mean, the druids have a pretty tenuous claim to Stonehenge as their historic place of worship but I really have no idea where drumming and the blowing of luminous whistles attached to strings comes into the legend of a stone circle that is as old as the pyramids of Egypt. This was age-old ritual reduced to bad 1990s rave and about as spiritual as a trip to an out-of-town shopping centre. But then, I suppose if you have necked enough pills, both could be pleasurable days out.

For most of the evening the druids were conspicuous by their absence. There was the odd man with a druidic outfit and a staff standing around but there was no sign of any large groups of them. I imagine that samba is not their thing. But if you are attending the annual pilgrimage to what you see as an important religious monument and you find it full of dancing youngsters, then I guess you may not exactly want to dive straight in.

Despite the various claims and counter claims from religious groups, archaeologists, historians and crystal-wrangling spiritual leaders, no one actually knows why Stonehenge was built nor what its purpose was, or is. Speculation runs from ancient computer to astrological map, sundial to UFO landing site and market place to place of worship, with the stones being claimed as a holy temple by everyone from druids to sun-worshippers and pagans to Buddhists.

I must admit that marking the rising of the sun on the solstice in the twenty-first century seemed pretty much like an irrelevant chanting, tie-dye, robes and spliffs custom to me. We know that the earth is not flat, our enemies are unlikely to curse our livestock with a plague of boils (tactical chemical weapons strikes aside) and the sun rises each morning over Stonehenge, numerous less-hip stone circles and everywhere else, so what the hell is the fuss about? If it is just a party people want, then why not say so? I'm not sure that I would want anyone partying on my ancient monument, but I am confident that English Heritage would be understanding if everyone just levelled with them. Maybe.

However, I was determined to see or experience something that might change my mind, so I set about wandering around the perimeter of the circle and the rest of the field. The police officers gathered in clumps by the fence didn't seem too keen on offering any kind of spiritual guidance, but

I did strike up conversation with a few people who seemed to have a vague notion that they would be experiencing some kind of wisdom-giving ancient rite, but weren't entirely sure what it was. One woman I spoke to, who had driven up from Brighton, assured me that the first ray of morning sun over the stones would be quite something; though what that something was she seemed unsure. And anyway, she had to leave before dawn to makes sure she got back in time for work the next morning.

Most people wished me a happy solstice as we parted, which is one card-selling opportunity that Hallmark seems to have overlooked, though I am not sure that any of us knew what this meant. Others offered 'aveyougottasparefagmate' in a kind of slur. Assuming it was some kind of ancient English greeting adopted by solstice regulars, I smiled back and walked on.

At the far end of the field from the stones, adjacent to the gate where men with rope-like dreadlocks and ropier dogs were still arguing about their pets not being allowed in, was a veggie burger stand. I'm not sure if this truly reflected the Stonehenge of old but whoever did come here in the past must have brought food. And as the 'no fires' regulation precluded the possibility of grabbing a local sheep and cooking it *al fresco*, this was as close to authenticity as we could hope for.

In the queue, the man in front of me was trying to persuade his girlfriend to ask if they had any burgers with meat in.

'Look, it says up there: vegetarian and vegan,' she said. 'I'm not asking, you ask.'

He looked sheepish and full of woe. He heaved the heavy sigh of the man who knows he has to stop in a strange village and ask someone he will never see again for directions. Men are just not wired for that kind of thing. Asking people we will never see again for sex is one thing, but asking which way to the King's Head, Anfield or the M3 is something quite different, as is asking staunch vegetarian caterers if perchance they have a beefburger or a doner kebab secreted under the counter, just in case of emergencies. In the end he did the decent thing and went off in a huff.

The burgers looked quite nice, but my appetite had been somewhat spoilt by my recent visit to the toilet. You would think that a group of people largely of the 'let's do away with authority and live as one' persuasion could at least get it together to actually crap *in* rather than *on* the toilets provided. Okay, okay, so it could have been the cops or an MI6 infiltrator who deliberately delivered the nut-brown delicacy to the rim of the already stinking plastic portable toilet in an effort to discredit the possible post-revolution toilet situation, but it seems somewhat unlikely. I settled for a coffee with lots of sugar, hoping that the caffeine-sugar kick would keep my eyes open for the four hours or so until the sun rose.

I headed back to our base camp, where I found John sitting alone on our bin liners. Fisheye had disappeared off somewhere with an old friend saying that he would be back in fifteen minutes, but that was over an hour ago. Maybe he was shopping with his Special Brew.

Since I had been away, more and more revellers had gathered around us and the drum-driven disco at stones central was getting more crowded and more raucous as the night progressed. This area was well lit by the ambient floodlighting provided by English Heritage, which prompted the odd call of 'Turn out the lights!' from those who wanted to experience their club night in the pitch black. I am sure that ancient visitors to the stones did without a clinical green glow to light their way, but then there were only about 20,000 inhabitants of England when the stones were erected and it seems unlikely that the majority of them would have consumed vast quantities of strong lager, Es or dope and then arrived at the stones en masse.

Meanwhile, around the outside of the stones arguments were breaking out because most people couldn't see where they were putting their feet. The lights shone right in your eyes and were casting shadows over anything below knee height, which is where most of the sleeping children tended to be. Rather than move their children to safety, mothers and fathers were bickering with innocent passers-by trying to get back to their friends, and shouting 'Watch my fucking kids!' at anyone who came close.

It was apparent that similar incidents were going on all around us. There is a limit to universal harmony and understanding and that limit seems to be allowing a pissed-up crusty to stomp all over your blanket and potentially tread on your kids. I am sure there is some kind of metaphor for global conflict in there somewhere. As far as I know, no one launched

42

a tactical assault on anyone else's blanket and children in retaliation for any incident but there was a lot of shouting, pushing and shoving going on.

Perhaps the cheesiest chat-up line in any repertoire is the 'Did you hurt yourself when you fell from heaven?' routine. In my case, though, it was the angel who hurt *me* when she landed square on top of me in the dark. And she arrived with a chat-up line of her own, proving that Stonehenge is indeed a strange and perhaps mystical place.

'Would you like to see my dog bites?' said the bottle blonde whose bony backside was beginning to dig into my thigh.

'Sorry?' I offered. There really didn't seem to be any correct answer to the question.

'Look,' she said, holding my hand and offering a bare arm with a large lump of flesh which looked as if it had been gnawed out and then stuck back in the casualty ward.

'I've got some more on my back,' she said as she clambered off my lap and found a space on the floor to lie down next to me. 'They're from a Staffie-pit bull cross,' she told me, just to make sure I knew they weren't from anything as common as a regular mongrel or as wimpy as a Chihuahua.

I didn't catch her name, but to be fair so much came out of her mouth in such a short time that I really couldn't have remembered it anyway. Let's call her Sharon. I did find out that she was a local who was here for the first time and had brought her eleven-year-old son with her.

'Aaah, look, there he is. He's having his first alcy-pop,' she said as she pointed her cigarette towards the youngster swigging a bottle of orange Hooch. I started to edge away. She gripped my leg in an affectionate but threatening manner, while John tried to contain his mirth at what was happening before him and thanking his lucky stars that my new friend had landed on me instead of him.

Once Sharon had released the grip on my leg and we had talked for a while, I actually started to warm to her. I felt I had a lot more in common with her than with many of the other people I had spoken to. Like me, she wasn't too big on the whole mystic significance of the stones, but we agreed that they were a stunning monument and an amazing feat of ancient construction. Everything was going quite normally until she started, for some reason, to talk about her ideal man. I really hope that it was the beer talking, as she described him as a cross between Bart Simpson and the DJ Chris Moyles.

'So, fat and yellow, then?' I asked.

'Yes,' she said, leading me to the conclusion that it was actually Homer Simpson whom she had her eye on. Perhaps it was his rock-solid marriage to Marge that stopped her from admitting this, even to herself.

'So, who's your ideal woman, then?' Sharon asked me.

I'm really not that good at this type of question. I am more of the type who forms lots of fleeting attractions based on the rear view of women walking in front of me down the high street rather than committing to one particular film star, soap character or cartoon-DJ crossover mutation.

'What about Homer's wife, Marge?' she tried.

I didn't reply before she had time to draw breath again so she tried a different tack.

'Would you like to get married to me?'

'Erm . . .'

'We could do it tomorrow. My sister is getting married up here tomorrow. It's a pagan wedding. What do you think? The marriage lasts a year and a day and then you are free. Sounds good, doesn't it?'

Well, in general terms the year and a day thing did sound a pretty sensible length for a marriage, especially one to someone whom you had just met. But in this case I had a feeling that even the 'and a day' part would prove to be a little too long. I was stumbling around in my brain trying to find the right words to let her down gently when a scuffle broke out just behind us between an extremely drunk man and a slightly less inebriated woman. As they pushed each other the woman stumbled close to where we were sitting, which for Sharon perhaps seemed a little too close to the tactics that she had used to snare me.

'Oi!' she shouted as she leaped up.

The woman, decked out in the regulation traveller fashion of combat trousers and para boots, stood her ground.

'What's your problem?' screeched Sharon.

Traveller woman, who was built like one of those squat ex-SAS instructors who you see on reality TV shows, brushed off Sharon easily before peacemakers, those who wanted to see a good fist fight and those who fancied joining in moved in. John and I took this as a sign to abandon our post and move to safer ground, further away from the circle and my would-be fiancée. Some things just aren't meant to be I guess, but we'll always have Stonehenge.

Further from the maelstrom of the mid-stone rave, things were a little quieter, though they weren't exactly normal. I witnessed a man wandering around showing people a giant cake that was shaped like one of the stones, as well as one rotund, naked reveller standing amid the crowd arcing streams of urine into the air before being led away by the police. There was also a nasty – though, looking back, quite amusing – incident in which a group of twelve-year-old boys gathered around a man shouting 'Hippy!' before proceeding to attack him. He managed to kick them away from him pretty swiftly, but this incident did make me reflect on what a violent atmosphere the whole event seemed to have for a festival largely steeped in the 'love and peace' spirit of the hippy era. Perhaps it would have been understandable if the boozing led to resentment-fuelled confrontation with the police or stewards, but the underlying conflict was individual against individual and marked the event out as more of a piss-up in a field than anything spiritual.

There were those who were trying to hold it all together. Some of the pagan groups displayed their elaborate wooden effigies and the large group of orange-robed Hare Krishna devotees were chanting throughout the night. I spoke briefly with a lonely-looking man who seemed to be in a Buddhist splinter group all of his own. He too was chanting for peace, harmony and a ticket to nirvana, though I imagine that getting some friends may have been a better path to follow, at least in the short term.

As the night wore on, I circled the stones several times in my efforts to stay conscious. There were controlled fires near the perimeter fence for anyone who wanted a quick warm-up on what was becoming a chilly night, and I was surprised not to see the guy I had spoken to earlier in the evening, who was clad only in shorts and a T-shirt, by one of them. When I last saw him he had been wandering around trying to beg blankets from families who were sitting on them. I'm sure that the naked pissing man must have been only too pleased with his warm police cell at around 3 a.m., when the air became increasingly cold and damp.

With the forecast arrival of dawn around an hour away, large numbers of druids began to appear, as if from nowhere, and gather in groups outside the stones. This caused a good deal of muttering as well as the odd heckle from the rest of the crowd. A lot of people seemed to resent the fact that revellers were being told to make way at the centre of the stones to these Johnny-come-latelies who had not been hard at it getting down to the beats for the last six hours or more.

'Keep religion out of it,' one man shouted, despite the fact that, in one way or another, religious and spiritual significance is what has made Stonehenge such a crowd-puller. I guess he may have been one of the few who believe that the stones actually used to function as a market place and was here to celebrate commerce, but that did seem somewhat unlikely.

At first the growing druid procession seemed solemn and brimming with ancient significance. There was a ceremony around a stone, torches held high and bats sweeping overhead. It was hard to see exactly what was going on through the throng, but as the druids began to walk around the circumference of the stone circle they were joined by some samba drummers, which gave things a slightly surreal, Pythonesque air. It was unclear whether the band were druids who had simply been infected by the samba beat and forgotten how to play anything else, part of a pre-arranged druid-samba collaboration or if the sambanistas had just decided to follow them around as a joke. Some of the druids looked a little perturbed, but not having seen any before I can't really say whether they always look that way.

As the procession made its way around the stones, the floodlights were finally switched off so that the sun could be seen in its full magnificence as it rose over the heel stone. The disappearance of the green glow was greeted with a huge cheer of the 'now we're free to get naked, smear ourselves with mud and copulate like wild beasts' variety. But no one actually took the opportunity to get primitive on a cold damp stone, at least not to my knowledge. The switching off of the lights was actually a bit of a letdown for all, as instead of being plunged into darkness, ready for the ascent of the sun, we experienced something akin to God turning the dimmer switch down a touch. With the dawn rapidly approaching, it was starting to get quite light anyway. At this point we were also treated to the first light rain of the night. The squib was literally as well as meta-phorically damp.

The next cheer from the crowd was a little like one of those that greet the arrival of midnight on New Year's Eve. This was the sound of the dawn solstice chorus briefly before 5 a.m. A few, those with their watches set a little fast, started early and some just joined in, while the sticklers waited and watched their own atomically set, accurate-to-within-one-second-per-millennia timepieces confirm that it was indeed dawn. There was no sun over the heel stone, no dramatic illu-mination of the sacred megaliths and no ancient equivalent of the Big Ben chimes to announce that dawn had, in fact, dawned. The sky remained grey, the rain still drizzled down and after almost eight hours of spiritual, alcoholic and phar-maceutical foreplay, the earth, and indeed the cloud cover, did not move. Most faked it though, whooping and cheering their way through the first five minutes of 21 June as if it somehow really did have some significance to their lives.

After one last look around the stone circle and a cursory search for Fisheye, John and I joined the long procession back to the car park and our eco-unfriendly drive back to the land of wonder, warm baths and dry clothes that is the great indoors. As we headed across the field to John's car, others were preparing for the second major spiritual event of that day – England's World Cup match against Brazil, which was to be broadcast live at 7.30 a.m. You may not have your average hippy, traveller or Stonehenge-goer down as football fans but the number of big screens that were being set up outside converted ambulances, magic buses and VW campervans illustrated otherwise. I should point out that the average traveller 'big screen' is actually a twenty-inch 1979 Mitsubishi television that has been salvaged from a skip and propped on two folding chairs, but that didn't put off the crowds that began to gather in small huddles all around the car park.

Once Fisheye returned to the car and we had exchanged some of the tales of our night at the stones, we decided to head off to nearby Salisbury to watch the match in the dry and warmth of a pub. We exited the car park, being careful not to run over any of the packs of dogs or feral children that ran with them, and headed south.

Fisheye slept in the car while John and I went in search of a pub. We found one in the high street but there wasn't actually room to get through the door. It was a similar story at another hostelry a few yards up the road on the opposite side of the street, but it was third time lucky as we found a big pub with two bars and two large screens.

Being in any pub at 7.30 in the morning is an unusual enough experience in England, but the crowd at our chosen venue made it even more strange. The main bar was jammed to the rafters with regulars, but our overspill bar had an eclectic mix of hippies, travellers, locals on their way to office jobs and two tables-full of elderly German tourists. The Germans, who were staying at rooms above the pub, were busy tucking into their breakfasts and even the threat of exuberant fans splashing beer and Smirnoff Ice onto their cornflakes when Michael Owen scored for England was not enough to prompt them to look up from their cereal bowls.

Shortly after Owen's goal, something occurred to me. We had waited all night for the rising of the sun on a significant day, now England were engaged in sporting combat in the land of the rising sun on that same morning. Surely that must be some kind of a positive sign, mustn't it?

Luckily I didn't have any money riding on the game, because my theorising was completely wrong. I had chosen to look at the positive signs rather than the negative. I should have been focusing on the promised sunrise that never delivered its potential, the naked man pissing pointlessly into the sky (which was surely a signifier of the ineffectiveness of the long-ball game) and the dominance of the samba beat. Brazil's victory really should have been easy to foresee. The signs were all there.

The summer was still only beginning, but with the World Cup effectively over, the days growing shorter and the sense of national excitement quelled, it seemed for a moment as if autumn was already drawing near. But such thoughts were extinguished as John and I opened the pub door to leave and the sun, which had finally appeared, almost melted our retinas (if indeed a retina is a thing that can be melted). After hours spent in half-light at the stones and in the dark of a pub set up for big-screen television, we were not used to real light and spent the next quarter of an hour squinting and blinking like new-born kittens as we wandered through the town in search of the train station.

I had a date with a train back into London for a good long bath, a well-earned sleep and a change of clothes. At £23.10 for a single journey, my ticket really should have included a massage, a meal and a cigar, but as it was I just had to be thankful for the chance to nod off for half an hour at an impossibly uncomfortable angle among the half-cut commuters on their way to work after witnessing England's defeat over a beery breakfast.

3. TRAINS, PLANES AND THE SPECIAL BUS

When you tell your friends that you are off to spend a weekend in Lincolnshire with a group of trainspotters, you get some pretty strange looks. But if you then tell them that you will be camping out with the nerds next to the East Coast Main Line railway tracks and engaging in a game of cricket for the prize of a small plastic train full of cigarette butts, then they stop including you in their rounds and start asking if you are going to be okay getting home.

I hadn't even told them the bit about the event – known as the Tallington Ashes – being a kind of trainspotter Glastonbury Festival, with the entertainment provided by two spotter-fronted bands that sing songs about locomotives, signal boxes and ticket inspectors. It may have seemed odd to outsiders, but how much more English can you get than a game of cricket, slightly dishevelled men with notebooks and a pint of good, warm beer at the Tallington village pub, which was hosting the event? This is the kind of event that John Major must have been fantasising about in the 1990s when making prime ministerial speeches about the state of our nation.[1] In fact, someone really should have invited him along, I'm sure he would make a great umpire.

Trainspotting is generally something that you pick up by the age of ten or just completely ignore. No one I knew as a child ever got into taking down train numbers, though this may be something to do with the fact that the railway lines in Margate use the electrified third rail system. If we weren't hearing in morning assembly about some kid getting fried on the tracks, then we were being brought together in the school hall to watch safety films about other kids getting fried on the tracks. So the incentive to go trespassing by the side of the railway lines was somewhat diminished. The childish delight of pissing over the edge of the bridge just beyond the allotments on to passing trains below was also something that I missed out on, having heard a particularly nasty apocryphal tale involving urine hitting the third rail, conductivity and screaming.

Aware of my lack of childhood experience of the hobby, Joseph Porter, the forty-year-old singing spotter who organises the Tallington Ashes each year, sent me an essay he had

---

[1] 'Fifty years on from now, Britain will still be the country of long shadows on county grounds, warm beer, invincible green suburbs, dog lovers, and – as George Orwell said – old maids bicycling to Holy Communion through the morning mist.' John Major to the Conservative Group for Europe, 22 April 1993.

written about the pastime that has ruled his life since the age of six. The point of doing so was to make sure that I didn't simply reiterate the stereotypical 'anorak' view of trainspotting, or worse still think that it bore some relation to the Irvine Welsh book/film/T-shirt of the same name. Of course, it also gave him the chance to wax lyrical about locomotives and impart yet more train-related data.

Joseph's highly informative treatise detailed the large number of sub-groupings of trainspotters. I learned that, far from being a one-dimensional hobby that involves merely underlining the numbers in the National Railway Enthusiasts Association's *Spotter's Companion*, there are scores of specialists – such as bashers. From Joseph's description these seemed to be malodorous, hard-drinking obsessives with a fully developed spotter language, who travel as far as they can behind certain types of locomotive, preferably on the way to a beer festival. This practice is often undertaken by those who also spot beer, or 'scoop', on the side. Scooping involves 'spotting' all the beer you can drink at a real ale festival and decanting those brews that you can't manage in order to drink the regulation half-pint later on so that you can officially put it down in your book. I'm not making this up, honest.

More worrying still than the description of the bashers was that of track bashers, whose mission is to seek out obscure lengths of seldom-travelled track and the wagon spotters, who ignore the locomotives but instead try to collect all the numbers of the long lines of freight wagons as they career by. These strange creatures implement video cameras or dictaphones so as to do away with the risk of RSI from scribbling down so many numbers so quickly.

As I travelled by train (naturally) to Stamford, which is the nearest station to the village of Tallington, on a warm Friday evening, it dawned on me that reading the lyrics of some of Joseph and his band, Blyth Power's, songs and the essay he sent me about spotting did actually have my train senses twitching. I had also been dipping into Nicholas Whittaker's charming memoir, *Platform Souls*, a surprisingly engaging portrait of the hobby that sets out to give the spotter the image of a kind of action hero battling against the odds and the derision of others to bring home the numbers.

As I stared out of the window into the fading early evening light, I began to notice the class numbers of trains and even felt a frisson of excited recognition when I saw a pair of Class 47 diesel engines in the sidings as we pulled out of Peterborough station. Earlier in the week, I had clipped out a newspaper story about a rail accident, not because of the human interest but because I noticed that the engine involved was a Class 56, the same model as the locomotive that Joseph had named his band after, 56076, Blyth Power.[2]

On arriving at Stamford station, I even took a cursory glance through the window of the Robert Humm & Co rail enthusiast's bookshop. It was getting quite worrying, but at least I hadn't actually noted down any of the numbers of the trains I had seen. This reassured me that I was reasonably

---

[2] The nameplate 'Blyth Power' has now passed on to 56134. Please, no letters.

safe from being dragged into a life of travelling around the country, sneaking into locomotive sheds or trying to befriend railway workers with access to the all-powerful TOPS computer – the system that can tell you where that elusive loco is located and where it will be going next.

Travelling by train to Stamford gives you a rather odd introduction to this attractive small town. At the centre of the town there are historic stone buildings, medieval churches and a collection of almshouse-style dwellings, but what greets you when you alight from the train is a pitiful selection of Barratt-style new homes fashioned into a mini estate. This is neighboured by a car park, some recycling bins and one of those modern pay toilets with the sliding door that always seems to be occupied. You could be forgiven for taking a cursory glance and then getting the hell out of there.

I was expecting to see at least a few other likely candidates for the Tallington Ashes as I stood outside the station, surveying the depressing mock-something or other estate but, as I found upon my arrival at the pub garden campsite, everyone except me had decided to come by car. I had thought that a part of the romance and adventure of trainspotting was the freedom from slavery to the internal combustion engine. But most of those attending just thought that it was easier to get there by road, especially as there were engineering works due at Stamford station on Sunday and the dreaded replacement bus service would reign.

The atmosphere at the campsite around the back of The Whistle Stop pub was not exactly at Glastonbury levels (though I imagine that the ability to go about one's business unhindered by fire jugglers, unwashed trustafarians and stupid people selling 'smart drinks' is why a lot of people would rather be at Tallington). By the time Joseph wandered onto the stage of The Outback – the inexplicably western-themed stage building which was 'out back' of the pub – to play a short solo set at 10 p.m., we were about fifty strong.

Joseph's acoustic strummings – a catchy, if somewhat odd mix of songs about trains, demolishing Stonehenge and ploughing salt into the fields of farmers who protest about fuel prices – were followed by various offerings from other happy campers who took advantage of the open mike policy, including an act calling himself Gob Dylan. Gob performed a notable version of the Sex Pistol's 'Anarchy in the UK' in the style of his namesake Bob. We were treated to a finale by Joseph and Blyth Power's guitarist, Steven, performing a duet of a track entitled 'Goodnight', which as far as I know is the only song of unrequited love about a girl from Broadstairs[3] and which certainly must be the only piece of music ever to give a lyrical nod to Shrewsbury.

Before leaving the stage, Joseph gave a quick explanation of the following day's events for the benefit of the smattering of bemused local drinkers in the crowd. Giving a rundown of the bands that would be playing, he described Blyth Power

---

[3] Since writing this line I have discovered that, amazingly, 'Goodnight' is not the only song of unrequited love to feature Broadstairs. Indie-comic band Half Man Half Biscuit have a track on their *Camell Laird Social Club* album entitled 'She's in Broadstairs'.

as 'a cross between The Clash, Steeleye Span and The Rubettes, with a bit of Hear'Say thrown in'. From the looks on their faces, I could see that made it about as clear as mud.

Like many of my fellow campers, I went off to my tent regretting that last pint of Tiger ale, which was already nagging at my bladder. Being able to walk for less than one minute from bar to bed might be a wonderful thing come closing time, but the trip back to the toilet in the cold of the night would seem far longer. As well as prompting me finally to flee the tent and dispense with the ill-advised excess beer, the dramatic temperature drop between midnight and 2 a.m. reminded me that camping is far better if you have someone to share body heat with.

Camping next to the East Coast Main Line may seem like a great idea if you are a trainspotter. But for the few of us who were not, the constant sound of trains zooming past just ten feet away from our heads, with each arrival announced one minute before by the alarm connected to the nearby level crossing, it seemed more like a cruel and unusual punishment. Just when you thought that there couldn't possibly be any more high-speed passenger trains that night, the clunking, screeching freight trains began. You could hear spotters excitedly rustling in the undergrowth, trying to get a look at the train numbers, but fortunately there didn't seem to be any wagon spotters loudly reciting the numbers of the containers into cassette recorders.

Hair product manufacturers who design gels and waxes for

that 'just got out of bed' look do not, thankfully, often do their research in fields behind pubs in Lincolnshire. If they did, the streets would be full of men sporting slightly frizzy, sleep-squashed pillar box-red dreadlocks, possibly teamed with a Dennis the Menace-style jumper. This was the look sported by Jessi Adams, trainspotter extraordinaire and singer/guitarist in the world's second most prominent trainspotting band, Eastfield, that morning as he crossed the field to the toilet block at the back of the pub.

Jessi had been a member of Blyth Power until recently but was sacked from the band during one of Joseph's legendary megalomaniacal band purges. In a direct inversion of the history of spoof-rockers Spinal Tap, Blyth Power have retained the same drummer (Joseph) throughout their nineteen-year existence while guitarists, bassists, keyboard players and backing singers have come and gone like, and often with, the seasons. But it seemed that there weren't any hard feelings, as the pair were sharing a lot of the organising and taking turns at running the stall selling CDs, T-shirts and fanzines, as well as disappearing on the odd spotting excursion as time allowed.

Jessi was still pretty much a numbers man, while Joseph has forsaken crossing off the loco digits in his *Spotter's Companion* in favour of taking photographs. His current enthusiasm was for the Sprinter units, which to you or me look much like all carriage and no engine and run the short-hop commuter routes or take school children and shoppers between dismal towns in Hertfordshire. The complete opposite of the romantic and powerful diesels of yore, these electric buses on rails are generally withdrawn from service after twenty years and hence now excite the spotters who initially scorned them, as they race to take down their numbers before they are scrapped.

'I'm trying to photograph them all,' Joseph told me. 'I'm laying down a fine vintage of Sprinter photographs now so that in twenty years' time I will be able to brag about them.' He really wasn't joking about the bragging bit.

Unlike during the days of the nationalised railways celebrated in *Platform Souls*, the privatisation of the rail network has lead to an atmosphere of conflict rather than communication between spotters and those who run the trains. Where once a blind eye was turned to the odd spotter who found his way into a locomotive shed, now there is the risk of a brush with security guards and the danger of finding yourself in court for trespassing. For this reason, any spotter worth his salt carries a high-visibility vest at all times. As well as decreasing the risk of being hit by a train, this bright-orange bib acts as a backstage pass to the world of trains. As there are so many different contractors working on the tracks at any time, anyone wearing or carrying one is assumed to be officially sanctioned and can wander along at trackside and into locomotive sheds with impunity.

'If you have a vest sticking out of your bag you can even just walk straight into the staff canteens,' said Joseph, obviously a man with a strong stomach. 'No one really knows who is meant to be there and who is not.'

After ablutions and breakfast-time discussions about who

spotted what overnight, the stage was set up for the bands and Blyth Power ran through a lunchtime warm-up set to make sure that all the gear was working and sounded as it should. During this extended sound check, Joseph's cricketing nemesis and fellow spotter, a man who everyone seemed to know simply but lengthily as 'Chris from Bishop's Stortford', turned up at the pub, just in time for the annual cricket match which was to follow.

As the band clambered off the stage, Joseph took the role of games master and announced that anyone taking part should assemble on the field where teams would be picked, coins would be tossed and play would commence beneath the then blistering sun.

After some initial selection of skilled batsmen and natural allies by Joseph and Chris from Bishop's Stortford, the playground-style process of picking teams was dispensed with and the remaining thirty or so players were split down the middle. I ended up on Joseph's team and, as he had won the toss, we fielded first. This, so Joseph explained, was a cunning plan which would enable him to add latecomers to his side and provide an almost endless stream of batsmen and women should they be needed to defeat Chris and win back the Tallington Ashes, which had spent the last year in Bishop's Stortford.

Despite the image I had of trainspotters as those boys who were always picked last, and usually had some kind of note about their asthma when it came to games lessons, I was surprised to find that some of the spotter crew were actually fairly good at both bowling and batting. They were even unhindered by the silly hat chosen from a box behind the wicket that each player had to don before their short walk to the crease. Things were looking bad for Joseph as Chris's team racked up 102 runs before being all out, with Chris himself scoring six runs and out for whacking the tennis ball we were using on to the railway tracks. Luckily we were among those who spend a good deal of their leisure time running across railway lines, so it was no trouble to get the ball back.

I was sixth up to bat for Joseph's team, following our captain's fine six runs (scored while attired in a witch's hat), and managed a feeble zero after being caught out on the third ball. I blame the stupid jester's hat I had chosen to don while at the crease. The fact that I had fluffed an earlier catch made my contribution to our eventual victory negligible to say the least, but it was still nice to join the team as our captain received the plastic train filled with cigarette butts and, quite possibly, the remains of someone's grandfather.

The cricket segued almost seamlessly into the musical proceedings that the non-spotting, non-cricketing campers had come to witness. There were Beefheart-like hippy bands, performance poets, goth rockers and tight punk rock trios. But all of these were, at some point, upstaged by passing trains, be it due to the deafening rattles of the freights or the sudden exodus of half of the audience towards the level crossing in a desperate attempt to catch the number of a passing express. The high spot of the day for most was the arrival of an enthusiasts' special pulled by both a Class 92 and a Class 37 locomotive – the trainspotting equivalent of being invited back to Anna Kournikova's place to find the Williams sisters there already waiting for you.

As the sun began to go down, Eastfield took to the stage and launched into a kind of pop-punk shoutiness, which I imagine is what The Ramones would have sounded like had they spotted trains, come from the Midlands and grinned a lot. The songs were a mix of anti-authoritarian tracks to jump up and down to, mildly confusing numbers about artificial sweeteners and, of course, plenty about escapades on foreign railways, bust-ups with security guards at loco sheds and paeans to the trains that nearly got away. I suppose when you give your songs titles like '47002' then at least you can be sure that no one else is going to steal them.

Having said that, Eastfield's is not, as you might expect, the only song about a Class 47 locomotive, or even the only one played that night. When it was Blyth Power's turn to entertain the 150-strong crowd that had, by then, gathered, Joseph introduced 'Probably Going to Rain' with a solemn explanation about the song's origins as a tribute to 47009, which had been destroyed in test crashes. A cruel end to such a magnificent beast, apparently.

Later in the set, Joseph implored fans to 'imagine he's a Class 37' as he sought their appreciation for a solo the band's guitarist, Steven, had just completed. 'Oooh,' they cooed as they summoned up the collective mental image of a powerful locomotive on the stage before them. There was also a spot-ting-related interruption to play as a freight train rumbled by and Joseph downed drumsticks to ask 'Did anyone catch that?' A brief discussion about the number of the engine pulling the rattling wagons ensued before the music could continue.

The band did indeed sound like a cross between The Clash and Steeleye Span, but I'll have to take Joseph's word about The Rubettes, as the only thing I can recall about them is that they wore white suits. I don't think there was much of the Hear'Say about Blyth Power either, though, as with The Rubettes, I have trouble humming a single bar of their material in my head, so I can't be entirely sure. I don't imagine that either band ever felt the urge to do any songs about Saint Augustine, Cecil Parkinson or the cod war, as Blyth Power have.

One odd thing that I witnessed was that when Eastfield played, five devotees flailed wildly and sweatily around the outdoor dance floor wearing Eastfield T-shirts, yet when Blyth Power were on the same people were leaping about in T-shirts bearing that band's name. They had actually brought band T-shirts with them for both bands and changed between sets, as if dancing, cheering and clapping were not enough.

One of the practitioners of the T-shirt switcheroo was Chris from Bishop's Stortford, who at least had the excuse of guest drumming on a track by each of his favourite bands that night. I have to say that these percussive interludes were a blessed relief from the geography-teacher-meets-Morris-dancer–on-a-step-machine freak-outs that he executed while he wasn't on stage. It really was quite disturbing, though perhaps not as much as the sight of the stick-thin chicken dancer who sported a mouse-hued bowl cut and looked distinctly as if he had been dressed at random from the reject bins of the local Cancer Research shop. The overall look was similar to that of the undernourished refugees you see on news programmes wearing cut-off shell suit bottoms paired with a well-worn pound shop T-shirt, both of which have recently arrived in an overseas aid package.

Blyth Power efficiently finished off the night's entertainment just as time was called at the bar, so that everyone could, once again, be faced with the head and bladder versus heart decision as to whether they should order one final drink. The sedative effects of alcohol versus the almost certain knowledge that you would need to get up to pee in the night. It was a tough call, but with the prospect of freezing again and the threat of another night of train noise, everyone but the hardiest of spotters hit the bar.

Thankfully, both the need for the toilet and the freight trains held off for the night, leaving me to wake the next morning feeling at least partly human. When I unzipped my tent I found that Joseph, Jessi and Chris were already up and bedecked in high-visibility orange for a trip to the depots of Peterborough.

'It's a little easier on a Sunday as the security is usually more lax and there is also less traffic on the lines,' said Joseph, who, despite his slightly chimp-like gait, could easily pass for an old hand on the railways. I supposed that they would have to excuse Jessi as a 'you can't get the staff nowadays' agency worker if questioned as to their business.

I wished them happy hunting and set about demolishing my weekend home and stuffing it back into its bag. I then begged a lift back into Stamford and made my way to the station to wait for the rail replacement bus service, which would take me slowly and uncomfortably part of the way home. The air-free, overcrowded journey made me more than happy to see the Sprinter waiting to take me home once I was back in the land of two rails. I was so glad to get off the foul-smelling coach that I even forgot to express inner concern that I knew the type of engine that would be transporting me. I was glad that my notebook and pencil were safely tucked away in my bag; after all, it is of moments of emotional weakness such as this that addictions are born.

The next time I saw a Sprinter I was not, however, quite so delighted. Had I taken up the noble art of jotting down train numbers I probably would have thrown down my *Spotter's Companion* in disgust at the woefully inadequate bright-green Central Trains monstrosity that rolled into Cambridge station that afternoon. It was not even close to rush hour but the two-carriage train, which was going all the way to Liverpool Lime Street, was filled to twice its seated capacity as we left the station. Some people on the platform couldn't even get on the train, as there was no room left even to stand.

Thankfully I was only travelling as far as Ely, a journey of fifteen minutes, and I had bagged a prime standing spot, next to the toilet. Also sharing my wardrobe-sized floor space was a trio of fifteen-year-old girls in shell suits who were

having an intellectual discourse as to the meaning of the illuminated 'WC' sign with an illustration of a wheelchair next
to which we were standing.

'It's Wheelchair Case.'

'No, it means toilet.'

'No it doesn't,' said the tallest finally. 'It stands for Water
Centre.' This conjured up a wonderful image of a Tardis-like
lavatory that housed one of those swimming pools with slides
and wave machines, rather than the dismal piss-drenched
closet that was the reality.

Once I had managed to elbow the teenagers to a distance
that enabled me to reach into my hip pocket for my telephone,
I decided to put some forward planning into action and call
ahead to Ely for a mini-cab. I was on my way to Mildenhall
and, as the village had no train station and a bus service that
only runs when the new moon falls on a market day during
an Olympic year, I was faced with the choice of a twelve-mile
walk or attempting to book a private hire vehicle. I had the
phone numbers for three cab companies and tried them all
in succession. Each offered a not unreasonable rate, but when
it came to the 'When would you like it, sir?' question the
problem was the same.

'Ah, you see, it's the school run,' said the fat controller. 'I
could do you something after five.'

It was, at that point, 2.15 p.m. I declined his gracious offer
and tried another number.

'I can maybe do you one after four.'

Do any children in Ely walk to and from school? And what

are all those 4x4s in the driveways of local houses for if not traversing the hazardous Cambridgeshire terrain on the way to the school gates?

I called another.

'Sorry, guv. School run. Got nothing doing. Could get you something about four-thirty.'

'Couldn't they just walk for once?' I asked. 'You know, get a little exercise. Some fresh air maybe.'

'Sorry, guv. Do you want me to book you one in?'

'Er, no, I think I'll leave it, thanks.'

Luckily, when I exited Ely station, a taxi was waiting in the car park. The old lady in front of me was heading straight for it – the only cab in town not being utilised for ferrying the local brats about. Luckily she walked straight past it and towards a car that had just drawn up, thus dispensing with the need for me to employ my shin-kicking skills on such brittle bones.

Twelve miles later and £20 the poorer, I stepped out of the taxi and wandered across the road to the pub where I would be staying. I was in Mildenhall to meet up with some planespotters, or more specifically some of those who had been imprisoned in Greece for spying when they were on a spotting expedition. Paul Coppin, who was out on bail pending appeal over his three-year sentence, had instructed me to be at his house in the village at the highly militaristic 'o-six hundred hours' the next day, so I had decided to travel up early and take a look around Mildenhall.

As I discovered, a look around Mildenhall takes exactly

five minutes. All I had known about it before I arrived was that Roald Dahl wrote a short story about someone finding some buried treasure there and that there is an American airbase. The airbase is the reason why Paul Coppin bases his Touchdown Tours business and his home there.

It turned out that those two things are all that there is to know, as the lack of any leaflets about the town in the rack of tourist information by the entrance to my hotel betrayed. There were pamphlets and flyers for various attractions all over East Anglia, including nuclear power stations and cold war fallout shelters, but no one could think of anything worth committing to glossy paper about Mildenhall. After all, there is not much that you can talk up about a curved piece of A-road with a scattering of average pubs, a good selection of boarded up shops and an economy so depressed that even the charity shops were moving out.

At least the Indian restaurant had survived, which meant that I wouldn't have to forage in the countryside for my dinner. Indian restaurants outside London are a complete mystery to me. I have had some of the best Indian food I have ever tasted in small towns in Norfolk and villages in Hampshire, but some rural curry houses seem able to prosper for years by serving up little more than the sordid remains of battery hens or reheated frozen vegetables that have been microwaved in a glutinous supermarket curry sauce. It took me until I was about twenty years old to realise that I actually liked Indian food, as my first takeaway had been a wretchedly foul combination of third-hand cooking oil and burned curry powder with some unidentifiable stuff floating around in it. Thankfully, The Ghandi served up a passable dupiaza with a portion of channa massala and some rice, which came in at under £10 with a drink.

After a pint in The Bell, I retired upstairs to my room to try to get an early night. I set my various alarms for 5 a.m. so that I would make it to Paul's in time for our arranged meeting and subsequent trip to the Waddington Airshow. The website for the show promised 'nine hours of non-stop flying'. I was hoping that we wouldn't have to witness every single one of them.

Outside my window, on the High Street, those too young to get served in the pub hung around chatting and waiting for those who had cars to drive past with the windows down and the volume on the tape deck up. Sometimes they would stop and provide me with a heavy bass mobile disco, but at least this was a momentary distraction from the pub's jukebox speakers, which were situated somewhere just below my bed.

It would have been easy to get pissed off at the kids racing up and down the High Street and keeping me awake, but I just felt a tiny bit glad for them that they had learned how to drive and discovered the main road out of town. Now, if they only learned how to use it properly and got the hell out of there, then I would have been even more happy. I would also have got to sleep before 1 a.m.

If Paul Coppin and his wife Lesley are, in fact, spies then they are obviously in very deep cover. The judge who handed down the guilty verdict and the three-year sentences to the couple and six other planespotters two months before our meeting had decided that Lesley, a fifty-three-year-old grandmother, was the ringleader. She was completing a crossword puzzle in the group's minibus when the authorities swooped, marking her out as an obvious master of subterfuge who must have been in charge of the whole operation.

When I arrived at the Coppin household at just before 6 a.m. on a Saturday morning, Lesley was out in the back garden watering the plants. This, of course, could have been the perfect cover for her using the top-secret garden-based transmitter to send news to her spymasters in Turkey, but it seems unlikely.

One of Paul's sons let me in and I was greeted by Paul, an amiable teddy bear of a man in his mid-forties who was sitting at the kitchen table with two fellow spotters, Tom and Tony. Tom was a furtive-looking stereotype of a spotter. A little younger than Paul, Tom had the regulation mother-administered haircut with a supporting cast of beige anorak, blue slacks, white socks and black school shoes. Tony, on the other hand, was tall, lean and tanned, looking every bit the ladies' man. A mini-cab driver who looked as if he would be likely to get a call back for the lead role in the next Bond film were he to go for the audition. He was a good ten years older than Paul and Tom but looked a great deal younger. I think it was the jawline that did it.

A few minutes later, Ray, a porcine forty-something postman from London, turned up and we were ready to roll. Paul climbed into the driving seat and Tony, by then sporting his aviator sunglasses, took shotgun, while Tom, Ray and I battled with Tony's fourteen-year-old son and three of Paul's young boys for the remaining seats in the mini-bus.

As we left Mildenhall, we briefly swung by the US air force base to see if any new planes had arrived since Paul had last looked, which, intuition told me, had probably been the previous evening. As it turns out there were some new planes and Paul got out his pole and made a Hercules, jotting down its number, 80075, in his notebook.

I should, at this juncture, point out that while trainspotters 'cop' engine numbers planespotters 'make' aircraft numbers. And a pole is a telescope. I thought that planespotters used binoculars, but Tony soon put me straight.

'Binoculars are for turkeys.'

Turkeys being amateurs – those new to the game who haven't invested in some decent kit yet, or those who don't take it seriously enough.

I also found out that a fudger is someone who claims to have seen aeroplanes that they haven't, just so that they can cross the number off in their book to finish classes of aircraft and show off to their peers. Shameful behaviour. Did these people never listen to those lectures before school exams about how 'you are only cheating yourself' if you were the kind of person who wrote all the answers on the inside of your pencil case or on your arm?

On the way out of Suffolk, Tony pointed out a low piece of fenland to our right, explaining that it is reclaimed land that used to be under water.

'Don't let the locals tell you that they did it though,' he said. 'It was the Dutch, they know what they're doing.' He then explained that most of the locals are inbred anyway, so I imagine that it was perhaps their over-fingered hands that prevented them from doing whatever it is that you do to reclaim fenland. It seems that wherever you go in the country, there is always an area where the locals allege that this love that dare not speak another family's name is rampant, though, of course, it is never the exact one that they live in. I think it may be time for a government enquiry into the matter, or at least the addition of a question to the next census: 'Do you and your spouse share A: Grandparents, B: Parents, C: Genetic mutations, D: All of the above.'

Despite his enthusiasm for Dutch dyke work, Tony was less complimentary about planespotters who hail from the Netherlands.

'They're the bottom of the heap. A bit too enthusiastic at climbing fences and the like.'

At this point it struck me that I was actually being driven along in a mobile plot for a sitcom pilot. Here were four middle-aged men – the dependable driver, the tanned Lothario, the bowl-cut spotter stereotype who was the butt of the others' jokes and the Alf Garnett character that Ray was proving to be. They were all trapped and/or united by a single calling and travelled the Continent in their trusty mini-bus, seeking adventure, love and plane numbers. With hilarious consequences, obviously.

On arrival at RAF Waddington, we joined a lengthy queue

of aviation enthusiasts waiting to pay their £12 admission fees and be waved into the car park. It was not yet 9 a.m. but I could see that the air base was already crawling with spotters. In the van, Ray was explaining how planespotters, just like their train-chasing counterparts, sub-divide into smaller special-interest groups. There doesn't seem to be any airborne equivalent of the boozy bashers, attempting to down obscure ales in as many 757s as possible, but each spotter usually finds a methodology that suits them and settles into it as they become more experienced. Ray, for example, is strictly a military man and has no time for civilian planes, whereas Tom would probably write down the number of a paper dart if you scrawled one on the side and then threw it at him.

'The spotters on Queen's Buildings at Heathrow are pond life,' said Tony, talking about one of the most popular vantage points for spotters of passenger aircraft. 'They're real spotter stereotypes with dandruff and—'

'Lobotomies,' Ray chipped in.

Tom, who lives near Heathrow, kept quiet. He was slightly worn down, being the subject of a large percentage of the banter on the way to the air show, most of it about his sex life.

As we reached the front of the queue, Paul passed our money to the RAF airmen in charge of the gate, while Tony engaged one of them in conversation about their work. Tony would do this constantly throughout the day and seemed completely oblivious to the fact that their eyes glazed over within five seconds of his initiating the conversation.

Prior to meeting Paul, Ray, Tom and Tony, my only experience of planespotters had been from afar. To be precise, it was from the roof of my girlfriend's old flat on Holloway Road in North London, which just happened to be right opposite the Aviation Bookshop, a specialist bookseller dedicated to all things airborne. It was actually the morning after we had met at a film show in the East End, which blurred into a lock-in at a pub and a walk back to Holloway, with a few friends and me crashing out on her living room floor.

Being unable, or unwilling, to move when everyone left in the morning, I stayed behind and we made the precarious climb out of the window and up on to the roof. From there we had a clear view of both the Aviation Bookshop and the sex shop a few doors down. And so it was that we bonded over hangover-soothing coffee and the great game of guessing whether passing men in anoraks would go into the sex shop or the bookshop. By the end of an hour we actually became quite good at judging – it was always the seediest-looking ones who were there to satisfy a lust for Spitfires, Boeings and Cessnas.

With this in mind, I was most surprised to see a large number of women in the exhibition area as we took an initial walk around the site. Most did seem to be with boyfriends and husbands, but it was still a shock to see so many at what I had thought would be a men-only event. Tony wasn't quite so surprised, intimating that if he didn't have his son and fellow spotters in tow, he may well have got lucky.

'The ladies still find me attractive you know, Iain,' he said.

There were a huge number of stalls at the show, selling everything from vintage Airfix model plane kits to over-priced bacon rolls and foul-tasting coffee. There were videos of air shows that you may have missed, books, pilot uniforms and some of the most horrific knick-knacks I have seen in my life, many of them involving plaster teddy bears in flying goggles. Our contingent grabbed breakfast and caffeine to go and set about the business of making a circuit of the planes that were on show.

Paul and Tony, who had children to entertain, took a slow walk around, stopping along the way to pull them away from expensive flight simulators and placate them with candyfloss and giant lollipops. But Ray and Tom simply raced round taking a cursory 'got' or 'not got' glance at the aircraft and noting the numbers they needed before heading back to the mini-bus to doze the rest of the day away. Within an hour of arriving their work was done and having seen every kind of aerial display you could imagine over the years, they weren't particularly interested in paying too much attention to the various fly-bys that were by then under way.

On the way to the show, Tom had been keen to dwell on just how boring his hobby was. I could now see why he thought so. But that would not stop him from joining Paul and Ray for a trip to France as soon as this show had finished. He told me that he expected to see even fewer planes that he needed for his log books there, which would be even more boring. Here was a man who hated his hobby but was still driven by the need to collect more and more numbers. It was difficult to see what it was that he got out of his desire to gather numbers, which seemed totally unlinked to any enthusiasm for the aircraft to which they were attached. Sure, it was never going to be the most thrilling of pastimes, but Tom had long since managed to suck it dry of any enjoyment it may have held.

Paul still had some enthusiasm though, pointing out details to his sons, who had spotting books of their own and had been all over Europe on number-crunching trips with him. I secretly hoped that this would instil an interest in travel or geography in them as they trekked off to Bratislava and beyond, rather than cursing them with a lifetime of chasing aeroplanes to no particular end.

Whoever had sorted out the pitches for traders at the show obviously had their business head screwed on. Near to the runway where the display aircraft took off and landed was a row of enormous bouncy castles, which were interspersed with booths selling beer. This meant that parents could sink a pint while their offspring, by now full of candyfloss and Coca-Cola, wore themselves out by leaping around for five minutes. This perfect arrangement allowed Tony and me to share a drink while we watched his and Paul's children throw each other down inflatable stairs and roll head-over-heels down bouncy slides. Paul had gone off for a meeting with some of the other spotters who had been locked up with him in Greece to discuss their impending legal appeal against their convictions and sentences[4], so we had agreed to supervise his brood.

Once the bouncing and the drinking had ceased, we strolled across to the airstrip to watch a few planes take off and caught a Battle of Britain fly-past zooming low overhead. I correctly identified the Lancaster, Hurricane and Spitfire. But one of Paul's sons made the junior spotter *faux pas* of misidentifying the Lancaster as a B-52, which gave Tom someone to tease when we arrived back at the mini-bus later.

Amid a display of vintage cars was a small camp that had been set up by military enthusiasts. This featured an armoured car and a Jeep, as well as a group of Brummies speaking intermittently in cod-American accents. They weren't exactly historical re-enactors, as they wore a mish-mash of US service uniforms, jeans and trainers, but they did seem to enjoy playing at being GIs. This was pretty incongruous seeing as there were actual, bona fide American servicemen showing off military hardware at the event.

'Those kind of people are highly dubious if you ask me,' opined Tony, pointing at a member of the group who looked a bit like Sinn Fein's Gerry Adams to ram his point home. 'They've probably never even been in the forces.' Tony's world definitely divided into those who had and those who hadn't, with RAF pilots being right up there at the top of his fantasy

---

[4] On 7 November 2002, Paul and Lesley Coppin, along with the rest of the convicted spotters, had their convictions quashed on appeal in Kalamata, Turkey.

society – mostly for their ability not to disintegrate when flying a Harrier jump jet and enduring six times the force of gravity.

We had arranged to meet back at the mini-bus at 3 p.m. so that we could get back to Mildenhall in plenty of time for the evening's trip to France. But by the time midday had past, I was already beginning to feel as bored as Tom with the whole thing. It was true that some of the aerial displays were good, especially the bright-orange Swiss Air Force trainer air-craft – which sounded exactly like the Stuka dive-bombers in World War II films as they careered towards the runway before climbing rapidly and looping the loop – but there is only so much flying you can watch.

Thankfully, Tony and the kids were tiring too, so we all made our way back to our parking space, where Tom and Ray were snoozing happily in the van. By about 1.30, Paul had returned from his meeting, as had the youngsters, who had got bored of sitting in the van and gone off to discover the funfair. A brief discussion between the spotters ensued and it was decided that we might as well leave, everyone having collected the numbers they needed. After all, who wants to stay at an air show and actually watch it? Even if you have paid £12 to get in.

On the way back to Mildenhall, Tom expounded on his theory that there should be a planespotting game for the PlayStation.

'It could be a bit like Grand Theft Auto,' he said, telling a still comatose Ray about the car-theft and shooting game on which he had based his idea. 'You could get points for breaking into hangars and finding secret planes. I think it would do pretty well.' I'm not sure that I share Tom's enthusiasm for the idea, but if you see magazine covers featuring a pixelated, anorak-clad man with headlines stating 'NUMBER-CRUNCHING PLANE GEEK IS THE NEW LARA CROFT', remember where you heard it first.

When we arrived back at Mildenhall, master-spy Lesley Coppin was busy making strawberry jam and a flan. The flan base could have been a disguised satellite communications dish but it did look pretty spongy from where I was standing. As soon as we had all sat down with a cup of tea, everyone got out their spotting books, notebooks and lists of planes from the show and entered data. Tony allowed himself a triumphal cheer when he realised that some of the transporters he had seen were not ones he already had. Paul seemed delighted with the eight new planes that he had 'made' on our trip and went off to enter them into his computer database, while the others discussed the merits of underlining spotted aircraft in their books using a ruler.

It's the thing to do if you want to be taken seriously. No one will respect you if you have smudged, scruffy underlining.

When he returned, I asked Paul what had got him spotting in the first place.

'I think it was just in the school playground,' he said. 'Though I had been into trainspotting a bit before that.'

Tony also expressed a prior interest in trainspotting, though he seemed a little embarrassed to admit the fact. From these revelations it seems clear that trainspotting is a gateway pastime to a harder, more expensive hobby. One that can, ultimately, see you imprisoned on foreign shores. The tabloids really should run exposés on this kind of thing, you know. Especially if it is being pushed in the playgrounds of our nation's schools.

Once the totting up was done and all the plane numbers were in order, it was time for Tony and me to depart, along with his son and one of Paul's boys, who were both keen to engage in healthy teenage pursuits such as lying on the sofa battling on the PlayStation and eating the burgers that Tony had promised them. There was at least some hope that they might somehow avoid a life spent globetrotting in search of that final Hercules well into their retirements, even if it was to become couch potatoes.

Tony had offered to give me a lift to Ely in his cab for a cut-price rate. After my previous difficulties with taxis in the area, I was more than happy to accept and to speed my exit from Mildenhall. One night was more than enough.

Something that had become clear during my excursions was the hierarchy of the spotting world. The planespotters look down at the trainspotters who, in turn, look down at bus-spotters – who really have no one much to look down on. I suspect that they may look down upon the groundhoppers, though – men who attempt to travel to a match at all ninety-two Premiership and Nationwide League football grounds. These hobbyists are much derided by all, mainly for the crime of combining a spotting technique with a sporting pursuit, as well as for their obsession with cataloguing the quality of the Bovril and meat pies provided by the in-ground caterers. Such esoteric matters are beyond the hard-and-fast methodology of the collation of raw, unquestionable data.

Being English, I am imbued with the desire to root for the underdog. I was born with the ability to identify with those who show effort instead of skill, pluck instead of grace and bloody-mindedness above the rational desire to quit. For this reason, I wanted to go out and try the lowliest form of spotting that I could. To get a feeling for the loneliness of the long-distance obsessive. To go it alone and try to understand. As I was travelling through the summer and ground-hopping is more in season in the winter months, then bus-spotting it was.

My plan was not actually to take down any numbers. I'd only have to throw them away later. My desire was just to go along and discover if I could see the appeal and be stirred to any great emotional level by seeing a large group of buses in one place. I wanted to find out if there was some nobility in the art of bus-spotting or if those who derided it were right and the whole lot of them were just number-obsessed freaks.

One of the major events in the bus-spotter's calendar is the annual bus rally at the North Weald Aerodrome. This is located out in Essex next to the M11 motorway or, if like me you are travelling by public transport, at the far eastern reaches of the Central Line on the London Underground.

As I travelled out through Bethnal Green and Mile End, I was actually beginning to quite look forward to the event. I can see any number of ageing Routemaster buses within spitting distance of my flat, but the idea of seeing them in some kind of cultural or historical context did seem like it could be interesting, despite the fact that I have never got round to visiting the London Transport Museum. I was hoping that maybe they would have a rusting double-decker that had been pulled out of the Thames after a whole fleet that had been sold to Fidel Castro was sunk, so the legend goes, by the CIA.

Somewhere around Stratford, my romantic notions were shattered by a man who got on the train and sat down a couple of seats away from me. If you ordered a bus-spotter from Central Casting, this is the guy they would send. He was in his mid-forties, slightly balding, had a bit of a hunch and was holding a thick and tattered ring-bound notebook. On his feet he wore the Englishman's favoured summer footwear – well-worn brown sandals with black socks – and his hair was obviously self-cut, varying, as it did, between about half an inch and two inches long in seemingly random clumps. His trousers looked slightly damp around the crotch and his non-matching jacket was the kind of sorry-looking garment that you see hanging out of a torn bin-liner outside a charity shop on your way back from the pub on a Friday night.

Initially I tried to convince myself that perhaps he wasn't a bus-spotter at all, but who was I trying to kid? All thoughts of gleaming Routemasters and bus-related espionage went out of my head and instead I was transported in my mind to a field filled with similarly diminutive forty-something men slavering over something with uncomfortable, hard plastic seats. I wanted to get off the train and go home, but I reminded myself of my mission to walk the walk, even if it was the walk of someone who looked as if they had a problem controlling their bladder. I also comforted myself by remembering that I have friends who live in North Weald and, if it all went wrong, I could at least escape to their place for tea and sympathy.

I tried to ignore Central Casting Spotter, let's call him Nigel, and get on with reading my book, but then I noticed that each time we reached a tube station he scribbled something down in his notepad. At the next station I leaned over slightly and saw that that he was actually noting down each tube station we travelled through in tiny, tiny writing so that he could fit about three station names on each line of his pad. Between stations he sat staring out of the window, but as he sensed we were drawing into a station he poised his pen above his pad. Only when he saw the whites of the station signs did he put pen to paper. As he wrote he read from the overhead tube map to make sure that he got the spelling right.

Nigel could, of course, have just read the stations from the overhead map and jotted them all down, leaving him the rest of the journey to relax and stare out of the window. But he didn't look like the kind of man who would enjoy just sitting back and relaxing, he needed to be constantly doing something, so he noted: 'Snaresbrook ... South Woodford ... Woodford ... Buckhurst Hill'. To not do them in turn would not be spotting and what if our train were to have careered off the rails somewhere outside Loughton, killing all on board?

85

Someone may have found his spotting book laying by the trackside and read in it that he had been through Debden, Theyden Bois and Epping, even though he never made it that far. He would go to his grave derided as a fudger by his peers, the lowest of the low in the world of spotting. There is probably some kind of 'fudger's grave', a spotting community equivalent of the unmarked burial plots of paupers or the executed. So he sat recording the inevitable as if it were an adventure.

I did wonder what Nigel was doing taking down tube station names when he was on his way to a bus rally, but later I discovered that there is a good deal of cross-spotting when it comes to London Transport. Anything with their distinctive circular logo on it is fair game for writing down in a notebook and later committing to ledgers or computer databases.

As we arrived at Epping station, our destination stop, Nigel went the opposite way to everyone else leaving the train. I assume that this was to spot a rarely used or obsolete exit from this end-of-the-line station. I left by the more conventional exit and was pleased to see that, as promised, a bus was waiting to take us to the aerodrome and the rally.

The bus was labelled 'special' on the front and certainly lived up to its name. In short, the passengers already on the bus gave it the appearance of the bus for Rampton after a particularly busy day at the Old Bailey. In fact, I was pleased when Nigel got on, as he looked pretty normal compared to the rest of my travelling companions. They appeared to have been assembled from the spare parts of stereotypical paedophiles that just happened to be kicking around in a tabloid editor's mind. There were anoraks in every colour, an almost full compliment of cheap-but-functional brown shoes, a good deal of home barbering and a lot of strangely distant stares.

This being a bus-spotting event, the bus journey to the airfield formed part of a bus route. So, despite the fact that we were all obviously on our way to the event, we were treated to a tour of the locale on our one-day-only service. I had expected our bus to be something a little more glamorous than the modern single-decker we got to travel on, imagining we would be transported by something a bit more Enid Blyton, in blue or green. Even Nigel seemed a bit disgruntled.

'This is an old Red Arrow, isn't it? I used to hate these,' he said.

The fully kitted-out volunteer bus conductor he addressed this to didn't question the 'used to' of Nigel's statement, just nodded in agreement. The conductor looked strangely out of place in his archaic uniform on what was obviously a driver-operated bus. He had the air of a man who had been laid off years ago when this kind of bus came into service and who has travelled around on them ever since in some kind of daze, in memory of better days for both him and the bus industry.

Disembarking at the aerodrome, I was pleased to see that not everyone looked quite as scary as my travelling companions. I did spot one large man with his shirt open to the waist and what appeared to be either far-from-fresh blood or shit stains all down the front of it, but the rest of the crowd was uniformly normal in their Marks & Spencer's garb.

There were about a hundred buses on display on the airfield, but most of the activity seemed to be going on around the stalls, which were selling all kinds of bus memorabilia. I overheard one stallholder telling a customer that he had, sadly, sold out of all his bus driver's shirts already and the Tannoy announced that all this year's 425 limited edition commemorative bus models had sold out as well. The bus nostalgia business seemed to be booming and I witnessed frenzied activity around the photo stalls, with one man climactically crying 'Yes! Yes!' while holding a photograph of a bus that he had obviously been trying to track down.

I didn't quite leap in the air and exclaim, but I did enjoy my own nostalgic frisson when I spotted a cap badge from East Kent buses on sale for a couple of quid. At once an image of the face of the grumpy bus driver who used to insist on checking every single bus pass on my ride home from school popped into my head. He was the most misanthropic man I have ever met and I couldn't help hoping that the badge was the one that they made him turn in after he finally snapped and leaped from his cab to give some snotty thirteen-year-old a good pasting for attempting to travel a slightly different route from that specified on his pass. The stallholder selling the badges was in full busman's uniform and looked a little like something out of a *Carry On* film, or maybe an extra from a low-budget German porn rip-off of *On the Buses*, so that put me off a bit and I moved on.

A few stalls later, I was momentarily back in bus nostalgia heaven as I spied a series of spotters' guides to East Kent buses that went back to the 1980s, when I would have been travelling on them. I did wonder whether they might contain details of some of my back-seat graffiti or my after-school smoking prowess but somehow doubted whether spotters would record such socially interesting information. I picked one up and sure enough they were far more concerned with model numbers and registration plates than with unsubstantiated rumours about heavy petting at the back of the bus and who had been throwing orange peel at pensioners on the trip home. Anyway, seeing all those numbers reminded me why I was there in the first place – to feel what it was like to be a spotter and to strike up some kind of enthusiasm for the buses on view – so I left the traders in old bus tickets, bus stops and driver's caps and strode across to the concrete airstrip where the buses stood.

The first thing I noticed as I reached the display area was the considerable number of men hanging around the gate that separated the rally from the rest of the airfield. They were actually spotting planes in the middle of a bus rally. This threw up all kind of questions, such as what these elite spotters were doing slumming it with the bottom feeders, or vice-versa. Surely planespotting and bus-spotting couldn't mix, could they? As I approached, though, I saw that most of the group had just ambled across to watch some of the planes take off and were not taking down fuselage numbers. Some did have binoculars, but as Tony had pointed out to me on our trip to Waddington, they must be turkeys if they were using binoculars rather than a telescope, so the natural order of things was still intact.

Wandering up and down the double line of parked-up buses, I noticed that there was quite a commotion going on near to what seemed to be the grottiest bus on show – a cream, orange and blue modern double-decker that looked as if it had seen better days. Everyone who came past stopped to take photographs and some of the lone spotters even struck up enthusiastic conversation with others, gesticulating excitedly towards the uninspiring model.

I sidled over to one spotter to ask what all the fuss was about, ill-advisedly opening with: 'I'm not a bus-spotter as such, but . . .'

The spotter looked quizzically at me.

'Well what are you doing here then?' he asked.

I couldn't be sure if he meant 'get off, this is our territory, mate' or 'go, flee; get out now while you can. I only popped in for a look eight years ago and look at me now.' I struggled for an explanation and, as is always best in such situations, opted for a lie.

'Oh, it's just my dad used to work on the buses and I live nearby and thought I would come along for a look.' I said. 'Anyway, why is everyone so excited about this bus in particular?'

Thankfully, my bow to his superior knowledge stopped him from issuing further questions.

'This one is from Dublin,' he said. 'That's why it is a bit of a rarity. We don't often get to see them.' He shuffled away before I could flummox him with questions about the intricate workings of the Irish bus system.

Next to the Dublin bus was another bland modern double-decker, but it grabbed my attention when I overheard two spotters having a heated discussion about whether the paint that had been used on the bus was authentic Stratford blue, or whether it was an inaccurate paint job worthy of scorn from the serious enthusiast. The bit that tells you where the bus is going – the 'blinds' if you are an enthusiast – said that the bus was a rail replacement service.

On the way back from the cricket match at Tallington, I had been reading an interview with Eastfield's Jessi Adams in a punk fanzine I had bought while the bands played. In it he cited the rail replacement bus service as the place where the worlds of trainspotting and bus-spotting collide. The trainspotters suffer like the rest of us as their journey to a locomotive shed is delayed, while the bus-spotters delight in a new route to ride and the chance that a rarely seen bus will be dragged out of semi-retirement to do the job. This does, as Jessi asserted, seem a little disturbed, but then trainspotters are just as guilty of exactly the same thing, as every historic steam excursion is openly cursed by diesel enthusiasts who pray that the 'kettle' will break down and have to be replaced by a Class 37 locomotive or something equally romantic. Perhaps ground-hoppers live in hope that modern football stadia cease functioning and Derby County are temporarily forced to go back to the Baseball Ground or Manchester United to some long built-over municipal park where they once had a kickabout in 18-something-or-other.

Leaving the paint enthusiasts to argue about the exact

correct shade of blue that the bus should have been painted, I headed for a big gang of bright-red Routemasters, the royalty of London transportation, and allowed myself briefly to be caught up in the heroic elegies to their utilitarian functionality that were attached to their side windows. There were stories of buses being in service nineteen hours a day and details of their birth, death and resurrection by enthusiasts, complete with pictures of every stage of their existence. Most of the serious spotters were ignoring these though, as they had seen them all before and were more interested in getting snaps of the variety of buses that had been painted gold in honour of the Queen's Golden Jubilee before they were returned to their more traditional liveries once the celebrations were over.

After grabbing a coffee, which seemed to have been made to 'keeping bus drivers awake' strength, I found myself drawn back to the market area by the thought of the East Kent driver's badge, which was nagging at me. Something was telling me to buy it, even though I was unlikely to attach it to any item of clothing for fear of being seen as some kind of spotting nerd in the real world, away from the rally.

On my way across the market area, I witnessed two men bickering about the picture of a bus in the book that one of them was holding.

'I'm surprised that you don't have that one, John,' said the book holder in a disparaging tone to his companion.

'Oh, *that* one,' his companion replied. 'I didn't recognise her in that livery, I obviously saw her in different colours, long before she had that one.'

This was not so much a heated discussion as a subtle form of playground one-upmanship concerning which of the pair, who were both in their fifties, was the best spotter. A childish argument that could well have been going on since their childhood.

I took this as my sign to leave. After all, if I were to buy the driver's badge, where would that leave me? I certainly didn't want to stumble accidentally into starting a collection, let alone one that might lead me to be in their position in five or ten years' time. So I hopped on the next bus out of there, this time the one servicing imaginary route 304, and went off to enjoy the rest of a pleasant, if a little showery, late summer's afternoon. Taking my seat, I breathed a deep sigh of relief, thankful that I was unencumbered by the need to take down the number of the bus as I boarded it, glance admiringly at the bus conductor's badges or even criticise his pairing of a 1972-issue pair of trousers with a 1981 jacket.

4. SLURPING WITH
THE ENEMY

As far as I know, the Germans never bombed our chippy. They may well have struck the one in Hull where my grandmother used to work, but I'm sure that it was nothing personal, as they seemed intent on flattening most of the town.

For this reason, I was feeling pretty open-minded as I set off to meet a group of historical re-enactors who spend their weekends and holidays dressing up as members of the Luftwaffe and parachuting into various European countries. I was, of course, suspicious that they might be a foaming-at-the-mouth, extreme right-wing splinter group or some kind of decadent fetish club which enjoys goose-stepping across the Continent in rubber thongs, but a phone call to the group's chairman and co-ordinator Andy Clark, or – as he is known to the troops – Oberleutnant Schreiber, had at least partially dissuaded me of the former.

'The Luftwaffe regiment we portray were a non-political,

élite force,' said Andy. 'We are very clear that we are a historical group and have to be careful to discourage anyone with extreme views from joining. Anyone found involved with any of that would be removed immediately.' He sounded very serious and a little tired of having to defend the reputation of the Luftwaffe Historical Group all the time, so I thought that it was best to leave the questions about the thongs to a later date. I should point out, however, that the formation of the Luftwaffe did come about under Hermann Göring during Hitler's rise to power, so it does seem fair to say that those who joined the real thing, élite or not, knew who was buttering their bread and why.

When I rang the National Rail Enquiries line to find out about train times to Bletchley, where Andy's group were taking part in a re-enactment, my illusions about never having to deal with bus-spotters again were cruelly shattered.

'Because of the engineering works you'll have to change at Hemel Hempstead and join a replacement bus service from there to Bletchley,' said the woman on the phone. The place would surely be swarming with be-sandalled, bickering men noting down new numbers in tiny script and whooping with delight before turning to suicidal thoughts.

I had completely forgotten about the ongoing maintenance programme on the West Coast Main Line which meant that any passenger, other than Labour Party members travelling to their conference, would be unceremoniously de-trained (a new verb that I learned on my travels) somewhere north of London and sent by bus to Milton Keynes to join the world of trains once again. Virgin Trains supremo Richard Branson, whose desire to upgrade his fleet was the main reason behind the maintenance, promised that the buses would be 'luxury coaches' and that passengers would be given free drinks to ease their discomfort, but then he had also promised to rid the streets of litter and die horribly in a ballooning accident, neither of which he had come good on.

On alighting at Hemel Hempstead, passengers were split up into two groups – those who were travelling to Milton Keynes and beyond and those, myself included, who were not. The Milton Keynes crowd were pointed to a group of smiling Virgin staff bearing water bottles and dressed in air stewardess-style garb, while the rest of us were shoved in the direction of a gang of surly-looking bus drivers at the far end of the station car park. It was then that I found out that I was not a Virgin customer at all, but the property of Silverlink. If there was something worse than being a Virgin Trains customer, then this was it.

It was no surprise that our 'luxury coach' turned out to be one of those cramped, air-free coaches that you associate with school trips and the smell of vomit mixed with sweaty children and sweatier sandwiches. There was no free drink, but there was carpet on the ceiling, which I guess must be the 'luxury' part. I mean, I bet Branson has carpet on his ceiling. You just would if you were him, wouldn't you?

There had been a few likely bus-spotters among the crowd as I crossed the car park and a good number of them had got on to the same coach as me, but by earwigging on conversations I worked out that most of them were not bus-spotters at all but either on their way to the same re-enactment as me or a computer geek's event that was taking place at the same venue.

I hate travelling by coach at the best of times, but with a hangover, no air and no water it is even more unpleasant than usual. Just writing about it is making me feel slightly nauseous. My stomach wasn't eased by the fact that our driver appeared to be about fourteen years old and had probably learned his driving skills behind the wheel of a hot-wired Sierra. I imagine that this job was part of one of those police rehabilitation programmes. It was possible that he and his fellow reprobates had even built the coach as part of a community service order using bits of old Volvos and some leftovers from *Scrapheap Challenge*. The youthfulness of the driver was doubly vexing as, in addition to making me fear for my safety, it also negated my theory that all coach drivers are born aged fifty and very bitter about the world.

The young, spotty driver certainly seemed to be enjoying the experience of being out on the open road with a cargo of brittle bone and delicate tissue, as he zoomed straight past our first station stop, only bringing the bus to a halt about half a mile later when the passenger who wanted to get off there managed to get the point across to him. Instead of turning back he just let her off at the side of the road on a country lane – less annoying for the driver and us, but fairly inconvenient for the passenger.

When the bus finally arrived at Bletchley station, I stumbled off like a booze-cruiser after a particularly rough Channel crossing. I imagine that my complexion was, by then, that distinctive shade of ivory with a green tinge of someone who is about to hold a very important conversation with God on the big white telephone. Thankfully, I managed to keep my corn flakes down and as I followed the Geeks Reunited crowd up the path to Bletchley Park my stomach began to settle slightly.

Bletchley Park is, of course, famous as the setting of the Kate Winslett film, *Enigma*. Apparently, they also did some code-cracking stuff there during World War II and invented the programmable computer too. At least this is what I was told as I took a tour of the mansion house and the surrounding huts, where Alan Turing and various other oddly wired eccentrics were housed during the war while they crunched numbers, drank tea and, occasionally, went a bit mad. I could fully understand the going mad part, as trying to absorb the information about the billions of possible settings that the German Enigma encryption machines had, and the fact that the messages sent via them had to be decoded from a fresh range of settings each day, had already given me a throbbing headache after just five minutes. I think the coach journey, the alcohol poisoning, the bagpiper we had passed on our tour and the gunfire coming from the re-enactment groups hadn't helped, but at that point the idea of decoding even a bus ticket was enough to make me want to lie down in a darkened room.

With bright sunshine being my only option, however, I bravely strode down the hill, away from the house and towards the gunfire. As I arrived, an English regiment was just about finishing off Jerry. They had cornered the troops of Fallschirmjäger-Regiment 6 – Andy's re-enactors – and were picking them off in a very English, jolly-good-sport kind of way, while a man with the air of a physical training instructor gave a running commentary to a crowd largely consisting of armed forces veterans.

'We wouldn't have wasted ammo like that,' commented one of the veterans, who had a beret and blazer both covered with medals and badges, tut-tutting at the sporadic gunfire before turning to his friend. 'The sergeant would have had our guts.'

Sadly, none of the Germans cried *'Achtung! Gottim Himmel!'*[5] when they were gunned down, as they used to on the pages of *Battle* comic and, invariably, when we played 'war' at school. Just as in this battle, the girls in the playground were only allowed to join in if they were happy tending to the injured. It was generally the less popular kids who ended up playing the Germans.

The skirmish was, apart from the appearance of one rather weighty and obviously pension-drawing German soldier, very realistic. Being largely of the 'I don't fancy having my head blown off' disposition and not one for carrying weighty manual typewriters through war zones, I have never had the

---

[5] My very amateur and very English translation for this, using *Collins German-English Dictionary*, is 'Attention please! Heavens above!', which I think we must all agree is exactly the kind of thing that we would shout upon being shot.

urge to become a war correspondent and witness combat close-up, but the noise and the chaos did seem to portray how frightening such an experience would be.

While the English soldiers buried their dead and tended, again very sportingly, to the German wounded, I took the opportunity to take a walk around the encampments of the various re-enactment groups and the stalls selling all kinds of military memorabilia. In the marketplace you could buy anything from a British army belt for a couple of pounds to a German Luger pistol for £450. There didn't appear to be any weapons of mass destruction on sale, though it was hard to say what kind of 'under the counter' deals might be available if you said that you knew Big Dave.

'Oh, you know Big Dave? Why didn't you say earlier? I've got some very nice uranium on offer at the moment. You should have been in last week, I had a lovely anthrax in. Limited edition, signed, numbered and in a presentation case it was. Beautiful.'

As the event had a special forces theme, there were plenty of men strutting about dressed in a semi-militaristic manner trying to affect an 'I am a human killing machine' look, though often this came off more as 'I have very painful haemorrhoids, please help me.' These are the men who have read every Andy McNab, own several field craft manuals and probably had a big row with their mum when she taped *A Touch of Frost* over their footage of the Iranian embassy siege. Instead of playing air guitar in front of the mirror these men imitate Ray Mears building a shelter out of twigs, ant shit and snake venom that can double as a midnight feast should the need arise.

Some of the members of this ersatz élite had set up their own individual stalls away from the main body of the re-enactors' living history displays, which were located in the shadow of the mansion house. These mostly had the appearance of a re-enactment society of one, where the overweight or under-height wannabe had laid out an array of his favourite weapons, webbing or helmets on a blanket in a show-and-tell fashion. They could, at least in theory, kill a man with a single blow and then make a bridge from his entrails, but it seemed that basic, elementary interaction was beyond most of them.

When I came back round to the Luftwaffe encampment, Andy was addressing his troops in the kind of pseudo-German made famous by the World War II comedy *'Allo, 'Allo!* This was, perhaps, not surprising as he had portrayed a German soldier in the programme that made Herr Flick a household name. To be fair to Andy, though, I think that the En-Ger-lish was more for the benefit of those watching than a necessity due to any inability to speak the language. After all, he had been in charge of the group for thirteen years.

The troops had all come back from the battlefield, the field hospital and their graves (though sadly not as undead flesh-eating zombie super soldiers) and were undergoing a de-briefing and the award of honours for the most outstanding recruits. Among the decorated was the rotund man in a jump-suit who I had seen take a mortar round in the earlier battle. I later discovered that he was actually a genuine former member of the Luftwaffe and had fought in World War II at Monte Cassino. I also discovered that his name was Gerry. Gerry the Jerry. Who said the Germans have no sense of humour?

Once Andy had finished and the troops were dismissed, I clambered over the rope fence and into the Luftwaffe headquarters, where the troops had spent the night camping out under authentic period canvas. The serious re-enactor would not be seen dead in a regular polyester igloo with Day-Glo panels and built-in groundsheet. Groups such as Andy's also tend to spend their weekends dining on authentic food and drink, which explained the foul-tasting coffee that one of his underlings brought us both as we sat down. Though I am not so sure what excused the tub of I Can't Believe It's Not Butter that was sitting on the mess tent table.

It was abundantly clear that Andy was very much in charge of his regiment, with all those present acting as they would if Andy, with his big trousers and diminutive stature, really were their commanding officer, giving due deference to his rank when addressing him. They also came round and offered cake, stew and pieces of asparagus to him as we sat and talked.

'I'm sorry about the coffee,' said Andy, seeing the face I was making as I tried to down some of it. 'It's authentically bad. We do like to get as close as possible to what would really have been eaten at the time, so it's mostly potatoes, cabbage, sausage and black bread – the kind of rations that the troops would have had. You do stop going to the loo after a while though, which is just as well as we are pretty busy.

'The hardship is all part of not being misread. If you are having to camp out and eat this kind of food it makes it more clear that we are not some kind of Nazi group. In a way we are the pantomime bad guys – we have to be there or the Allied troops would have no one to fight. But at the same time we don't want to dishonour either them or German troops by being incompetent or amateur, because that is not how it was. If you ask some of the veterans out there, they will tell you that the Germans were fine soldiers. It tends to be the younger generation who have objections. Most people respond positively, those who don't tend to be ignorant of the fact that what we do is about respect and remembrance.'

I tried another sip of the coffee from my grubby tin cup. It tasted like something brewed from rolling tobacco with the dregs of a can of Dr Pepper added, more for spite than flavour.

Andy regularly interspersed explanations of the history and procedures of the group with yet more reasons why they could not and would not tolerate right-wing extremists in their ranks. My initial reaction to this was to think that no one would really want to get involved in this kind of activity without at least a bit of interest in the politics. But then I remembered Gerry the Jerry who, having lived through Nazism, could probably do without playing at soldiers just to let the Reich live on. And if he did want to then he surely wouldn't be doing so under the tutelage of a thirty-five-year-old business analyst, even if he was sporting those strange balloon-thighed jodhpur-type trousers that Hitler used to wear.

'He actually came up to me at the para veterans' meeting

in Germany that we attend every two years as guests and was taking the piss out of my German accent. But his was a bit odd too, as he had been living in England since the war. We hit it off from there. He has been so useful to the group because he has actually done it for real, so he can say, "No we didn't do it like that, it would have been like this." He's amazing to have around.'

On their encampment, the group had set up a tower from which to practise parachute jumps and demonstrate the technique to the public. I had been surprised when Andy first told me that one of the prerequisites for being allowed into the group was a willingness to leap out of aeroplanes, with five completed jumps being required to become a fully fledged Luftwaffe paratrooper.

A major part of the group's calendar is the two annual jumping expeditions, usually to Holland, where they pile out of an aircraft dressed in full period kit. In the Netherlands they tend to substitute American or Polish uniform for their regular Luftwaffe issue so as not to offend the locals, or the odd farmer who may have an overlooked, but nonetheless operational, anti-aircraft gun in his field.

I had thought that Fallschirmjäger-Regiment 6 may be pariahs in the re-enactment world for their commitment to playing the bad guys, but as I was talking with Andy, re-enactors from various other groups, such as the US Marines, were more than willing to come over and fraternise with the enemy. There were even Wrens and women civilians in flattering 1940s dresses dropping by for a chat and a laugh – the kind of behaviour that could have earned them a tarring and feathering or at least a head-shaving in the past.

When Andy was called away to chat with one of the civilian women, presumably to trade stockings for Allied secrets, I went into the mess tent, where the troops sat 'enjoying' some coffee and bread. The atmosphere was positively jovial inside, which contrasted with Andy's serious dissection of the world of being a re-enactor and trying to explain to all and sundry that you are *not* a Nazi.

The main players inside the mess hall were Alison – a large, cheery woman who was in charge of the group's anti-aircraft gun – and Richter – a slightly camp, skinny man with straw-blonde hair who was dressed in the Luftwaffe's sand-coloured tropical dress, which included voluminous shorts. If there had been a German version of *It Ain't Half Hot Mum* then this is what they would have worn. And I imagine that Richter would have been a character in it.

'I'm mostly here for the leather and the sausage,' he said, giggling suggestively with Alison. 'Oh, and the Joy Division,' he said, pointing to her. For which he received a playful slap.

It was surprising to see women troops in a German fighting unit but, Alison explained, this had become more and more common as the war continued and the leadership was forced to abandon principle in favour of numbers. Women were employed in the Luftwaffe as *Flakhelferinnen*, whose job it was to assist with the use and maintenance of anti-aircraft guns.

'We really want to get our own gun and searchlight,' said

Alison, briefly sounding like the quartermaster of some hard-line guerrilla outfit. 'The one that we have at the moment is on loan, but to buy one would cost about £3,000. But then, I suppose that is what student loans are for.'

Richter was still more ambitious. Obviously aware of the fact that he was part of an air force without any air power, he was keen to get hold of a Messerschmitt 109, the only problem being that they cost upwards of a million pounds to purchase.

'We actually want to make one,' he said, 'I work in vehicle restoration, so I've actually absorbed my hobby into my job. It wouldn't be a flying one but it could move around on the ground with a car engine.'

Even though Richter was clearly very dedicated to his hobby and extremely knowledgeable about the history of the Luftwaffe, it was extremely hard to take him seriously, with his jauntily angled cap and those enormous shorts. His comic potential was not helped by the fact that he was a dead ringer for either Armstrong or Miller from the TV comedy duo. I'm not sure which one is which but Richter, with his golden locks, resembled whichever one that the blonde one is. Oddly enough, another member of the group, another Andy, could have been a convincing stand-in for Jimmy Nail. Maybe it really was them and this is what celebrities do to unwind of a weekend. I can definitely see Geri Halliwell enjoying a role as a malnourished prisoner of war. As long as the gruel was carbohydrate- and gluten-free, that is.

During our conversation I kept wondering what Tony, my

planespotting acquaintance, would make of people dressing as Germans and building their own planes. I imagine that a self-built, non-flying Messerschmitt must be some sort of aviation enthusiast heresy, even without the dressing up in uniforms that Tony had found so disturbing at the airshow we had been to.

One thing that really came across from Alison and Richter was that, despite the fact that their hobby was bordering on the obsessive, they were really enjoying themselves by taking part at every opportunity. Where Tom the planespotter had lamented everything about his sorry lot, these two talked excitedly, going back and forth with recent reminiscences of 'really great' weekends and gentle-natured, jokey squabbles about whether Richter had been 'dead' during one of the private battles that the group take part in each year.

These private battles are, according to Alison, where the real re-enacting goes on, away from the eyes of the public. Various groups co-operate to carry out military exercises complete with the taking and interrogating of prisoners, and the group tries to communicate only in German. Being under attack and having to work guns or just function with the kit and the clothes gives important lessons in what they may have right or wrong. This is especially important to Alison, as there is very little written history of the *Flakhelferinnen*.

As we were talking, one of the other re-enactors ran in shouting something garbled in German, which, at the time, sounded as if it may well have been '*Achtung! Gottim Himmel!*'

Upon hearing this, Alison rushed outside towards the flak

gun, which was set up at the edge of the camp, while Richter and I exited the tent at the other end, just in time to see the same fly-past that I had seen at the airshow – a Lancaster, Hurricane and Spitfire. What the soldier had been shouting about was incoming enemy aircraft, though obviously there was no exchange of gunfire or bombs dropped, as even blank bombs may well hurt when dropped from a great height.

While we were standing outside the tent, I asked Richter what had made him join the group.

'Were you unpopular at school and forced to be the German?' I ventured, hoping that he wouldn't be too offended.

'Not really, though all my family were in the British Army and the RAF and I am the black sheep, I suppose,' he replied. 'But I think it's for the adrenaline rush, like I got just then with that fly-past. I like to be doing something. I can't understand those people who just set up dioramas with dummies wearing uniforms like some of the people here. I mean, that's just weird.'

Alison, on the other hand, came to the Luftwaffe on a long and winding route that started with reading Tolkien and took her through mediaeval costume, eighteenth-century food and eventually lead to her wearing black overalls and polishing an anti-aircraft gun.

'Reading *Lord of the Rings* started me off,' she said. 'That fundamentally changed my life. I joined the Tolkien Society and went from being an elf and having furry legs to becoming an archer and being second best in the country at the longbow through re-enactment. I've just moved on through periods. I am always me though. No matter what period I am in, I am just myself as I would have been then. I never play a part, just think how I would be in that situation. I now have five different period tents at home for living history events. Moving on to this just seemed a logical step as I've always been interested in artillery.'

'And leather and sausage,' interjected Richter.

'Yes, and leather and sausage,' she continued in a mocking monotone, giving Richter a hard stare but then cracking into a laugh.

At this point, Oberleutnant Schreiber came back from fraternising with the enemy women and gave his troops a 'please settle down and stop showing up the unit' kind of a look, but this just came over as another *'Allo 'Allo!* moment. The uniforms of the Luftwaffe may have struck fear into some during World War II, but viewed today they come across as incredibly fey and flamboyant. And it wasn't Andy and Richter's fault. I took a look in some history books and the photographs and illustrations in them made the flying fighting men look like an early prototype of the Village People. If the war had gone on for three or four years longer, they probably would have been dressing like Elton John by the end of it.

By contrast, the women's outfits were just plain, simple black overalls. Like many of the rest of the outfits, these have to be made by the group members from scratch. Details such as buttons and insignia are painstakingly researched and sought out through online traders and the various cottage industries that have sprung up around the re-enactment scene.

The bi-monthly re-enactors' magazine, *Skirmish*, advertises a treasure trove of moth-eaten army greatcoats and Napoleonic bayonets and keeps enthusiasts up to date with who is fighting who and where. Sadly, no one ever seems to try out the kind of battles that I would like to see, such as Romans versus Vikings, Luftwaffe against Roundheads or even mods and rockers. The possibilities are endless. You could even re-enact battles of the future, such as goths versus space aliens.

The previous year I had seen an artist-staged re-enactment of the Battle of Orgreave from the mid-1980s miners' strike, which featured baton-wielding police against rubber brick-throwing miners, but most re-enactment societies stop recreating history at 1945. I imagine that the PlayStation generation may be more likely to be dragged away from their sofas by something a little more modern that they can relate to, so now may well be the time to form the Poll Tax Riot Re-enactment Group or the Brixton Riot Society.

Once Andy had returned to the tent, the troops in question made some attempt to take things more seriously again, but as it was near to packing-up time and Andy had taken to tidying things away in preparation for the taking down of the tents, he didn't seem too bothered about formality.

'So what happened to military discipline?' I asked.

'Well, we do all let our hair down in the evenings as the regiment would have done,' he said. 'We sing a few songs and that. Songs that may have been sung at the time, of course, but nothing about marching into Poland or anything. Just pop songs from the time.

'One of the funny things with discipline is that it is much harder for me to break someone who has actually been in the armed forces in Britain as the drill is so different from what we do. They usually have a lot of trouble with the step of the marching.'

It was actually quite a surpise to me that any quantity of ex-soldiers would want to get involved in re-enactments, never mind a German regiment. But after finding out about Gerry the Jerry joining to more-or-less re-create a job he did in his youth, I suppose nothing should have been too much of a shock. Andy himself had actually been in the RAF and is still a reservist.

'I am a Territorial Army paratrooper,' he said. 'Though I don't really like to talk there about this stuff that I do. Some would get it, but I think some may misunderstand.' He did make it clear that those in authority were fully aware of his hobby and had, fortunately for Andy, raised no objections.

As the event drew to a close, I found myself really not wanting to leave. It had been refreshing to meet Andy, Alison and Richter. I had come with the idea that they could well be secret Nazis but was pleased to find that was not the case – they were just a tad eccentric and there was plenty of room for levity and a touch of campness in the camp. Most of all, though, my lack of desire to depart was linked to the fact that I knew that to do so would mean subjecting myself to the ride back on the bus.

I walked down the lane to the station with a heavy heart and an already turning stomach. I tried to remind myself that it was just a short journey and that people regularly travel from Glasgow to London on similar coaches, but nothing helped. As soon as I stepped aboard the waiting coach, a tide of nausea swept over me and the bile rose and fell constantly as we travelled back to the train and civilisation. Thankfully, I just managed to stave off the desire to vomit copiously. If Branson had been at the station taking part in a 'sorry for any inconvenience' PR stunt I am not so sure that I could have kept it down, and I doubt that I would have tried too hard.

Foxed by the cheery nature of the Luftwaffe Historical Group and their ability to enjoy themselves, I began to wonder if all re-enactors were actually secretly having fun while the rest of us lamented their sad and miserable existence. I suspected that it was the German-ness of the group that allowed them a deal of escapism others could not achieve. The obvious thing to do was to find a very English event and see how it compared.

As luck would have it, I found that just the event was taking place in the far from English-sounding Ashby-de-la-Zouch, combining battle re-enactments and living history encampments with a celebration of the Queen's Golden Jubilee. This seemed a happy coincidence, as so far I had managed to avoid any Jubilee festivities – if you don't count a few bus-spotters gathered round a gold-painted bus with some regal insignia pasted on its side.

Never having been to Ashby before, I decided to take a quick look around the town when I arrived. I was surprised that it was so small and, being a Sunday, everything but a few pubs and a newsagent was closed for the day. For some reason I had expected it to be on the scale of Leicester or Nottingham, but it was essentially a one-street market town that just happened to have a ruined castle – which was where the re-enactment was to take place.

As I approached the castle entrance, I could hear the strains of some Beatles hits being given the brass band treatment and I envisioned a bustling event already in full swing. I kicked myself for lingering over my lunch and quickened my pace.

Reaching the entrance gate by the castle gift shop, I looked out across the grounds and saw, well, no one. It's true that it wasn't the nicest of days, but it wasn't raining and this was supposed to be Ashby's big Jubilee event. All the big names had been advertised: Queen Victoria, Queen Elizabeth I and even Boudicca and the Celtic warriors – which sounded to me a bit like one of those soft-rock/ballady-metal Irish crossover bands you see playing the pub circuit – but no one had come. I hoped that the actual Queen didn't decide to do some kind of impromptu visit to see what was being done in her name by the good subjects of Ashby. She'd probably spend hours asking me 'and what do you do?' and I would have to sustain a huge lie for the whole afternoon.

Once inside the castle grounds, it was clear that there were some people at the event – they had been hidden down the hill – but most of these were re-enactors. As far as a crowd goes, there were about twenty children and a similar number of adults. The size of crowd that a soft-rock/ballady-metal band might play to on the pub circuit.

The whole event had an air of desperation about it. Where I had found the makeshift stalls of the loner-SAS types at Bletchley Park amusing, the same set-ups here – offering Jubilee memorabilia or period jewellery – just seemed sad and forlorn. Stallholders disconsolately tried to catch your eye so they could tell you about their wares, re-enactors wandered around with next to no one to re-enact to and it seemed that several of the day's events had been abandoned due to lack of interest. The planned fancy dress street party went the way of many other street parties that summer, as no one could be bothered to participate.

One man who did seem to be enjoying the day was PC Nathaniel Ringwood, the village policeman, who was running a display of local police history. He had an array of hand-cuffs, batons and guns on show, but his favourite exhibit was hidden beneath a blanket on the ground.

'Go on, take a look,' he said.

'What is it?' I asked.

'Lift the blanket, it won't harm you,' he replied, in the manner of a fairground freak show proprietor.

I gingerly lifted the corner of the blanket, expecting the sizeable lump beneath to be a severed head or something equally horrific.

It was a mantrap. A grisly-looking metal device used for catching poachers, much as a poacher might trap a deer.

'So did the police use these, then?' I asked, shocked.

'Oh no, it was just the landowners. They were outlawed but it was a long time before they actually stopped using them.'

His excitement seemed to betray the fact that this was more of a personal interest than strictly a piece of police history, but I had not heard of a recent rash of unsolved cases of people being caught in traps around Leicestershire, so it was safe to assume he was harmless. Anyway, it helped to pass the time and I was getting the feeling that this was something that I would be in need of at this event.

Walking around the ruins, I bumped into a very convincing Queen Victoria and a pretty good Queen Elizabeth I. They were with another queen, but I couldn't work out who she was supposed to be. The ermine-trimmed gown suggested our current monarch, but the fact was that the ermine was actually more Cruella de Vil than Queen Elizabeth II. She could have been the Norman Queen Mathilda, the only other monarch on the bill, but as I had missed her opening address to her Albini household, I really couldn't tell.

If she were the Norman queen, and I suspect that she wasn't, then I think she really should have been spending more time with her troops, rather than swanning about in a historically inaccurate way with Queen Victoria and her entourage. Mathilda's troops were based at the bottom of the hill situated, rather confusingly for any children attending, next to Boudicca's Iceni tribe. The Iceni, in turn, seemed to be sharing their camp with their natural enemies, the Romans. In fact, when I first went down into the living history camps area, a female Iceni druid was jumping up and down on top of one of the Roman soldiers.

'It's his armour,' she said, affecting that pleading tone that people use when they have been caught doing something they shouldn't. 'It needs a bit of straightening out.' The Iceni version of 'mummy and daddy are just tickling each other', no doubt. The kids seemed to buy it anyway, though I doubt that they would have been able to justify it to their teachers when writing and drawing a 'what I did in my holidays' report. 'And then the lady wearing the car rug was on top of the man in the feathery helmet and the funny skirt. They were both laughing a lot.' It's the kind of thing that keeps educational psychologists and social workers in jobs.

Hopefully, the later battle between Boudicca's army and the Roman soldiers would at least have sorted the sides out for the children. Though seeing the same four Romans rising from the dead to fight again in Colchester, London and St Albans may have raised more questions than it answered. It seemed that the Silures Iron Age Society, who were playing the Iceni, had a shortage of re-enactors who wanted to play the bad-guy Romans. And who could blame them when it almost certainly meant being regularly jumped up and down on by the druid with the booming voice?

Booming druid, who did, indeed, seem to be wearing a car rug thrown over one shoulder, was the narrator of the Iceni historical display. She was, with her theatrical voice and great presence, made for the role. But it did rather confuse matters that the great warrior queen Boudicca was played by a shy and retiring young woman who wouldn't say boo to a goose, never mind to booming druid.

The Norman drill display was far more interactive, as the re-enactors invited children to join them to learn how the Normans became feared warriors. This was great for the more adventurous youngsters, but one girl did object to being shouted at by the soldier in charge of the drill, and ran away crying to her parents. I think he had seen one too many boot camp reality TV shows and concluded that discipline can only be instilled at ear-splitting volume. The other kids didn't seem to mind, though, and he soon had them arranged into an efficient fighting machine that could run as a unit and defend itself from blows from attackers. So I guess he may have been right.

A passing shower made the afternoon drag a little more, so I was glad to see Queen Victoria take to the central arena for the final event of the day. No, it was not the part where the fat lady sings, although I would have liked to have seen a kind of Victoriaoke act, but the presentation of the prizes for best fancy dress costumes. I had been hanging on for that, as I really wanted to witness how they would deal with the fact that no one, re-enactors aside, was actually attired in anything that could be described as fancy dress.

I imagine that the organisers at English Heritage must have envisioned a real 1950s, or even 1970s street-party atmosphere when they organised their Jubilee event. The apathetic response of the locals spoke volumes about the general air of indifference that the Golden Jubilee had engendered. People were generally willing to turn up if they thought they may get a glimpse of a royal, but if it was just celebrating with friends and neighbours then no one could be bothered.

In the end there was a bit of a fudge. The boy's prize went to one of the re-enactor's children and the girl's prize to a youngster who just seemed to have had a couple of Union Jack flags attached to her at some point during the day. If I had known, I would have worn a hat or something. After my tragic defeats in the shin-kicking and the toe wrestling, it would have been nice to win something. There was no prize at all announced for adults. I could have cleaned up.

5. A FÊTE WORSE THAN DEATH

When Margaret Thatcher famously declared that 'there is no such thing as society' it showed that she had been neglecting to attend any village fêtes. If there is one last bastion of Englishness that is still waving a flag and putting out the bunting for society, then it has to be the annual summer fête, with its charitable bent and ability to bring people together in the name of tombolas and marrow-growing competitions. If she had spent more time trying to guess the weight of cakes then perhaps she would not have so badly misjudged the mood of the nation and brought about her own downfall by introducing the poll tax. Things could have been so different. She may not even have gone mad quite so soon.

The fête, be it village, garden, church or parish, is the most English of events. Ostensibly a very normal annual celebration, it is actually a hotbed of eccentricity, unfettered creativity and, perhaps most of all, overblown petty bureaucracy. As far as organisation goes, the average fête has a hidden administration that would make even the most overstaffed of quangos blush. While you are reading this book, someone in a small village in Oxfordshire is reading the minutes of the last meeting of the 'Entertainments Sub-committee (Beat the Goalie)' and drawing up plans for Friday's obstacle race brainstorming session. And in the corner of a Herefordshire whist drive a triumvirate of seventy-eight-year-olds are cooking up a plot to overthrow the refreshments secretary and install a puppet regime that will allow them to cream off any unsold Rich Tea biscuits for themselves.

I knew that I wanted to go to as many fêtes as I could in the summer, but as they are, by their very nature, rural affairs I was faced with the choice between dealing with the vagaries of 'one man and a Mondeo' taxi services or begging a lift. My inability to drive may seem sensible when having a hayfever sneezing fit while being driven up a motorway by a friend, or even noble when conversing with hard-line cycling activists at a party, but it quite literally doesn't get me anywhere.

I decided that Norfolk was probably the county with more fêtes per capita than any other, so that was to be my target area. This ruled out Chris, as I think that the drive would have been a little too far for him, even after our groundbreaking county-crossing trip to Staffordshire. The obvious candidate was my girlfriend, Christina, but she had been in and out of hospital while I had been gallivanting about

England resisting the advances of comely dog-bitten maidens. I didn't know if she would be up to it.

'Does it mean we get to stay in a hotel?' she asked.

'Yes, we would be going to fêtes on Saturday and Sunday, so we'd have to.'

'Okay, I'll do it, as long as I can pick the hotel and you don't talk about box junctions all the way out of London.'

I must admit that I do have a bit of a thing about box junctions. The one piece of driving knowledge that has actually lodged in my brain is that you should not enter these cross-hatched yellow areas before your exit is clear. As this is the only thing on the road I know about, it is also the only transgression I ever notice. I imagine that their inventor spends much of his time sitting at home with his head in his hands muttering 'When will they ever learn?'

To keep box junctions out of my mind, Christina set me the task of finding us a hotel as she drove us both to Norfolk, setting off at 8 a.m. She had provided me with a list and it was my job to call them as we travelled. This seemed like a fine, simple plan, but as I had not arrived home until well after 4 a.m. that morning, its operation was somewhat hampered by my constantly dozing off.

Between naps I tried about a dozen different hotels and B&Bs, but to no avail. Everywhere Christina wanted to go was full. We would have to put ourselves at the mercy of whatever a randomly chosen B&B could give us. Hopefully it wouldn't be some kind of lice.

Our first fête target was the village of Colton, which is

situated in the heart of Norfolk, not too far from Norwich. We had been drawn by the promise of ferret-racing, which conjured up images of straw-chewing locals with string around the bottom of their trousers or hessian smocks and floppy hats. Christina also claimed that there was a good pub in the village, which was an added incentive to visit it.

Thankfully, Colton was relatively easy to find on the plethora of differently scaled maps that Christina had given me to navigate with. Flipping between a large road atlas and one of those Ordnance Survey maps where houses, shops and even household pets are marked can be a little confusing when you are trying to find the correct turning. I still have nightmares about the moment I thought we were driving into the alimentary canal of a Doberman that was marked on the 25:1 scale OS map. Luckily, I was looking at the wrong map and it was actually just a B-road.

As we entered the village, it was a nice surprise to discover that the fête was actually taking place at the pub that Christina had told me about, rather than at a school or village hall. The Ugly Bug's bar was being used to house some of the stalls, while its gardens brimmed with tombolas and other games of chance.

Our first priority after the long drive was to get a drink. This is usually a simple task, but as the pub was combining the fête with a mini beer festival the choice was somewhat harder. I knew that I should probably avoid the Essex Boys with its promise of malt and hops that shine through 'just like the girls' white stilettos!' but there were twenty-seven other beers to choose from. In the end I plumped for a pint of Woodford's Great Eastern, bought Christina a half pint of Moon Dance and went to take a look round the stalls.

On the far side of the pub garden, by the ice-cream seller, a man of about seventy was drawing quite a crowd with a game made from 150 old match boxes piled up in stacks of fifteen and held together by a wooden frame. The idea was that you poked the matchbox drawer with your finger and if there was money inside then you won it. It was twenty pence for three pokes at the boxes but it seemed that no one was winning. Either the old guy had fixed the boxes or the punters were getting the psychology wrong. I handed over my money and proceeded to play.

Poke. Five pence. Poke. Two pence. Poke. Ten pence. A hit every time. I was three pence down but on a roll. I felt the kind of rush that a seasoned casino gambler has when he gets the urge to put his house on evens at the roulette table. Here the options were a little less dramatic so I simply handed over another twenty pence. This time it was poke ten pence, five pence, ten pence. I walked away a total of two pence up. I didn't want to outplay my winning streak but I knew that the matchbox guy was a beaten man. That was enough for me.

While I had been taking far too long making decisions about which matchbox to poke, Christina had wandered off to the pub, where the cake stall was. She returned eating a fairy cake.

'What about me?' I asked.

'Oh, sorry. You were busy,' she replied.

I went over to the pub to check out the cake stall myself, leaving Christina to queue for an ice-cream to wash down her cake.

At the stall there were two middle-aged women doling out the cakes, pastries and fancies and another to take the money. The stall could easily have been run by one of them alone, but I imagine that there was a strict chain of command to be adhered to and protocol to be observed at such an important outlet. Whatever the hierarchy was, it seemed to be having a lot of trouble delivering my cup of coffee. In a far from unpredictable turn of events, the hot water urn had run out, but none of them knew how to refill it. I would have thought that this kind of basic training would have been covered in some kind of government-recognised fête tea lady training scheme, but it was clear that none of the tea ladies in question had attended any such course. I had visions of scalding, screaming and the smell of skin melting onto support hosiery, but luckily a younger woman came along and smoothed things out.

As I went outside an announcement came over the Tannoy.

'One hour has now passed at the Colton village fête. We still have the Punch and Judy show, the doggy gymkhana and the chance to win an Internet television in the grand draw. I hope that you are enjoying yourselves.'

There was no mention of the ferret-racing, which was disappointing, but I assumed it would be one of the many events later on in the day. I resisted the temptation to try to win the Internet television. I am not sure exactly what an Internet television is, but together those two words sounded very much like 'unwanted gift' and suggested a gadget as useful as a refrigerator iron or mobile phone carriage clock.

I found Christina and we sat down together. All around us children were arguing with their parents, mostly about wanting to go home because they were so mind-numbingly bored. These kids looked on jealously as another of their peers was told that he would be sent home if he didn't shut up about wanting his dad to buy him tickets to win the Internet television. It seems that fêtes are entertainment for children organised by those who have no idea what they enjoy. What self-respecting eleven-year-old wants to throw wooden balls at crockery in a damp pub garden when he can play *Plate Smash 3* on his Game Boy?

An elderly couple returned from the bar and sat down opposite us.

'It's magic for the little ones, isn't it?' said the woman to Christina. She was probably one of the organisers. Although perhaps she meant 'magic' in the deathly dull, watching David Blaine standing on top of a pole sense of the word. That must have been it.

I took this as our cue to depart to the Punch and Judy show, which was due to start at any minute. The puppet master (as I am sure he insists on being called) was still preparing as we arrived, giving us ample time to examine his green Robin Reliant three-wheeler, which was parked up next to the deckchair-striped red and white tent that he did the show from.

The show was standard Punch and Judy fare – sausages, mild violence and the policeman turning up to save the day – with a bit of balloon animal making thrown in for good measure. The kids seemed fairly uninterested in the whole affair, even when the balloon animals were being given away. Their indifference was easily matched by the Punch and Judy man himself. I imagine that a lifetime of working with children and saying 'sausages' in a funny voice is a lot to bear. It's fairly surprising that there are so few incidents each year of Punch and Judy men pulling out automatic weapons and gunning down their entire audience.

As the show ended there was another announcement.

'We are now two hours into the Colton village fête and we still have a lot more for you ladies and gentlemen . . .'

There was still no mention of the ferrets.

'I wanna see the fewwets,' said Christina in a mock child crying kind of voice.

'Okay, okay, I'll find out what's going on,' I said.

We wandered over to where the organisers had been making the announcements from. There we found a man who was the personification of a middle-aged English man enjoying the summer. He wore a Union flag plastic bowler hat, a checked 'dress down' shirt, sand-coloured shorts and brown sandals with grey socks. The kind of look that can repel Eurocrats, government ministers and those who want us to measure stuff in kilos at a glance. I imagine that even Trinny and Susannah from BBC2's *What Not To Wear* may have turned and fled if presented with this John Bull in July look. Not even a little something in neutral tones cut on the bias could have saved him from the sartorial depths.

His co-organiser and, I assumed, wife was draped in a full-size Union flag and wore a gold crown with her floral frock and sensible shoes. This gave her the look of an absent-minded grandmother on HRT who had got lost on the way back from the Last Night of the Proms and stumbled into a branch of Burger King to wait for her husband to come and find her.

'So what has happened to the ferrets?' I asked.

'Sorry, the ferrets have cancelled,' said the plastic-bowlered organiser. 'We've got the model helicopter display instead.'

'Oh. Right.'

All that way to see ferret-racing and we had been done. The scrawny creatures were probably racing and nipping the fingers of curious children at another fête, or running up the legs of hapless yokels. They could at least have put some cock-fighting or bear-baiting on in its place. Helicopter display? Have these people no sense of tradition?

With the chance to see ferrets gone, we decided it was time to move on to another fête. We headed out past the strange man with the matchboxes and the picturesque duck pond feeling very conspicuous to be leaving so early.

Once we got back to the car park, it was easy to pick out Christina's rusting seventeen-year-old Honda Accord among the rows of Jeeps and 4x4s. The next destination I had in mind was the Aylmerton Horticultural Show and Fête. If there were giant marrows and slightly risqué vegetables to be seen, then I wanted to get a look.

Once we had got back onto an A-road and had travelled about one mile north of Colton, the heavens opened. I immediately feared for the matchbox man and his finely crafted game of chance. If the rain kept up it would be papier-mâché within minutes. I was also concerned for myself, as I was only wearing a thin, short-sleeved cotton shirt and didn't much fancy wandering around soaked to the skin in search of the kind of deformed tuber that would excite Esther Rantzen. I did have my waterproof cagoule in my bag, but that would mean getting wet while I rummaged about for it in the boot of the car. There is some kind of logic in there somewhere. Just not the very good sort.

The downpour really drove home the Englishness of fêtes. All those planning meetings in draughty church halls, all the committees and coffee morning conflicts – they were all for nothing if you chose the wrong day and everyone got drenched. But every year the fêtes are defiantly planned as outdoor events, even though we probably have more words for being sopping wet after a shower of rain than the Eskimos do for snow.

When we reached Aylmerton it was still pouring with rain. Christina swung the Honda into the car park. This was, essentially, a bog interspersed with stony bumps and it sounded like they were shearing off the exhaust each time we hit one. Neither of us wanted to get out in the rain to see if they actually had inflicted any damage, so we carried on until we found a space.

We sat and stared at each other for a moment.

'Do you really want to go out in this?' Christina asked, hoping that I would say that we should just go and sit by a fire in a village pub instead.

'Well, no, but I think that we should now we are here,' I replied, dashing her hopes of escape.

We got out of the car and tiptoed gingerly across the bog to the road and then crossed to the village hall, where we were rewarded with a vision of misery, human suffering and enough chutney to cause a sticky tidal wave that would engulf most of East Anglia if it were all unleashed at once.

The scene in the garden at the back of the hall looked like a cross between a Sunday league football pitch and a shop selling cheap sofas – a bit of grass, a lot of mud and huge swathes of polythene covering everything in sight. Despite the fact that it was tipping it down, defiant elderly stallholders stayed bravely at their posts – just in case anyone should need a second-hand jigsaw or pot of homemade jam to make their day slightly less miserable. Anyway, being first to call it a day and pack away your white elephant stall would be social suicide. You may as well wave goodbye to getting on the committee next year, even if you were carted away from the fête in an ambulance, suffering from pneumonia. In England it is acceptable to moan endlessly about your lot after the fact, but to complain audibly about discomfort, illness or inedible food in the here and now is tantamount to an admission of being French. We are inordinately proud of the fact that our upper lip is, and always will be, the stiffest that the world has ever seen.

I had no reason to save face and no 'spirit of Dunkirk' reserves to draw upon so I was only too pleased to follow Christina into the sanctuary of the village hall. I had managed to crane my neck and half of my body under her umbrella as we walked round, but one side of me was saturated.

'Wow, look at this,' said Christina, as she picked up what looked like a genetics experiment involving a cabbage and a baby that had gone horribly wrong.

'Put it down,' I half-whispered. 'Those old ladies will probably kill us if they catch you.' They had already started eyeing us with some suspicion outside, but I suppose that may have been because we were the only attendees under the age of sixty. We were also the only ones there who weren't actually stallholders.

The item in question was a head fashioned from a cabbage with cherry tomato eyes, carrot tops for hair and a bean for a mouth. It had been highly commended in the children's 'make a vegetable monster' competition. The winner was a marrow-and-courgette dinosaur-style creation. The creators of these sculptural masterpieces were nowhere to be seen.

Tables were set up around the edge of the small village hall containing onions, cabbages, potatoes and some very desperate-looking raspberries. Sadly there were none of the giant marrows or pornographic carrots that I had been expecting. But then there wasn't really a huge amount of entrants for the horticultural prizes. It seemed that everyone who entered won something, even if the fruit or veg in question looked like the sort of thing that you might find on the road at 5 p.m. after a street market. Some of it did look great, but the art of competition vegetable growing is obviously a dying one.

Within about twenty minutes we had 'done' the Aylmerton fête. There was no sign of the resumption of the promised open air bingo or any other activities, even though the weather looked like clearing up a little, so we decided that we may as well leave and see if we could get the car out of the car park with its underside still intact. As far as we knew, the exhaust could well have been the one thing that was holding the rest of the ageing car together.

We managed to extricate the Honda in one piece and all was going well until we were careering up the road towards Sheringham. Then the rain began to lash down, falling heavier than it had all day. Christina turned the windscreen wipers on but almost immediately the passenger-side wiper flipped over, making it completely ineffectual.

'Can you get out and try to flip it back over?' asked Christina, pulling into a small lay-by next to an old cottage.

'No problem,' I said, getting out into the torrent and feeling the rain go straight through my shirt and onto my skin.

I reached across the bonnet and grasped the wiper with my left hand, gently turning it over so the blade was flush with the windscreen. As I did so the majority of the wiper came off in my hand. I tried jamming it back on, but to no avail. The plastic join was severed.

I got back into the car, holding the piece of wiper in my hand. Christina gave me a look.

Luckily Christina is one of those practical people who carries things like string, spare batteries and plastic spoons around in the car with her at all times, just in case they should come in handy. I think it may be something to do with having been to art school. So within five minutes she had used the string to macramé the wiper back onto its metal arm and we had an almost fully functioning wiper that would take us as far as Sheringham and the nearest car spares shop.

Once we had reached the seaside town, Christina dealt with getting a new wiper while I visited the tourist information office to get a brochure about local B&Bs. Even though tourist information offices are often staffed by the people who charity shops turn down as too scatter-brained or rude, I can never resist visiting them wherever I go, if only to people watch. On this occasion, however, the staff seemed quite sane and even surprisingly helpful to a Dutch family who wanted some information about local cycle routes. Well, they didn't tell them to 'piss off' anyway. At least not while I was in earshot.

I met Christina back at the car and we fell into one of those arguments that isn't really an argument but you both get incredibly wound up by. I was quite happy to stay in Sheringham, which compared to my home town was fairly upmarket, but she wanted to stay somewhere smaller and inland, away from the tacky souvenirs and fudge shops – even though she had developed a recent liking for cheap seaside fudge. She was picking places in Northrepps, Trunch and Happisburgh, but I wanted at least a hint of a sea view. Eventually we decided on a compromise which would see us heading towards her desired stopping off points, but along the coastal road.

The first place we hit that looked as if it would fit both of our bills was Mundesley, a small cliff-top village with a village hall, a pub and not much more. We saw a grim-looking square building offering rooms as we drove into the village but ignored it, hoping to see something more appealing further on. Sure enough we soon came across a house with a 'vacancies' sign outside and decided to give it a go.

An elderly man in slippers came to the door.

'Do you have a double?' I asked.

'Yes, it's at the top of the house,' the landlord replied. 'It's not en-suite, mind.'

'Ah, that's okay. Can we have a look?' I said.

He got the room key and we followed him up the steep stairs. I wasn't sure that he would make it all the way. He did look a little fragile.

'There you go,' he said.

The room was a vision in pink-and-grey polyester frills. The kind of room that ladies of a certain age would lure grateful milkmen into in 1970s sitcoms. The double bed had that over-large look of two singles that had been pushed together and I had a sneaking suspicion that the wardrobe may well have still contained this man's mother's clothes. Perhaps her body as well.

'Okay, thanks. We'll think about it and maybe come back,' I said, neglecting to add the rider that we would only do so if there were no other vacant rooms, bus shelters or shop doorways in the whole of East Anglia.

We got back into the car and drove the short distance to the far end of Mundesley but no one else had any rooms on offer, so we decided to go back and see what was available at the large, austere house we had passed on the way in.

Christina pulled the car onto the forecourt of a run-down petrol station next door to the B&B. We walked back and I rang the bell.

Before long a cheery-looking man in his sixties opened the door. He informed us that he did, indeed, have a vacant double room and invited us to take a look.

'It's £20 each for the night, bed and breakfast,' he said.

As we walked up the stairs behind him the signs were surprisingly good. The whole place seemed clean and unfussy and there was even a telescope set up on the landing so that you could look out to sea. He swung open the door to the room and I half expected my hopes to be dashed by a mass of clashing floral patterns, but it was plain, polyester-free and looked comfortable.

'Great, we'll take it,' I said, looking to Christina to make sure she hadn't spotted a limb hanging out of a wardrobe door or anything. She was actually smiling for the first time since I had bought her a beer when we arrived at our first fête.

The room at Peel House, which used to be the police station, was not exactly the best I have ever stayed in, but it was everything that a B&B should be and that they usually are not. We felt welcome, the bed was comfortable and the en-suite shower worked properly. There were even nice little touches such as the biscuits and sweets alongside the usual tray of tea-making equipment and a hotel-style breakfast menu card that you could fill out to let them know what you wanted to eat in the morning.

With no time to sample the custard creams, we headed off to our third fête of the day in Burgh, Aylsham. I was initially attracted to the Burgh fête because I misread the location in the *Eastern Daily Press* events guide as 'Burgh Asylum', but even after realising my mistake my attention was held by the fact that it was to be held at a church and that various salads would be on offer. My hunch was that it was a posh fête.

As we left the B&B, it started to rain again. We travelled to Burgh via Felmingham, which had a wide selection of flowers and vegetables on sale outside houses, with an honesty box or jam jar next to them for you to drop your money into. It was not something I could see functioning in London, but the idea of being able to buy cakes, apples or potatoes from your neighbours anonymously does seem appealing to me. More appealing than having to do so at a fête in the rain, anyway.

As we parked in the lane near to St Mary's Church, where the fête was taking place, there was a certain something about the greenness of the trees and the shady walk down to the church that told me that I was right about this being an affluent area. My suspicions were confirmed when we were greeted with the cake stall at the entrance to the church. Before us rose a veritable K-2 of cakes, every one screaming 'I was baked in an Aga you know.' It was good to know that those hours between greeting the nanny, lunch and the personal training session with Giles hadn't gone to waste.

Further along, the barbecue was well under way and selling burgers made from local animals whose lineage could be traced back to the court of Henry VIII. There was also a huge array of salads and, of course, lashings of balsamic vinegar for all. Burgh was obviously the kind of place where petitions calling for the provision of a quality ciabatta outlet and the outlawing of instant coffee occupied the majority of parish council time.

In the church grounds there was a scene of dampened misery similar to that at Aylmerton, only here everyone was prepared with Barbour jackets, cagoules and golfing umbrellas. There was the usual array of games outside, including the fête staple of Whack the Rat, which requires you to hit a stuffed sock dropped down a drainpipe before it hits the ground. Who needs television?

Inside the church, the vicar himself was running a tombola of sorts. It was the kind where there is a board full of nails and you pay to pull them out, winning a prize if you pick one with a painted tip. I couldn't help thinking that the vicar could have made the stall far more attractive by using a picture of the crucifixion with nails to pull out placed at strategic points, rather than just a plain white board, but I imagine that may have upset some of the parishioners.

I invested a pound in four nails and drew them out. I had a fifty per cent success rate. I hadn't been paying too much attention to what colour on the end of the nail went with which prize, but it turned out that, along with my pack of fizzy chews, I had won one of the star prizes – a bottle of Chardonnay. The vicar didn't exactly look delighted for me. Maybe he had been reading my thoughts about the crucifixion scene idea. Is having a potentially blasphemous thought a sin when it could actually help church funds?

Back outside, the rain was pouring down again and people were seeking shelter beneath the churchyard's trees. Avoiding them lest there be a biblical bolt of lightning, I tried my hand at throwing darts at tiny envelopes to win a prize, but missed all of them. Meanwhile Christina was sitting in a plastic chair amid the gravestones, chowing down on a burger made from a lamb whose ancestors had been made Duke and Duchess of Cambridgeshire due to some foolish but irreversible seventeenth-century administrative error. Technically speaking, her snack was 267th in line to the throne.

The next morning we awoke with a renewed sense of optimism. The weather didn't look so bad, we had enjoyed a good night's sleep and we had a car boot sale to look forward to. We had spied a banner advertising one as we were driving around Sheringham and from the size of the field it looked as if it would be a big one.

After breakfast we hit the road and travelled to the boot sale, which was marked by a sorry-looking Union flag drooping from a twenty-foot metal pole that was bent at the top. Perhaps Napoleon's jibe about us being a nation of shop-keepers was sort of right, as it seems that we have all tried our hand at selling off our junk on a Sunday morning. We even have a television show that celebrates the fact and books that tell us how to make a living at it. This essentially means that the same crap circulates the country, gaining value as each new vendor allows themselves a wry smile at the four-pence profit they made on that mooing novelty cookie jar or postcard of the Queen's wool suppliers. I'm not complaining though, I love boot sales.

On the third stall from the entrance, I unearthed a minor treasure trove – a plastic bag filled with eleven small naïve portraits from the 1960s and 1970s (they were dated on the back) by an amateur artist who had attempted to capture the spirit of the popular prints of the day. Some were reminis-cent of the kitsch of Vladimir Tretchikoff, famous for his paint-ings of blue-faced ladies and African princesses that now line the walls of retro collector's shops and ironic Hoxton lofts, but these were one-of-a-kind originals and a little twisted to boot. I was particularly fond of the painting to which I gave the title 'Woman Behind Bars with Dove Flying Free'. Perhaps the artist was painting them for his shrink to examine. It cer-tainly had me participating in a moment's amateur psycho-analysis.

'How much for the paintings?' I asked the stallholder, trying to show a casual indifference to actually owning them.

'Two quid.'

There was no indication as to whether this was for the whole bag or for each painting. Some dealers sell any old oil painting for £10 or more, so I was getting a bargain either way. I reached in my pocket and fished out one of those hefty £2 coins that can double as clay pigeon substitutes.

'Here you go, mate,' I said, holding up the bag of paintings and passing over the coin. I waited for the outraged 'That's two quid a piece, guv!' but just received a cheery 'Ta!' Result.

After not finding much else at the boot sale, we took off to Sheringham's seafront, where we sat on some rocks eating chips in the sun and reading the Sunday papers between gusts of wind – a perfect English seaside moment. As we sat we studied our fête options, and decided to go for one big one and avoid all the driving around we had done the day before. Perhaps if we persevered with one whole fête then we would be rewarded with something enjoyable.

One event stuck out like a sore thumb in the local paper – the Lingwood Fun Day. It had to be fun with a name like that, didn't it? The preview promised piano smashing and said that the event was to be opened by the Black Thunder Girls. Neither of us had any idea who they were, but assumed, rightly as it happened, that they were some kind of local micro-celebrities.

We headed off in what we thought was plenty of time to drive south-east to Lingwood, but we had reckoned without that perennial country driving hazard – the tractor-driving farmer, pootling along at five miles per hour with a mile-long tailback behind him. By the time we arrived at the village hall in Lingwood, the Black Thunder Girls had already opened the fête and a troupe of young dancers were springing around the central arena.

Luckily, the Black Thunder Girls had stuck around, which gave me the chance to ascertain that they were the hired glamour for the local pop station, Radio Broadland 102.4 FM. I had been hoping they might be some kind of cheesy local pop outfit but their act seemed to consist entirely of being blonde and wearing black Lycra. Having missed their opening of the fête, it was hard to work out if they had any more strings to their bow.

The first event up after the dancers was a Punch and Judy show. I had been put off by the previous day's rather lacklustre affair but Christina wanted to see it, so we walked across the field at the back of the village hall to where it was taking place. It was far more violent and distressingly free of morals than the one at Colton and my faith in the traditional art form was restored, though we didn't stay for the finale as the dog show had started in the main arena.

Not being a 'dog person' my experience of dog shows is fairly negligible. I can kind of understand why people would want a slobbering, incontinent wolf-descendant as a house pet, but why anyone would want to tell them to 'sit', make them jump through hoops or parade them around a ring is beyond me. If dogs really were man's best friend, they would surely have found a way of telling us how stupid this looks by now.

'Ruff. Ruff. Grrruuff-ruff-ruff.'

'What's that you say, boy? I look like a complete idiot making you stand on a podium and shake paws. You think we're all arseholes? Oh, okay, I'll let the rest of the humans know.'

My worst fears were confirmed when I saw the first event – a race involving dogs running after a ball in relay over four jumps and back again. It wasn't so much the stupidity of the task as the fact that this kind of race is actually seen as a specialist event and even has its own name. It is called flyball. Who the hell thought of that? And, come to think of it, who spends hours every week training their dogs to do this? At least the elderly golden retriever taking part showed his disapproval by walking the course rather than running, despite the crowd's encouragement.

The children in the 'Kids' Obstacle Race' that followed had obviously seen the golden retriever as some kind of folk hero and proceeded to clamber under netting and around slaloms as slowly as was humanly possible. Not even the helping hand of a couple of Black Thunder Girls and the promised prize of a bat and ball attached by a piece of string helped.

After a slightly more enthusiastic display for the adult race (mainly by young men who wanted to impress the Black Thunder Girls) it was time for the event that we had all been waiting for – The Grand Piano Bashing Contest. Actually, this was a bit of a misnomer as none of the pianos were grands, but it was certainly worth watching.

The rules were fairly simple. Each team consisted of three young men and one Black Thunder Girl. The men had to smash their piano with the pair of sledgehammers provided, making sure that the pieces were small enough to fit through a small circle cut out of a large piece of wood leant against a skip. The spare team member and the glamorous assistant would feed the splinters and shrapnel through the hole.

Depending on your viewpoint, giving two trios of eighteen-year-old lads sledgehammers, especially on a warm afternoon in the vicinity of a full bar, is either the most stupid or the most sensible thing that you can do. I went with the latter and delighted in the Laurel and Hardy-style antics of the hapless trio on the side of the arena closest to me. One would lift the hammer to swing and another would suddenly lean down to pull at some wood, right where the blow was about to be delivered. I had already pressed two nines into my mobile phone's keypad as I wanted to be the first to describe the sound of splintering bone to the emergency operator.

Amazingly, five minutes passed without so much as a flattened finger, though not much of the piano had been bashed. The team farthest from our side of the arena seemed far more efficient and had started to feed a healthy amount of dismantled piano into the skip, but the others had just created a lot of dust and a few splinters.

Neither of the Black Thunder Girls were faring particularly well either. Protected by goggles and large gloves the girls looked far from glamorous. Their hair was lank, they were covered in dust and the sweat was pouring down their faces. It wasn't a pretty sight.

After about ten minutes of staring at a still whole piano, the crowd started shouting instructions.

'Knock the sides off, then it'll fall apart,' shouted one spectator.

Even with my D grade 'O' Level knowledge of physics, I was able to work that out. The lads were just bashing wildly, hoping to disintegrate rather than deconstruct the piano.

I was almost beginning to feel sorry for the Black Thunder Girl on our side. She seemed to be doing more work than anyone. While the lads flailed around, rubbed their now sore arm muscles and gesticulated a lot, she was scouring the floor for slivers of wood and running to and from the skip like a thing possessed. Eventually the message got through and the largest of the tragi-comic threesome managed to kick the back off the piano and hammer away the sides. By this point, though, the other team had almost finished. The Black Thunder Girl looked suicidal. As the opposing team finally collected their prize of a crate of beer, she was still desperately picking up splinters. I don't think it is an experience that she will be repeating next year.

With the main event over, Christina and I took the chance to have a good look round the stalls, which, give or take a couple, were all variations on the classic tombola. You could pull out a lollipop, hook a duck, hook a Pokemon character, pop a balloon or simply buy a numbered ticket to win any number of prizes that you would have stepped over if they were laying on the pavement outside your house. The tombola is the place where Brut 33 and Charlie gift sets go to die.

By the time we left I was the proud owner of a pair of vintage, unused St Michael bottle-green bri-nylon socks circa 1972 and Christina had her hands on an embroidered pastoral scene that featured a robin. At least that was two Christmas presents for relations we wouldn't have to worry about.

6. WHERE TH'OFFENCE IS, LET THE GREAT AXE FALL

As far as I am concerned, without Shakespeare there are three great things that England would have missed out on. These are, in no particular order of merit, the phrase 'methinks he doth protest too much'[6] – which modern language has been unable to better, B.A. Robertson's 1980 hit single 'To Be Or Not To Be'[7] and the legendary incident at my school when a man from the travelling theatre group was clearly growing something in his tights during a performance of *Macbeth*. All the rest you can keep. It's just not for me.

I have never had any inclination to visit the 'Shakespeare Country' of Stratford-upon-Avon, but as I was attending a fête

---

[6] The actual Shakespeare quote, from *Hamlet*, is: 'The lady doth protest too much, methinks.'

[7] Sample lyric: 'We are a couplet heaven knows. Undo my doublet baby. And I'll undo your hose.'

in nearby Welford-on-Avon, I decided I really should go along afterwards. Then I wished I hadn't.

Apart from being a fair bit larger, the Welford Fête was almost identical to the last fête I had attended in Lingwood. There were dog shows (where, disturbingly, the organiser kept referring to the dogs' owners as their 'mummies'), tombolas-a-plenty and instead of the Black Thunder Girls there was the Bear from Radio FM102 cutting a lonely figure as he tramped the field in search of someone who knew who he was. There was sun, there was rain and even a mini-tornado that whisked away one of the stalls, but most of the day was a dreary, over-organised array of morris dancers, karate exhibitions and displays by the local fire brigade.

One thing that did impress me was the old-school carnival operator who was running the Win A Goldfish stall, which was one enormous scam. All you had to do was get a dart in two separate pictures, which most eight-year-olds could manage, and you won a fish. Of course, the parents then had to fork out several pounds for a bowl and food so that the fish wouldn't be dead by the next morning. Every way you turned there were small children holding plastic bags containing fish and frowning parents with one hand delving for money in a handbag or trouser pocket.

Upon arriving in Stratford, I was surprised that it was not more like some of the old market towns of the Cotswolds, as I had imagined it, and instead was simply a replica of every other medium-sized town in the rest of England. The odd mock-Tudor beam aside, I could have been in the New Town of Harlow in Essex.

My impression of the town as a centre of English literary history was not helped by the fact that the first sign I saw in the town directed me towards 'Shakespeares birthplace'. You would have thought that the addition of an apostrophe in the correct place wouldn't have broken the bank of the local authority, what with all that tourist money rolling in.

When I reached Shakespeare's birthplace, I was somewhat shocked to see that he had been born in what looked like a 1960s library. By contrast, the nearby library looked like the kind of place in which you might imagine Shakespeare would be born.

As it turned out, the modern façade to the birthplace was just the entrance where you paid to get in. Fortuitously for those running the visitor attraction, this means that if you want to see it, you have to pay the admission charge, which seems a bit much if this really is such a big part of our heritage. However, you can get a sneak preview for free, as I did, by going around the back.

In the birthplace gift shop you could indulge your desire for any number of Shakespeare-related items, such as chocolates, babygros, tea towels or even a set of *Macbeth* finger-puppets. Out in the pedestrianised streets, things didn't get any less crass. Everywhere you looked, from the downmarket to the downright snooty, everything was Shakespeare-themed. You could have ice-cream 'as you like it', eat at the Thespian's Indian restaurant and no doubt get a mean Julius Caesar salad as well.

Even a card in a telephone box for a local call girl promised 'A Midsummer Night's Dream'. Another featured a picture of a Miss Whiplash type promising 'The Taming of the Shrew'. Well, that's what I heard, anyway.

After taking in the town centre, including an unexpected diversion via a fake sixteenth-century archway to an empty shopping mall, I was in need of a drink. I tried The White Swan first, but was greeted with a strong smell of rotten eggs as I walked through the door so decided to go somewhere else. I headed down towards the Avon and, against my better judgement, entered an obviously Shakespeare-themed pub called The Encore.

Now, given the right treatment, The Encore could have been an averagely nice pub, but the addition of fake beams, wood-effect radiators and large posters advertising 'buy one get one free' offers on Smirnoff Ice and Bacardi Breezers (if they really had thought it out they could have re-named them Bac-Bard-i Breezers) made it a miserable experience. The beer was fine, though, and it did at least give me a chance to catch up on the local news in the *Stratford-upon-Avon Herald*, which, of course, carried a quote from Shakespeare beneath its name.

The newspaper featured an article by genealogist Roy Stockdill, who attempted to dispel some of the myths about Shakespeare, including the 'fact' of the Bard's birth on 23 April 1564 – of which, he said, there is no proof. Instead he put this down to wishful thinking by historians who felt that our most famous writer should be born on St George's Day.

Stockdill also cast doubt upon whether the grain-dealing Shakespeare of which there are some local records at that time was the same man who wrote plays to great acclaim in London. Which would, as one correspondent to the newspaper's letters page pointed out, leave the town with little to distinguish itself from any other fourth-rate market town. A Weston-super-Mare without the sea.

Outside the pub, the river featured an array of brightly coloured narrowboats that had been converted into ice-cream parlours, restaurants and even an art gallery. On the surface that seemed pleasant, but underneath it betrayed what Stratford is all about – separating you from your money. The addition of the obligatory fire juggler and one of those infuriating people who pretend to be statues added to the feeling that the whole town was a vile mix of Covent Garden's mercenary appreciation of the arts and the inauthenticty of the Las Vegas 'Venetian' canals. They may as well have done with it and re-name the place The Shakeyland Theme Park and Food Court.

One thing that was authentic was my welcome at the Georgetown restaurant. The Malaysian eatery prided itself on its colonial style and I must say that if I were eating at a restaurant where my country had just installed itself as leader of the indigenous population, then the level of service I received that evening was exactly what I would expect. I was largely ignored by the waiting staff, my meal arrived with several promised ingredients missing and I had to pay well over the odds for the pleasure. It was almost perfect in its execution. My only complaint was that no one spat on my starter. Now that would have been true authenticity.

*   *   *

On my way back from Stratford, it occurred to me that it could afford to be phoney, overpriced and unwelcoming simply because it was on the established tourist route for American, Japanese and European tourists alike. Stratford, along with Oxford, Cambridge and Bath, has a historic gimmick, which means that every package fortnight includes a trip to Bardtown. Arrive at lunchtime, see the sights, catch a show, have a meal and then off to a hotel before moving west to Bath or south to Oxford. A lazy, predictable and most unsatisfactory way to see our country. A bit like an English tourist visiting Disneyland and New York and then claiming to have 'done' America.

It's little wonder that American television still portrays us as living in one never-ending period drama, full of butlers and maidservants with BBC accents, when all they see as visitors are bookish middle-class towns and the West End of London.

I wracked my brains for somewhere more authentic that could dislodge the disappointments of Stratford from the tourist map, somewhere foreign visitors were missing out on and from which their tour buses and loud shorts were absent. Suddenly it came to me. Blackpool. Of course, it is so different from the likes of Bath that it should be there for contrast, to complete the picture of England that visitors get. And, let's face it, if they do still insist on paying homage to Shakespeare then they could always miss out either Oxford or Cambridge. It isn't as if you need to visit both.

Then north-westward ho!

I had visited Blackpool twice before, the last time about

eight years previously, and have always had something of a soft spot for it, if only because I see it as the big brother of my own place of birth. In Margate we had a vaguely glistering 200 yards; in Blackpool they have the full Golden Mile of amusements and seven of sand.

Travelling to Blackpool from the south, you are, more often than not, required to change trains at Preston. This makes the station like some kind of border crossing to the north-west coast and gives you a great chance to check out who else is travelling to Blackpool with you. In the past it would largely have been families with rosy cheeks, accessorised with buckets and spades. Nowadays your travelling companions are far more likely to be elderly women or loud, half-cut stag and hen weekenders who have been drinking since Euston station and are far more interested in hitting the clubs than the beach. The town somehow manages to maintain an uneasy alliance between these two groups, though, with plenty of entertainment laid on for both, as well as some that other tourists can enjoy too.

Alighting at Blackpool, I made my way through the town to the tourist information centre, which is around where you catch your first glimpse of the sea. I picked up a tourist map and made my way south towards Charnley Road, which I had been told was a good source of cheap B&Bs. What I had not remembered from my previous two trips to the town is that the whole place is a good source of cheap B&Bs. You can easily get a room with breakfast for £12 a night and as little as £45 for a week.

But a cheap room was not my only reason for wanting to stay in Charnley Road. I had a 2 a.m. appointment at one of the other B&Bs in the street and thought I may as well stay close by.

The meeting in question was to be at The Lismaine Hotel, which caters solely for stag and hen parties. It is part of a burgeoning empire run by two brothers, and one of them, Rob Hatch, had agreed to let me come over and meet his customers after the clubs chucked them out. I assumed that Rob was completely insane to want to do that for a living, but figured it would be good to find out just how mad he actually was.

I had looked up the names of some B&Bs in Charnley Road and had set my heart on either the exotic sounding Bali Hi or the King's Cross, which had the seediest sounding name – sharing it as it does with the area of central London most associated with crack cocaine and prostitution. As it happened, the Bali Hi was full and the King's Cross seemed to think that I was too seedy to stay in their hotel. Their vacancy sign was up, but when I enquired they told me that there were no rooms left.

I picked another B&B at random and rang the bell. I was greeted by a woman in her late fifties who looked every bit as if she had been a model in the swinging '60s. She still had the looks there somewhere, but the garish carpet and wall-paper that clashed with her leopard-skin outfit weren't all that kind, especially under fluorescent strip lighting.

Thankfully she had a room and showed me upstairs. It was £23 a night, but it did have a small en-suite bathroom, so I took it. It was fairly standard B&B fare, with ill-fitting floral curtains, an overly large chest of drawers and a dripping tap.

Once I had settled my bill ('in full, in advance, if you wouldn't mind') I made a cup of tea and sat back on the bed. It felt a little odd. I lifted up the bedclothes and sure enough the mattress had been encased in a plastic protective coating. At first this seemed a neat and hygienic solution, but when I was tossing and turning later that night, swimming in my own sweat, I would be forced to reconsider that opinion.

As is usual for me when entering any hotel room, I had a good root around in the wardrobe and drawers to see if there were any remaining signs of previous visitors. On most trips all I turn up is a Gideon's Bible and a half-finished packet of Murray Mints, but this time I struck gold. Where the Gideon's should have been there was a copy of *Readers' Wives*. It was not clear whether this had been provided by a management that knows its customers, some new initiative by this Gideon guy to make himself more popular or was simply a low-tech porn equivalent of the music sharing software Napster, but I had a quick look through, just in case the wives of any of my friends were in there. It would be awful to miss out and not be able to compliment your pal on his shapely wife, their new Ikea sofa and the enterprising use of those candlesticks that you bought them from their wedding list.

Blackpool, like all English seaside resorts, has been going through a strange period of late. With the advent of cheap package holidays and budget airlines, visitor numbers have been plummeting since the 1980s. Despite being voted the third worst place to visit in Britain by a phone-in poll on Radio 4's *Today* programme,[8] Blackpool still attracts around eleven million tourists a year,[9] but most of these are daytrippers or weekenders rather than those enjoying the traditional family week or fortnight, taking in the shows, the piers and the Pleasure Beach. All the big talk in the weeks preceding my visit was of regeneration through changes in the gambling laws and the introduction of casino-hotels echoing those of Las Vegas and Atlantic City in the US.

To me, this seemed to miss the point entirely. Blackpool already is the Las Vegas and Atlantic City of England. You can throw New Orleans in there too. The gambling may be in the shape of two-penny falls and ten-pence slots, but it is the taking part, not the winning that counts – good value, grin-on-the-face working-class entertainment. The promise of being able to be someone you are not, of casual sex and cheap liquor is already there, as are the strip clubs and lap-dancing clubs. And what about the majestic trams that glide along the seafront, disgorging revellers along the way? Better by far than the motorised gondolas of the Vegas Venice.

If these mega-casinos were to work they would need a huge influx of well-to-do punters willing to stump up for the five-star hotels and a place at the roulette wheel and I really can't see that happening. Well, maybe if the Americans cross Stratford off from their tour schedule and fall for the charms

---

[8] The M25 and the Millennium Dome were first and second worst respectively.

[9] Figures: Blackpool Tourism, 1999.

of Blackpool. But even then I can't quite see it. Anyway, it just wouldn't be the same if high-rollers replaced those in 'Kiss Me Quick' hats.

I decided to try out some of the amusement arcades, just to make sure that I wasn't looking through rose-tinted spectacles at their charms, and headed towards the sea from my hotel. I was greeted with a huge selection, with names like Slots of Fun and Coral Island, and wandered up and down the front for a good hour trying out slot machines, ten-penny bowling, grab machines and roll-a-two-pence-piece games that screamed 'Oh so close!' when you didn't win. I really don't think raising the stakes or the prizes would have made a big difference to the fun factor. I felt quite happy throwing away three quid with, eventually, no return. I don't think I would feel the same about £300 lost at a blackjack table.

The gambling had given me an appetite, so I left the arcades in search of something to eat. Food is not Blackpool's strongest point. Drink? Yes, in every possible flavour, from lager and lime to toffee-flavoured alcopops. But food comes largely in one variety – deep-fried. It may send Californians running, but I am sure that the rest of America would be just fine with that for a few days. It certainly seems that the Scots are. They still travel to Blackpool in abundance and there is an annual Scots week and a good smattering of pubs displaying the blue and white flag of St Andrew. Even when they are not in town, they are there in the spirit of those who choose to buy the street traders' tartan caps replete with a tuft of red hair sticking out the back.

I picked a chip shop, ordered chips with mushy peas and strolled along the promenade eating the steaming pile of fat-sodden Dalek food, watching the steady build-up of Friday night drinkers, feckless youths smoking fags and the arrival on the scene of stags and hens.

In most of London it is a rare, head-turning sight to witness a gaggle of young women headed by a woman in a veil and L-plates or a group of lads wearing identical T-shirts with suggestive squad numbers and even more suggestive names printed on the back, but in Blackpool this is the norm. If there is one place to have that one last drunken binge, regretted fling or lost weekend, then Blackpool has to be it. All sin committed under the light of Blackpool Tower is not really sin at all. 'I know it was wrong, love, but it was Blackpool.' Can there be a better excuse?

Throughout the night, I flitted between pubs, bars and karaoke joints, witnessing Blackpool in full rage. In every one it felt like that perfect drink-sodden moment right before last orders was called – people were singing, chatting non-stop, laughing and throwing their heads back – even when it was only 8.30. I had come expecting bar brawls, arguments over spilt pints and exactly who was looking at whose 'bird'. But everything was surprisingly good-natured in this Sodom-lite. True, I saw a couple of men walking down the prom with bloody noses, but there was far less of a feeling of impending fisticuffs than there had been at Stonehenge. There was some antagonism between stags and hens from time to time, but most of that was just banter. There was a lot of leering and leching from the guys, but none of the mob behaviour went beyond that, apart from the one moment when a woman dressed as Wonderwoman lifted her top and shouted 'Come and get 'em!' pointing to her ample bosom. The gang of passing stags came and got 'em without needing to be asked twice.

All night long, stags and hens circled each other in packs. Mobs of twenty-five-year-old women, all dressed as Lara Croft, flamenco dancers or schoolgirls, paraded up and down in search of a similarly sized group of men dressed as soldiers, pirates or wearing those squad-numbered T-shirts. I was running through David Attenborough commentaries in my head as the wildlife locked horns, chose mates and went off behind the arcades for a quick one.

For those who haven't found themselves in a clinch by the time the pubs close, there are always the nightclubs, of which Blackpool has plenty, or the strip clubs, of which ditto. I am no great fan of nightclubs, so avoided The Palace and Jellies in favour of the (at least physically) faithful groom-to-be's option and headed down the stairs of Sinless.

I paid my £5 entrance fee, bought a bottle of Beck's for a further £3 and found myself a dark corner to sit and watch the action from. As a short blonde with artificial breasts that were almost the size of her head span around a pole, you could almost have heard a pin drop in the club. It was hardly what you would call empty, with about ten groups of four and a couple of groups of eight or more seated watching the spectacle, but these men in unfamiliar territory didn't seem to know quite how to react. The women ruled this space and the stags were well and truly tamed. When faced with scantily clad women on the street they had been all mouth, but when it was all out on show under the spotlights they were as meek as lambs.

Unlike in the sawdust-strewn strip clubs of East London and the mill towns of the north of England, no pint pot was passed round before the girls deigned to take their clothes off and there were signs pointing out that the dancers were not allowed to accept tips. This meant that they had to hustle private dances at a fiver a throw. These involved no physical contact, simply a lot a thrashing around topless on the chair next to you. For another £10 you could buy a video of the occasion to share with family and friends. Or not, as the case may be.

As I was the only one at the club on his own, every girl made a beeline for me as she worked the room. Each time they came by I made my excuses and stayed.

One, a slender six-footer – at least she was in her heels – whose breasts appeared to be all her own, came over and sat with me for a while. She tried to sell me a dance, but when I politely declined she stayed anyway. I expect it was a relief to get off the heels for a minute.

'So why are you here all alone?' she asked.

I reached for my trusty mental book of lies and spat one out.

'I'm visiting my grandmother who lives in Blackpool and I didn't think that she would want to come with me,' I fibbed.

'I guess not,' she agreed.

We chatted a while about her university course and her home life, but before long she was back up on her feet and selling a dance to a man who came by to purchase one for an unsuspecting friend.

'That's the one,' he said, pointing to a man in a rugby shirt with the number sixty-nine on the back, who was slumped on the shoulder of another friend.

I looked at my watch. It was almost two in the morning and time for my meeting with Rob at his hotel. I downed the last of the beer from my bottle and found my way out of Sinless and on to the street.

As I emerged from the subterranean strip joint, something very strange happened. The streets were, once again, filling up as people left the clubs and made their way back to their homes or hotels, clutching giant burgers, bottles of beer or bags of chips. But there seemed to be a mantra in the air.

'Knocking shop, knocking shop, knocking shop.'

As I walked towards the Lismaine Hotel, these seemed to be the only words on anyone's lips.

I heard it as I passed shop doorways, I heard a bouncer say it as I walked by a strip club that was just kicking out and I heard it from the mouths of a gang of lads outside the Tower Ballroom. It was like a ridiculous opening sequence to a musical.

'Knocking shop, knocking shop, knocking shop.'

For most stags and their parties, this part of the night was the do or die moment before the wedding festivities a week or so down the line. Should they try to get a snog off that woman from an equally rowdy hen party or should they stand by their mates and head for a kebab and then back to the B&B, where the bar may still be open? The stag to hen ratio was at least two to one, maybe three to one, so the chances of all of them being able to attempt to sneak a conquest back to their plastic-covered single bed was pretty slim, anyway.

So for most lusty young men hyped up by drink, pills or an evening at the strip club, the cheap seaside brothel became the Holy Grail. One last fling before the wedding, even if you are not the one getting married. Legends were being exchanged outside amusement arcades. Someone thought that it may be somewhere near the Pleasure Beach, another reckoned it was near the Tower, or even underneath – 'it goes as far down as it goes up, you know'.

'Knocking shop, knocking shop, knocking shop.'

I saw one man staggering down the street trying to text with his right hand while using the largest burger I have ever seen in his left hand as a kind of counter-balance to ensure he stayed upright. I couldn't be sure, but as he passed me it looked as if the LCD screen on his phone really did read 'nokin shp'.

As I arrived at the Lismaine and was greeted by its owner, Rob, I heard the now familiar refrain from the stag party that was gathered in the bar. One of the lads had just returned after spying what he swore was a knocking shop on his way back from the chippy. He was greeted by his fellow stags like a warrior returning from battle. Back-slaps and hearty cheers all round.

'Are you sure? A knocking shop?' said Groom-to-be.

Warrior replied in the affirmative, citing his extensive travels in the building trade as the mark of a man who is able to spot a brothel when he sees one.

'A knocking shop?' Groom-to-be asked again. It was hard to ascertain whether this was sheer incredulity on his part or whether he had forgotten that he had already posed the question. In the age-old tradition of the stag, he was hammered; he had already tried to buy Rob a drink three times in the last ten minutes. Rob just declined politely. After all, this probably happens to him every Friday night.

'I'll go and take a look,' said Warrior, as if some doubt had set in about exactly what it was that he saw back there. Could it have been a mirage?

Warrior was one of those annoying people who can drink more beer in one night than most of us can drink in a month and still give an outward appearance of soberness. Not so much as a slurred word passed his lips and he looked as fresh as a daisy, even after seven hours of drinking.

He bounded off through the door and was back five minutes later confirming that what he spied above a row of shops nearby was indeed a knocking shop.

This confirmation was the stag party equivalent of the second key being turned at the White House in order to launch a nuclear attack. There was to be no going back from that point. Pool players stopped mid-stroke, cigarettes were extinguished and the troops rallied, ready to receive orders.

Groom-to-be was first to raise doubts about the necessity

of the mission. It was hard to work out what exactly it was that he said, but he did attempt some kind of international sign language for 'we have all we could ever need here', spinning round and pointing at the bar and the pool table as he went. There was also the small matter of his future father-in-law, who was due back any moment and probably wouldn't approve of the man his daughter was about to marry nipping off for a quick frolic with a prostitute.

Luckily for Groom-to-be, he was saved by the bell. Some more of the party returned and couldn't find their keys. Warrior went to the door to let them in and returned looking crestfallen. It seemed that the returning group had checked out the alleged knocking shop earlier and discovered that it was nothing of the sort. Groom-to-be looked rather pleased that he wouldn't have to slur his way out of participation.

To celebrate he yet again asked Rob if he would like a drink.

I was impressed at the inner calm that Rob displayed. At least it looked like an inner calm. It could well have been the clenching of teeth and internal organs that would see him dead from an ulcer in the next five years. I suspect that it was the former, however, as Rob actually chose to earn a living this way. He should offer week-long stints behind his bar to any local Buddhist monks who are having problems with attaining humility and inner peace. Hardly anyone noticed as he swiftly and silently put a bar towel under the head of one of the older members of the party, who was fast asleep and snoring loudly. Each time the man drew breath his head moved back and whacked against the hard, wooden back of the banquette where he was sitting. Rob's good-natured act of babysitting ensured that he wouldn't awake with inexplicable bruising and neck pain to add to his hangover.

With the excitement about the knocking shop over and the stag party one by one falling into a boozy sleep, I decided that it was time to make my move the hundred yards or so from my seat to my hotel. Of course, there was one stag who suddenly wanted me to be his new best mate and stay drinking until dawn, but I managed to shake him off and head for bed. I thanked Rob for letting me witness how he made his living and pulled the door shut behind me, glad that I wasn't him.

Back at my B&B, all was peaceful. Everyone was sound asleep. It could have been a serene guesthouse anywhere in the country. Only the inflatable toy stag's head that I had to step over to get to my room betrayed the fact that this was very much a Blackpool hotel.

After the previous night's drinking and my fitful sweat-drenched sleep – thanks to the plastic-coated mattress and the thin walls that allowed my neighbour's snores to permeate into my room – I didn't feel up to much in the way of breakfast but decided that some toast and black coffee was in order.

The breakfast room resembled a scene from an as yet unmade zombie film – *Repast of the Living Dead*. Between mouthfuls of Frosties, grey-faced men held their heads in their hands and emitted low moans, while others tucked into full Englishes, wearing shirts with stains of many colours and dubious origins down the front. The hook-nosed waitress brought me my coffee. I let it stand for a while and then poured it from the pot. It was roughly the same colour as my urine. I wasn't sure which to be more concerned about.

I left before the toast arrived, deciding that this was not the best place to be eating anything. Returning to my room, I took a shower that fluctuated between kettle-hot and ice-cold, but it did start to bring me back to something resembling life. At least it did until the hook-nosed waitress, now in the guise of chambermaid, walked in on me as I was drying off.

In my mission to prove Blackpool more tourist-worthy than Stratford, I had decided to spend Saturday as any average tourist would, so I started the day by nosing around the town centre and checking out the famous Blackpool Tower. Shops and tower done, I headed back to the seafront for a walk from one end to the other and to take in the Pleasure Beach.

Before setting off, I found myself drawn back into the amusement arcades for another fifty pence-worth of the 'oh so close' roll-a-two-pence game, as well as a swift set of Virtua Tennis in which my video game Tim Henman was soundly thrashed by a man in orange who sported a David Seamanesque ponytail.

By midday the pubs were already buzzing, as everyone desperately tried to cram in enough hair of the dog booze to steady their hand and wash down their greasy breakfasts. Some of the pubs were serving all-day breakfasts for those who were careless enough to lose theirs earlier that morning or as a reaction to the first vodka-Red Bull of the day.

At one hen party-filled pub not far from the Central Pier, a fire engine had pulled up outside and the fire crew were unloading equipment before entering. The men looked genuinely concerned for their safety and waited until enough of them were ready before going inside to check out whatever it was they had been called for. None of them wanted to risk it alone.

Their appearance inside the pub was announced by an erupting roar of women screaming 'Geremoff!' and 'Phwoar!' which was loud enough to be heard as far away as the top of the Blackpool Tower. The world of Blackpool is so topsy-turvy that seeing a group of fireman doesn't signal 'Fire, danger, must escape!' but 'Great, here come the strippers!'

As a draw for tourists, nothing comes close to Blackpool's Pleasure Beach. In 2001 it was the most popular attraction in the UK with six-and-a-half million visitors,[10] outdoing the British Museum and the National Gallery by over one-and-a-half million. Despite the damning verdict by *Today* programme listeners, they are still packing them in. My only question was why, when the town has eleven million visitors a year, do less than two-thirds of them make it to the Pleasure Beach? Just then a man answered my question by throwing up in a bin about six feet from where I was standing. He then swilled out his mouth with a swig of beer and went on his way.

Of course. Some people are far too drunk to find their way, or to get past security if they do. That must be at least four-and-a-half million. Problem solved.

---

[10] Figures: English Tourism Council.

Because of its relative sobriety, the Pleasure Beach had a different atmosphere to the seafront. There were far more families, couples, young teens and even some of Blackpool's older visitors – no doubt wistfully remembering what they got up to in the ghost train with that girl from the cake shop all those years ago. These days the Pleasure Beach is far closer to the theme parks of Alton Towers and Thorpe Park than the fairgrounds of old, with their sweet scent of diesel and slightly scary ride operators. But despite the fact that your ride is now likely to be computer-controlled by a spotty McJobber, the free admission policy (you buy tickets or wristbands to ride) and the sheer concentration of rides and amusements does still allow for atmosphere where the theme parks have only sanitised, officially sanctioned 'fun'.

My main aim in visiting the Pleasure Beach was to ride The Big One, the giant roller-coaster that takes you up to 205 feet and then hurls you downhill at seventy miles per hour into a maelstrom of bends, dips and near decapitation. It had not been completed on my last visit and I always exploit any chance I get to ride a new 'coaster.

I bought a book of tickets from a kiosk and joined the queue for the ride, which snaked through a length of fences and barriers leading up to the point of no return, where the only way out was up. The queue included fathers and daughters, groups of teenage friends in tracksuits and a sprinkling of L-plated brides-to-be, though hardly any stag parties. But since I guess that they make up the majority of the lost millions, that should have come as no surprise.

After fifteen or twenty minutes, I reached the top of the queue and was corralled into position, standing with just one person between the track and myself. A minute later the 'train' pulled in and we both got on, to be locked into place with various belts and buckles.

The ride to the top was very misleading. Just as it seemed you were slowing down for the descent, the carriages climbed a little higher. 'Surely this must be it,' I thought a little further up, but no, there was still more climbing to be done. Once we had reached the top, the view was spectacular. I could see right across the Pleasure Beach, the seafront and the sands.

Then came the drop.

I have been riding roller-coasters since the age of nine and this was by far the scariest, bumpiest, most bruising ride I have ever been on. I learned then why people scream on roller-coasters. It was terrifying. The sheer speed, the pressure of the 3.5 G-force and the creeping suspicion that I could fall out (although in reality there was no danger of it) combined to give me the feeling that I was in threat of imminent death. It was great. No it wasn't. Yes it was. And then it was all over.

Walking down the ramps and away from the ride, I was suddenly struck by the desire to go on it again straight away, but on reflection this may have been a dying cry for help from the brain cells that had become dislodged as my head was shaken like an oversized backside in a rap video.

After sitting for a while and regaining roughly ninety-seven per cent of my senses, I started off around the amusement park with my brain still feeling as if it were rattling around in my skull. I foolishly decided to go on the old wooden rollercoaster. After the sheer scale of The Big One it looked fairly tame, but my disconnected brain didn't seem to think so, simultaneously crying out in pain and telling me what an idiot I was every time the carriage sped down a hill or took a sharp bend.

Eventually I felt stable enough to leave the Pleasure Beach and make it back to my B&B. I headed for the tram stop and jumped on the next tram behind a group of a dozen lads. The conductor came up to the top deck and counted the group.

'Eleven, twelve, thirteen . . . that's £13, please.'

One of the men dug in his pocket and pulled out a £10 note, another fished around and handed the conductor the balance. I really should have thanked them for paying my fare. The conductor had just assumed that I was with them and they were drunk enough by that point not to know how many of them there were.

As such a big part of going to Stratford is taking in a show by the Royal Shakespeare Company, I decided that I had to catch one of Blackpool's famous end-of-pier shows to see if they could compete. I was in luck, as appearing at the (more end of the high street than end of the pier) Grand Theatre were the John Gielgud and Laurence Olivier of light entertainment – Tommy Cannon and Bobby Ball. Pop comic act The Barron Knights were also on the bill, which sealed it for me.

The first record I ever purchased was their *Live in Trouble* LP in 1980, which featured a version of David Bowie's 'Space Oddity' as if sung by two cats. I did buy a Specials single shortly afterwards, which would have sounded much cooler during those 'what was your first record?' conversations. Instead I spent my birthday present money on a novelty record by a bunch of forty-year-olds. Damn.

The Grand Theatre certainly was, well, grand. The nineteenth-century theatre retains nearly all of its original features and recent renovation work meant that the chandeliers, painted ceiling and balconies were all shining as if new. It certainly put me in the mood to be entertained.

Watching the show was a bit like stepping back into a more innocent era. As The Brian Rogers Dancers did song and dance routines, I was transported back to the time of *Seaside Special* on television, Bruce Forsyth's *Generation Game* and all the other programmes I used to switch channels to escape as soon as I saw the titles come up. I have to say that the routines were good, though. I was drawn in. I sat back, kicked my programme under the chair and set about enjoying myself. 'Get Happy' they sang. So I did.

Just to assure some of the more confused members of the largely grey-haired audience that they were in the right place, Cannon and Ball came out early in act one to say hello and do a couple of short sketches. The crowd loved them. I knew that some of the material was older than me, but even I allowed myself a little chuckle. Though I think I may have laughed at the wrong bit when they were driving home their opinion that the reason they are no longer on TV is because they aren't cooks. I had read an interview with another ageing comic using exactly the same line. It sounded less like a part of the comedy and more a desperate plea to any commissioning editors from ITV, should they be in the house.

Before The Barron Knights could take the stage, something terrible happened. It was Danny Adams, an exuberantly youthful Lee Evans wannabe with unfunny comedy hair and a wacky sensibility. I made a note on my pad: 'Call solicitor, find out EXACT definition of justifiable homicide.' I was pretty sure I might have a case, especially when he finished his act with a lengthy build-up to the kind of unicycling and fire juggling that you can see performed any day of the week on the streets of Brighton or Covent Garden.

The Barron Knights were on great form. I'm not sure that changing the lyrics of 'Killer Queen' to 'Will Camilla be Queen?' quite worked, but the mixture of old rock 'n' roll standards and a few medleys of their hit material, including the 'Space Oddity' cover version – 'birth control to ginger tom' – certainly did. Who would have thought that a song about castration could be so funny?

After an interval, a few more song and dance numbers and a forgettable cruise ship comic, it was time for the stars of the show to do their thing. And they did it, exactly as they had the last time I saw them on television back in 1980-something-or-other. Bobby Ball played the hard-done-by zany one while Tommy Cannon took the role of serious straight man. Braces were pinged, catchphrases dusted off and old gags exhumed, but somehow it didn't matter. In this context, middle-of-the-road variety was what seemed right and the duo delivered the goods. I was beginning to worry just how badly that skull-shaking on The Big One had affected me. I was laughing at Cannon and Ball. I even started to think: 'Oh, they're probably all right blokes to share a beer with.'

It didn't last. As their set drew to a close, the rest of the acts began to join them on stage for a rendition of 'O Happy Day'. This seemed pretty cheesy, but that is what variety acts are all about. Then I remembered what I had read in the local paper – Bobby and Tommy had been 'born again'. They had found God and decided to drag the whole cast into a happy-clappy singalong finalé about love and understanding. Luckily, I was sitting at the end of a row, so my exit from the theatre and straight into the nearest pub was a swift one.

Not long after my nightcap, I was tucked up in bed and began to feel the sweat trickle down my spine and collect in a pool atop my plastic-coated mattress. Thankfully, my snoring neighbour had checked out and only the occasional banshee wails of passing hen parties disturbed my sauna-like slumber.

The next morning I woke early and decided to head for the station rather than face the possible horror show that lay in wait in the breakfast room. I left my key in the door and made a hushed exit from the B&B and on to the station, stopping to buy the Sunday papers on the way.

Between flicking through the sports pages, throwing away

the business sections and regretting sitting next to a group of travel bore RAF officers, I pondered the whole Blackpool versus Stratford thing once again. Yes, Blackpool was brash, noisy and crowded and the standard of accommodation is often only marginally better than that of the kind of cheap American freeway motel that has armed security guards and regularly dredges the pool for bodies, but it is *the* best place to see the English at leisure.

The theatres, piers, trams and Pleasure Beach contain just as much history, if not more, than Stratford, and at least you know you are getting the genuine thing, not just somewhere that may or may not have been the home of our greatest playwright. Blackpool is built for entertainment while Stratford is merely designed for dull, worthy tourism and the sale of fudge.

You can learn far more about Shakespeare by staying at home and reading one of his plays than by visiting his alleged birthplace, but to know Blackpool you have to experience it at full tilt – the only speed it knows. Sure, it may be hard to understand or just downright perplexing for any overseas visitor, but at least they can be guaranteed to come away with a story to tell that doesn't involve the line 'and then we saw the museum' or the word 'quaint'.

7. FLYING MEN
AND FLYING BRICKS

There is a tradition in end-of-pier comedy that you always make jokes about how bad the town you are performing in is. The weather, the hotels and the personal hygiene of the locals are all fair game, but none of it is really meant. Like a variant on Jewish humour, it makes you laugh because you know it's kind of true, but it's nothing personal, no harm intended.

Bognor Regis, however, has been the butt of jokes at every music hall and comedy club throughout England. And they really do mean it.

When a comic in Blackpool, Margate or Skegness really wants to insult a seaside town, they turn from the one they are in to Bognor, the whipping boy of the English coast. The story goes that it is all King George V's fault. On his deathbed he is reported to have replied 'Bugger Bognor' to the suggestion that he may soon get another chance to spend time at the town to which he had given the royal seal of approval (hence the Regis part of the name).

Growing up, I felt a bit of envy every time Bognor's name came up in a Des O'Connor TV special or a Terry Wogan radio show.[11] Everyone knew that Blackpool was the king of the resorts and Bognor the dishevelled court jester, which meant that Margate never got a look in. I was convinced that my home town must be *the* last resort, but not having been to Bognor to make comparisons I could never be entirely sure.

With a trip to the West Sussex town to witness the annual Bognor Birdman competition I had a chance to put that right and finally decide which was worst. It's true that I had shed my general hatred of all things Margate-related over the years and even like some of its crumbling features now, but I was willing to be truly objective in my judgment.

The Bognor Birdman is probably one of the most famous oddball contests in England and usually gets to hog that 'And finally . . .' slot on one weekend's news programmes each year. Competitors either build a flying machine or simply don a pair of home-tailored wings and leap from the end of the pier, the winner being he or she who manages the greatest distance. To add to the thrill of dressing up like a bird or a flying fish, there is also a prize of £25,000, put up by Butlins holiday camp for anyone who can fly over a hundred metres from the pier.

On the day that I arrived, Butlins' money looked fairly

---

[11] My parents' viewing and listening choices, not mine.

safe. It was damp, drizzly and there was a strong wind blowing in the opposite direction to that in which the competitors had to fly. The record flight distance of 89.2 metres was likely to stand for another year too.

My first impression, as I alighted from the train, was that Bognor was fairly similar to Margate, with its empty industrial buildings, boarded-up shops and general air of economic malaise. But, as I walked into the town, I succumbed to the creeping realisation that it was, indeed, worse. It had outdone Margate in the race to the bottom. And then some.

Fenced off parts of the pedestrianised high street sprouted copious amounts of straw-like weeds. The dispossessed had claimed the area as their own, from which to vent anger at imaginary attackers and the demons in their minds. It looked like the kind of place to which heroin addicts come to die unglamorous deaths in bedsits above fried chicken shops – and then change their mind as they find the whole idea too depressing, preferring to OD in Hastings or Hove instead.

As I reached the seafront, I almost gasped. I had been expecting something on the scale of Great Yarmouth, with rows of amusement arcades, model villages and perhaps even a funfair. Instead I saw a couple of fish'n'chip shops, a doughnut stand and a shop selling inflatables and postcards.

For such a big joke, it was a surprisingly small place.

To the west end of the esplanade was the pier and to the far east was the enormous Butlins complex, where, locked away, all the town's amusements lay. In the 1950s, in a misguided attempt to retain the genteel nature of the resort, local councillors had convinced Butlins to shift its amusements eastwards and amalgamate them into a new holiday complex. This, at one fell swoop, made Bognor into Butlins Regis and destroyed the town's reputation as a better class of resort anyway. It also left Bognor with a wide and windy gap between its now biggest draw and the pier. The council had well and truly buggered Bognor.

I went to take a look at the Butlins complex as the preliminary proceedings for the Birdman contest got under way. With the wind at my back and rain swirling around in the air, I wandered past deserted trampolines and forlorn windswept ice-cream stands, even finding an Asian family hiding in some bushes to seek shelter from the elements. For some reason I have still not worked out, there seems to be one Asian family having an awful time at every seaside resort I ever visit. Like the obligatory nun in the disaster movie, they are there each time, acting as a portent of holiday misery.

Butlins itself is surrounded by security. This is not, as the old jokes go, to keep visitors from getting out, but to ensure that anyone wanting to come in to use the facilities has to pay the £10 per adult or £30 per family charge. Though the list of regulations and strict rules about what times non-staying guests must be in or out by did make it seem slightly closer to Pentonville than paradise. The fact that the site had also been the recent striking ground of a serial rapist, who was, at the time, still at large, didn't help in terms of general cheeriness either.

I had originally planned to stay at Butlins, but my efforts

had been hampered by the fact that my three e-mails and two telephone requests for a brochure went unheeded. I received a postcard about a special offer, but nothing else. My initial impressions of the town and the holiday camp left me grateful for their inefficiency.

Back along the esplanade, Butlins Red Club 7, a dire indictment of the *Popstars* culture, were going through the motions of their boy/girl band routine on the stage that had been set up opposite the pier's entrance. Four-year-olds were bopping happily to them, but any child jaded by more than a term at primary school turned their backs, muttering something about the watering down of our pop heritage. At least they were better than the previous act, Weapons of Sound, one of those *Stomp*-alike 'let's play percussion on old sinks and bottles' acts that used to clog up the closing credits of *Blue Peter* and still could do for all I know.

The competitors in the Birdman contest were divided into three categories – Kingfisher being those in fancy dress and maybe a set of paper wings, Leonardo da Vinci for wacky flying machines and Magnificent Flight for serious hang-glider types. The latter, for me, seemed to go against the whole spirit of the competition. Surely the point was to take part and fail spectacularly, not to try to win the prize money at all costs. I took an instant dislike to the men in wetsuits with serious expressions who made up this group. We know that hang-gliders can fly, so what was the point? What we don't know is if a giant butterfly model or a polystyrene albatross can fly. I was pretty certain that a fireplace wouldn't have the desired aerodynamic qualities, but that was what the crowd were here to find out. I mean, if you don't try these things you will never know.

After the contestants had paraded in front of the crowd and been interviewed for local radio, they began to gather at the end of the pier in preparation for their jumps. A ramp and scaffolding platform had been added to the end of the pier to give extra height and the surrounding waters resembled the Channel at the evacuation of Dunkirk, with a dozen or so small dinghies, support vessels and camera boats stationed a few yards out to drag jumpers from the water, ferry them back to shore and photograph any triumphs, tragedies or fatalities. It was winter-coat cold at the top of the jump platform, so I hate to think what it was like in the water, especially for those wearing little more than trunks and a life-jacket.

The first to jump were the Kingfisher class birdmen and women, who included business-suited double acts, an IT manager dressed as a flying frogman and an artist in a Mr Potato Head outfit. All of them took good leaps with a look of expectation on their faces, but simply plummeted like stones, buffeted by the biting wind that threatened to dash them back into the legs of the pier. Quite a crowd had braved the weather to gather on the beach and watch the action via a giant video screen, but these fancily dressed displays of gravity didn't seem to impress them much. What they wanted were magnificent men in flying machines who would prove that flight really is for the birds – hopefully by messing up miserably in a tangle of balsa-wood, canvas and limbs.

The audience were in with a chance of seeing disaster even before many of the more outlandish da Vinci class inventions could make it up the slope to the jumping platform. With winds whipping straight across the pier, many competitors had to struggle to stay on it. Strong gusts ripped off wings, shattered wooden frames and almost sent many over the opposite side from the one they were to jump from.

This was much more like it, recalling as it did old newsreel footage of men struggling with contraptions that had more wings than a flock of geese flying south, all stacked on top of each other. Bloody-minded, hopeless, but inspired to continue nonetheless. It came as no surprise to read in the press pack that ski-jumping anti-hero Eddie 'The Eagle' Edwards had taken part in the contest in 1989, managing to leap eleven metres away from the pier. Another hurrah for the English love of the underdog.

Sadly, not quite so willing to take risks were the safety advisors for a pair of children's television presenters, who decided that the blustery conditions meant that the pair could not take to the air in their beautifully constructed gliders for fear of some kind of decapitation and the subsequent and changes to advertised schedules that would necessitate. Instead the CBBCers meekly dropped like stones from the platform into the sea, providing a wet slap in the face to former BBC daredevil John Noakes, who would rather shatter limbs than lose face. Shep must have turned in his grave.

As the more serious faces and serious flying machines

made their way to the head of the pier, expectations of lengthy flights raised, but so did the wind. Jumping into the gusts gave contestants a good lift away from the pier, but the next cold blast would simply send them down into the brine or back towards the pier, bringing an 'Ooooh' from the crowd and laughter from me. All that effort, matching track-suits for the support team and they still managed less distance than the people who had simply jumped off unaided. It was poetic victory for the spirit of the contest over the draw of the prize money.

In the end, the best that anyone could manage was 37.69 metres and just less than ten seconds in the air. It was Ron Freeman, hang-gliding instructor and the Michael Schumacher of the flying man competition, winning for the fifth year in succession despite being twenty metres from his best distance and nowhere near the all-time record of eighty-nine metres.

Sadly, a contest which should be all about unpredictability had become largely predictable. The mad inventors were being edged out by the professionals who merely tinkered with existing gliders. Still, at least the last flight out was reserved for genuine eccentric engineer Dick Chitolie, who had described his profession on the entry form as 'crusader'. His 'Hot Lips' giant butterfly may have spiralled to the sea like a swatted fly to the carpet, but the crowd recognised his vision with one of the biggest rounds of applause of the day. If they had just wanted to see some flying they would have gone home after witnessing the fly-past of the

Utterly Butterly wingwalkers (who seemed to be following me from event to event) or simply gone to Gatwick for the day. What had brought them to the pebbled beach was the promise of Herculean effort followed by the flailing and splashing of proud failure. Chitolie was able to deliver this in spades and you just knew that he would be back doing the same thing next year.

Eschewing the awards ceremony and the attendant chance to hear more dustbin-based percussion in favour of a further exploration of the town centre, I weaved my way slowly along the seafront and up towards the pedestrianised walkways. Around the tea shops and pubs, people were attired in the latest English summer uniform of fleece jackets and football shorts. We are never ready to admit full defeat to the weather, so goose-bumped bare legs with jackets suitable for arctic conditions it is. The fact that a cheap fleece soaks up rain like a towel and takes several days to dry out after a downpour seems to have passed everyone by.

One shop that intrigued me in the town centre was the sixty-pence shop. I had come across fifty-pence shops, pound and ninety-nine-pence shops, but never a sixty-pence one. Was it a fifty-pence shop after inflation or merely a pound shop in recession? I was tempted to ask a passing woman in unintentionally see-through stirruped ski pants that had obviously been purchased there, but as she seemed to have been saving the rest of her money to spend on steroids and protein powder for the Staffordshire terrier she had in tow, I decided against it and headed for the station. After all, I had seen what kind of damage a dog of that type could inflict on my near-miss wife at Stonehenge.

After the Bognor Birdman contest, there was really only one other place that my interest in the flight of unlikely projectiles could take me. Naturally, I had to head for Gloucestershire to witness the International Brick and Rolling Pin Throwing Competition.

In theory, getting to Stroud, in what many friends now refer to as 'Fred West country' (a title that has yet to be recognised on the county's signs and tourist leaflets), should have been easy. I had, through harsh interrogation techniques picked up in an episode of *The Bill*, managed to ascertain from the Stroud tourist information office that the event was actually going ahead. I had checked and double-checked my train times online and, via the telephone timetable service, found out which kind of ticket to buy and whether there were any ludicrous restrictions on its use – such as no jeans, no trainers or not to be used by anyone with vowels in their name. The woman on the phone at National Rail Enquiries assured me that I could get a Supersaver for £33 on my day of travel and sure enough when I purchased my ticket at Finsbury Park station that was what I was charged.

At Paddington things started to go wrong.

As I found my train on the departure board, I was less than delighted to read that Supersaver tickets were not valid on the train I wanted to use. Computer error, I guessed. I wandered over to join the queue for the First Great Western information booth, just to make sure. I looked at my watch. Ten minutes until my train left.

Five minutes later I reached the front of the queue.

'They are not valid on any train to Stroud, sir, not in July or August,' the clerk told me.

'So why did someone sell it to me, then?' I asked.

'I don't know, sir,' he said, in a way that suggested that he said that an awful lot and was, frankly, getting a bit bored of it now. 'You will have to pay the excess.'

'Okay, okay, just tell me how much it is and I'll pay it,' I said. 'I don't want to miss my train.'

'I think it is about £15.'

'Whaaat? You *think*?'

The clerk flicked through a book.

'Oh, no, I mean about £4.'

'Whatever,' I said. 'Just take it.' I thrust my credit card towards the slot in the Plexiglas.

'Sorry sir, you'll have to go to the ticket office. We don't take payments at this window.'

Without sufficient time to punch the window and start raging, I half-ran towards the ticket office. On my way across the station concourse I had a brainwave. Maybe I could just pay the excess fare once I was on the train. I grabbed another First Great Western employee, who was trying to get rid of a couple of German tourists with not much grip of English, to ask if this was possible.

'I don't know, sir,' was his reply.

'Well, can you find out?' I asked, gesturing towards his walkie-talkie.

'No, this is just for the train times,' he said.

I figured that any time spent arguing the point with him would be time wasted, so I made for the ticket office, where I found a queue of about thirty people waiting in the standard class queue to be served by just a couple of staff. It doesn't take a Carol Vorderman-esque grip of mathematics to work out that I would not make my train if I waited there.

Then I saw the first class queue.

Two booking clerks and only one person in the queue waiting to be seen. I figured that this was my best bet and anyway my need was now first class and I was just waiting for the First Great Western employee who would like to argue otherwise.

I reached the front of the queue and explained my plight to the clerk, expecting to receive some officious instruction to join the other queue, but he dealt with my request quickly and efficiently, leaving First Great Western £3.80 better off.

I ran for my train and made it with just thirty seconds to spare. Predictably, my train then sat static at the station for five minutes before leaving.

Although rail operators would like us to believe that rail travel is becoming more and more like air travel, this is patently not so. Some of our larger train stations are beginning to take on the appearance of Heathrow or Gatwick in terms of retail outlets, and the system of booking tickets is becoming similar, but the on-board entertainment on a train is very much stuck in the past. The choice is still: read, listen to Abba too loudly on a Walkman (as the woman in the seat next to me on this particular trip was doing), stare out of the window or get drunk on Stella Artois or Mckewan's Export. Children can replace the last option with eating industrial-sized bags of cheesy puffs or colouring in, or not, as the case may be. Surely a film wouldn't be too much to ask, would it? Even one of those specially sanitised aeroplane ones would do.

My own solution to the lack of on-board entertainment has been to make my own. Previous efforts have included telling horrendous lies about life as an adult to small children, engaging the person in the seat next to me with fictitious tales of my life as a cockroach exterminator and, most recently, eyes-only flirting. On this journey I managed to play the 'I'm looking at you, no I'm not really looking at you' game simultaneously with both a pretty henna red-haired Eastern European woman and a furrow-browed blonde woman who beat her laptop frantically between occasionally catching my eye. She looked like she had been up all night trying to finish a script or an important business proposal and was still desperately trying to get it done, though she may well have been composing an e-mail to a friend about the weird guy sitting halfway down the train who kept staring at her and was beginning to freak her out a little.

Arriving at Stroud, I found myself in need of a drink and went in search of a pub. The one nearest to the station, actually part of a hotel, looked empty and a little desperate so I wandered a bit further and decided to try the Weatherspoon's.

No matter where you go, these chain pubs are always pretty much the same. Though apparently modelled on George Orwell's idea of the perfect pub, far from being the spot to enjoy a foaming mug of nut-brown ale in the company of charming barmaids, they are more often, due to their bargain-basement prices, the place to share a pint with the local alcoholics in the company of a spotty young barman in a nasty waistcoat. The decor and lighting are routinely awful, but it must be said that the beer is incredibly cheap and usually pretty good.

After downing my pint of Spitfire while being observed by the local drongoes – who were checking me to see if I had any young that they could kill and eat – I headed off for the tourist information office to see if there were any must-see sights in town.

As it happens, there weren't. But there was a museum in the park where the brick throwing was due to take place later that afternoon, so I took a leaflet about it and headed off on the ten-minute walk to Stratford Park, to the north of the town centre. As I was walking out of the town centre, I encountered a group of peace campaigning pensioners who were handing out leaflets in protest at the air show that was due to take place at nearby Fairford.

Their leaflet was headed:

FAIRFORD WAR TATTOO
A CELEBRATION OF DESTRUCTION

Oh dear, I thought. Tony and his planespotting pals wouldn't like that. Lucky for the peaceniks that Tony wasn't actually with me, as they would have received a stern and lengthy lecture about the RAF, with huge amounts of technical data thrown in for good measure.

Their leaflet betrayed the fact that they seemed to have got a bit bogged down in complex minutae themselves, even without Tony's assistance.

> THE US HAS A FLEET OF 21 STEALTH
> BOMBERS, WITH A COMBINED WORTH OF
> **£27.7 BILLION**. THEY EACH CARRY 16 X 2,000 lb.
> BOMBS, COSTING **£17,388**. PER BOMB.

> IF MARY HAS TWO STEALTH BOMBERS, EACH
> ARMED WITH A FIFTY PER CENT CAPACITY
> PAYLOAD, HOW MUCH WILL IT COST HER TO
> DESTROY BAGHDAD?

Actually, I made the question part up, but you get the idea.

As I reached the main road out of town, the heavens opened and big glops of warm rain fell slowly down. I sheltered in a doorway with a couple who proceeded to argue as to whether one of them should go back into town to buy an umbrella or whether the umbrella shop was actually farther away than the distance to their car. When they had decided that they could actually do without an umbrella the rain had passed, and by the time I reached Stratford Park the sun was out and it felt like a real summer's day once again. The outdoor pool was rapidly filling with children, families slurping ice-cream cornets strolled or cycled, and a man in a pair of well-worn tennis shorts hung around by the toilet block looking a bit shifty. I swiftly moved on to the museum, noting the man's face just in case it should crop up on *Crimewatch*, or if I did as one of those people that the police wish to eliminate from their enquiries in relation to something nasty.

Like most local museums, the Museum in the Park was pretty dull. One member of staff told me that they have 5,000 items on show and another 50,000 in storage. I resisted the urge to tell her that I probably had a similar number of carrier bags stuffed in the drawer underneath my sink and just smiled politely until she went off to chase some children who were having too much fun with the exhibits upstairs.

Mind you, if you do feel the urge to see the football shirt of a non-playing reserve from Forest Green Rovers's appearance in an obscure non-league cup final, then the Museum in the Park really is the only place to go.

Out on the field behind the leisure centre, brick throwers were beginning to assemble. Their presence was announced by a gathering of cars at the top of the small hill at the far side of the park and the appearance of the event's sponsors, who were setting up a table and pegging out the arena with red, white and blue bunting emblazoned with the words 'Bombardier Bitter'. I briefly considered running back into town to inform the peace protesting grannies about the event in the park, with people hurling missiles and the beer company with the aggressively named product, but decided that they may not have got the joke. They'd probably spotted me sinking my pint of warmongering Spitfire earlier, anyway, and had me down as some kind of fighter plane nut.

As I reached the top of the slope, I spied a man in his seventies standing and staring at the collection of men and women organising trophies and unpacking bricks, rolling pins and sandwiches from their cars. I walked over and said hello.

'How did they get up there?' he asked me, pointing at the cars.

'Well, I guess they drove across the grass,' I told him, hoping to rule out any doubt in his mind about flying cars having been invented while he was enjoying his mid-morning nap.

He seemed happy enough with my explanation, though slightly miffed at the idea of people driving across the grass when there was a perfectly good car park a hundred yards away.

'So, have you come to see this, then?' he asked, pointing at the throwers.

'No, I was just passing by. What's going on?' I asked, forming my teeth into a nice wide grin so that I could lie through them easier.

'It's brick throwing,' he said, making a throwing motion with his right hand. 'They throw American bricks because they are lighter than English ones and the women throw rolling pins. They've been doing it for forty-two years and they do it on the same day in the towns called Stroud in America, Australia and Canada. Though they didn't start throwing rolling pins until 1962.'

'So have you come along especially to watch, then?' I asked.

'No, I was just out for a walk.'

He then pulled a small piece of paper with some figures scribbled on it out of his pocket, and read them off. 'The record for brick throwing is 142 feet and 6 inches and the record for rolling pin is, oh . . . 156 feet 4 inches. Longer than the men.'

It was at this point that I gathered that he was not, in fact, the stat-mad John Motson of the brick-throwing world, or even an expert on the subject. He had just read the same article in the *Stroud News and Journal* as I had in the pub that morning, shortly after my arrival in town.

While we were talking, several of the competitors limbered up by throwing bricks and pins around, some to quite impressive distances. The basic technique was somewhat similar to shot-put or discus throwing, with a couple of spins by the thrower preceding the release of their gender-designated projectile. Considering the record distances thrown, some of them seemed to be standing rather closely together as they tossed bricks and pins in each other's direction, much as you might do a Frisbee on the beach. Still, I thought, at least it's not my head at risk. Knock yourselves out guys, literally as well as figuratively speaking, should you so wish.

When I saw how far some of the female competitors could throw the rolling pin, I decided that to take part at all would be to open myself to all kinds of ridicule from the locals, but as the announcements were being made at the start of the contest, I realised that this was not an option anyway. The competitors make up teams that compete for distance against their overseas counterparts, who would have their own contest in their own Strouds later in the day.

Unlike the noble art of shin-kicking, this was not a free-for-all that anyone could take part in. People actually spend time training for it and there is no room for outsiders. Many throwers even had specialist athletic footwear of the kind that javelin or discus throwers might wear. I was glad that I had not made more effort in my attempts to secure somewhere to try out a couple of practice throws. I had called one of those golf driving ranges, thinking they would be ideal, but they had just laughed uproariously and put the phone down on me when I told them what I wanted to do.

Instead of a slightly eccentric English pursuit, brick throwing seemed to have developed into some kind of serious white trash shot-putting that will, no doubt, be vying for Olympic status in a few years' time. Just like the hang-glider types in Bognor, these people were trying too hard. I wanted to grab some of them and shout 'For God's sake, you are throwing bricks, lighten up a little!' but thankfully my English reserve kicked in just in time to save me from potential embarrassment, and a probable hail of well aimed, forcefully thrown bricks.

As the throwing began, and the woman who seemed to be the hub of the brick and rolling pin throwing world announced the competitors' names and stats, it became clear that the old man and I were the only spectators there who were not in some way related to one of the throwers.

The throwers, in turn, seem to be related to each other and ultimately to the woman doing the announcing.

'She's one of mine,' she said proudly, announcing a daughter's throwing bests.

'He's another one of mine.'

'That one's my granddaughter, give her a bit of encouragement.'

She reeled off the names of various sons, daughters and grandchildren who were either throwing for the team today or were former champions.

It seemed that some kind of genetic experiment to breed the perfect thrower had been going on in the area for some time. There were about forty of us present in total and it seems that at least half that number were directly related to this woman, with the rest being relations by marriage, junior discus champions from local schools or brewery sponsors.

I'm not sure that plugging their product to what was, in effect, an audience of two made sound financial sense for the marketing people at Bombardier Bitter, especially as they didn't deign to entice us with any free samples while the throwing took place. But I guess they must have known what they were doing, especially as the woman from the brewery had a clipboard with extensive notes attached. That's always a good sign.

Note to the brewery's branding department: You may need to work harder on product name recognition. One woman near me kept referring to your beer as 'Bumraider'. I'm not sure if this was a misreading or some kind of derogatory reference to the after-effects of over consumption, but I think it may require investigation.

One thing that the old man hadn't told me was that brick throwing was actually an American invention and came to the town in 1960 via the mayor of Stroud, Oklahoma, who somehow managed to blag his way into a fact-finding mission to his town's namesake in Gloucestershire. Nice work if you can get it, I guess.

Like his Stroud, our Stroud had a brick-making factory, so he told his English counterpart about the brick throwing contest they had back home and an international event was born. Of course the namby-pamby Yanks insisted that they carry on using their lighter, five-pound patio bricks rather than our hefty house bricks, though at least they did show willing by allowing another country to enter the 'World Series' of chucking stuff.

The rolling pin throwing was brought in by Australian women who wanted to throw things too and, I assume, were already well versed in lobbing pastry-tamers at their errant husbands as they legged it out of the house in search of more of the foul, pissy lager that they specialise in producing there. For competition throwing a standard two-pound pin had been adopted.

After such a build-up and so many factoids the actual throwing itself was fairly dull, though that's not to say that it wasn't impressive. Even the mother hen's eleven-year-old granddaughter could heave a rolling pin an impressively Imperial eighty feet and her son managed to lob a brick 140 feet and 7 inches, which was just two feet away from the world record. These people would be really handy to have on your side in a riot, especially if they could learn accuracy alongside their ability for distance.

If you have ever watched shot-putting on television during the Olympics, you have a pretty good idea of how things went. A throw, a man with a tape measure, announcement of the distance – though in this case via a small child running back to the organiser's table rather than by electronic scoreboard – and the final presentation of medals to the winners. Actually, you may not know all of that, as no one I know has ever sat through the entirety of the Olympic shot-putting coverage on television and I suspect that few people not related to a thrower have. Anyway, they tend to hold it while something more interesting is going on elsewhere in the stadium, like a couple of stewards having a kickabout behind one of the stands.

The brick- and pin-throwing winners were, of course, rewarded with beer from the sponsors, so some of the younger competitors had their parents collect their prize for them. They had to make do with a bottle of flat Coke that had been warming gently in the car for the past couple of hours.

The atmosphere at the end of the contest was decidedly odd. It just seemed to fizzle out without much of a bang and descend immediately into a family picnic. Perhaps the brick throwing was just an elaborate ruse so that the family could drive their cars across the grass, park on top of the hill and get all that free Bombardier Bitter. Hats off to them if that is the case. After all, there is nothing so English as a scheme that involves the procuring of free beer.

Sloping away, I went back into town through the Merryweather shopping centre, or the Miserableweather centre as I am sure that the locals must call this mess of sad-looking retail outlets and security guards chasing off scooter-riding ten-year-olds. The town centre itself was actually bustling and fairly attractive, despite the any-town pedestrianised high street. There was really no need for such a soulless, climate-controlled abomination. Still, I guess baiting the security guards keeps the kids off the streets, leaving the rest of society to go about its business unhindered.

Arriving back at the station to catch my train, I checked the timetable to make sure that the information that National Rail Enquiries had given on the phone was correct. Of course it wasn't. The timetable said that my train would be ten minutes later than I had been told, but at least it was going directly to Paddington. I called National Rail Enquiries again, just to make sure that this was the right information. It's not that I have much faith in them, but the best way I have found to work out what is going on is to ask as many sources as possible and then work out a kind of average probability from all the clues I have gathered.

The other option is just to get on the first train you see at any station and see where you end up, which is often a more efficient way to travel than trying to work anything out in advance, especially as most train companies only announce where a train is headed once you are on board and leaving the station. Almost every time I had to change trains during my travels, I had to find a member of staff to assist me, as there was so little information available on the platform. I'd advise you to avoid the sign that says 'information' on suburban stations, as this generally leads to an unstaffed desk with a handful of bus timetables, a leaflet about joining the National Trust and yesterday's copy of *The Sun* left lying around. I really have no idea how any foreign visitors find their way anywhere in this country by train.

After listening to a series of pre-recorded messages about travel mayhem elsewhere in the country, I finally got through to a member of staff at the timetable call centre.

'No, it doesn't go direct. You have to change at Swindon,' said the voice at the other end of the phone.

'So why does it say that the train goes to London, not Swindon, on the timetable at the station, then?' I asked.

'Oh, I think they just do that to make it simpler,' she said. By telling the passengers the wrong information they were actually helping us. How stupid of me not to realise.

8. IT'S PIXIES, YOU IDIOT

In reading about the crop circle phenomenon, I was pretty sure that I had heard all of the possible theories as to how and why these strange formations mark the wheat and barley fields of England each summer. At one end of the scale are those who insist that the complex geometric designs made by flattening cereal crops are far too out-of-this-world for humans to have a hand (or indeed a foot) in and are actually messages from other galaxies, and at the other are those who claim that they are the work of thirty-something pranksters who prefer the company of lengths of rope and planks of wood to that of women.

The space between these two polar positions is filled with a whole raft of conspiracy theories, crackpot science, and speculation about natural magnetism, sheep, wind and top-secret government weaponry. One theory that I was not prepared for, however, was the one that would be divulged to me during a religious pilgrimage to Exmoor.

But before reaching Exmoor and the revelation, I had first to get to Barnstaple, where I would be staying while in Devon. This sounds a fairly simple task, but it isn't as easy as you might think. Especially if, like me, you try to do so with the 'help' of the train operator WAGN. The main part of my journey would be with First Great Western, but as it started at a WAGN-run station near to my home, I had to book through the WAGN ticket line. All part of the dumb-ocracy by which our rail system operates.

As a result, I had to spend forty-five minutes arguing at some volume with the WAGN ticket office staff at Finsbury Park station before I was finally given the ticket I had paid for by telephone some days earlier. You would think that for £63 upfront you might be entitled not to be treated like some kind of fraudster for being cheeky enough to expect that you could pick up your ticket as arranged.

I'm pretty sure that the incidences of master criminals breaking into ticket buyers' flats and then demanding the booking code and credit card number used to make the purchase at knifepoint in order to score a ticket to Devon are pretty few and far between. Even in Finsbury Park.

Planning ahead for the stupidity of others, I was picking the ticket up a day early so, thankfully, I was not in danger of missing my train and hence managed to remain relatively calm and limit my use of the f-word to single figures, I think. Once I had got my hands on the ticket, I headed home to do something that we English are very good at. I wrote a letter of complaint.

With the anger out of my system and down on paper, I was feeling pretty good as I travelled to Barnstaple the next day, a journey of just over four hours from the door of my flat to the door of my B&B in Barnstaple. My cheery mood was slightly surprising, as shortly after the ticket incident I had looked up Barnstaple on the Knowhere.co.uk website. The site is one of my favourites for getting the lowdown on towns I visit as it is an open forum which is mostly contributed to by teenagers whose main interest seems to be skateboarding, snogging, cider and arguing about whether Burger King is better than McDonalds. In the entry for Barnstaple the word 'shithole' was used more than once. One semi-literate contributor was also inspired to add 'NOTHINK IS GOOD ABOUT BARNSTAPLE' in the section entitled 'The Best Things'. The most flattering entry was one that claimed: 'Barnstaple is full of mutants. However it is not as bad as Bideford.' Agreed, it didn't look good, but then this was the kind of thing that all teens said about their home towns, so I was prepared to give it the benefit of the doubt.

On arrival at my B&B, I was greeted, eventually, by a woman who seemed less than happy to see me. I would have been likewise inclined had I known what the inside of her B&B looked like.

As is standard with many B&Bs, upon entering I was bombarded with a plethora of instructional signs telling me what I could not and should not do. The signage continued into my room and a large notice above my bed informed me:

SMOKING ALLOWED
IN BEDROOMS
7 AND 8 ONLY
DUE TO FIRE
REGULATIONS

This was almost enough to make me decide to take up smoking and head on up to room seven to see if they would let me in to share a Marlboro. I imagine there must be a really good, old-fashioned behind-the-bike-sheds vibe going on in there of an evening.

My room contained an aged desk with a reading lamp on it that used to belong to one Paul G, or so the name scrawled on it in Tippex implied. It also contained a badly tuned television set that could be re-tuned for about ten minutes before needing attention again. My view was of one of the main roundabouts out of the town. How I came to envy the passengers on the buses and the truck drivers that roared past during my short stay.

The room also featured one gent's urinal. Actually, you might call it a sink, but any male who has stayed in accommodation without en-suite facilities will know only too well that, when faced with the prospect of getting dressed and leaving the room to take a leak at 3 a.m., it is, in reality, a toilet.[12]

---

[12] Actually, the in-sink piss is not solely a male pursuit. I once had a girl-friend who nearly pulled the sink off the wall in my room in a shared house when trying to balance on it during a post-pub pee. Being a gentleman I ignored the sound of straining plasterwork and refrained from shouting 'get your fat arse off my wall-urinal'.

Examining the corroded chrome around the plughole, I made a mental note not to wash my face in the sink the following morning but to stick with the shower in the hallway. At least any traces of urine there would be swirling around my toes rather than my mouth.

After I had put down my bag and pondered the discovery of a golf tee and a butter knife in the drawer of the desk, I decided to escape the hotel and see what Barnstaple had on offer – which, on reflection, was not a lot. In fact, most of it was as grim as the surly teenagers on the Knowhere website had claimed.

One of the other major tourist pulls for the area is the *Tarka the Otter* industry. The train I had arrived on after changing at Exeter St David's had been christened The Tarka Line and there was a Tarka Trail and endless Tarka-themed gift shops, museum exhibits and knick-knacks celebrating the life of fascist sympathiser and author of *Tarka the Otter*, Henry Williamson. This whole concept seemed fairly flawed, as the book is as dull as dishwater and last caught the public imagination over twenty years ago, when it was turned into an equally sleep-inducing film. A rather desperate ploy for a town that really has no justification for a tourist industry.

Walking through the town, I became pretty sick of Tarka the Otter within about three minutes, to the point where I initially avoided going into the Ottakar's bookshop after misreading the sign as 'tarka's' from a distance. Thankfully they had avoided the temptation to have a pool of otters and a cardboard cut-out of Williamson in Blackshirt garb as a promotional stunt and had even decided against stocking Williamson's follow-up flops *Moseley the Mouse*, *Himmler the Heron* and the little-known *Tarka, Quite Justifiably, Annexes Poland*.

The town's cavernous tourist information centre concentrated solely on the area *around* Barnstaple, including The Big Sheep Family Entertainment Park in neighbouring Bideford, which, in another case of literary theming, offered horse whispering shows. Now I haven't read *The Horse Whisperer* but I am guessing that these shows consist of someone whispering to a horse, which could hardly be classed as entertainment, could it?

Meanwhile, The Milky Way adventure park near Clovelly looked positively terrifying from the publicity material, which showed a man in a kind of alien gimp mask mounting a bumper car with some rather uneasy-looking kids trying to get away from him. This made more (or perhaps less) sense when I read in the literature that the gimp in question was the 'Clone Zone' alien, which I imagine means he must have been kitted out in the Soho gay men's sex shop of the same name.

The map of Devon given away by the tourism office pinpointed exactly zero attractions in Barnstaple, bar the actual tourism office itself. However, the smaller map of Barnstaple on offer did highlight the Spar convenience store as well as the soullessly depressing Green Lanes shopping centre, where Skodas were being sold in the 'Town Square'.

The area of the town that overlooks the river Taw seemed

to be enjoying something of a renaissance, with a modern glass café and new bars springing up. However, the visitors' centre and gift shop didn't seem to be faring too well in its waterfront location. The only visitors enjoying the sunken garden in front of it were the local skateboarders who, judging by the amount of worn-down concrete in the immediate vicinity, had clearly made it their home. By comparison, the benches looking across the river to a lorry park were in pristine condition, despite having been installed eighteen years ago. Either the locals and visitors were a dainty bunch who made sure not to sit down too hard or carve their initials into the wood, or no one ever came and sat on them. I sat there with no one else but the skaters in sight, thinking that maybe it picks up at the height of the holiday season. Then I realised that it *was* the height of the season.

There was something about the pointlessness of Barnstaple that made me feel ill at ease with the world. I am pretty sure that John Betjeman would have written a nasty poem about the town, to rival his one about friendly bombs falling on Slough, if only he could have thought of a suitable rhyme for 'Barnstaple'.

One of the very few saving graces of the town was the pasty shop. The Presto store was part of a chain and looked much like any member of the various coffee shop multiples, but it did sell divine, still-warm pasties in an amazing array of flavours, including spicy chickpea and potato with mango chutney. I am not sure how this kind of creation would go down with traditionalists over the border in Cornwall, but their presence in Barnstaple would just about make me think twice about ordering a strategic strike on the place, should I ever have the power to for some unexpected reason.

The existence of the amusingly named Pathos Beauty Salon might also help persuade me to keep my finger off the button. The only other shop that made any kind of positive impression was the school outfitters, Gover in Joy Street, which had a window display of original, un-ironic, un-postmodern Dunlop Green Flash tennis shoes.

After the pasty, I decided to try out the local pubs and plumped for the Rising Sun, as it served the local Usher's beers and there did at least seem to be some people inside it. Sadly for me, those inside were stuck in some kind of 1970s hard-rock time warp and I had to endure Hawkwind's 'Silver Machine' followed by 'Smoke on the Water' and 'The Ace of Spades' while I sipped my pint and listened to the man next to me at the bar blather on about seeing Black Sabbath back in the days before house music, boy bands and personal hygiene were invented.

A decision to move on to the Three Tuns was initially rewarded by the sight of the pub's magnificent wooden bar, which incorporates three 'tun' beer barrels. However, things started to go awry when Phil Collins came on the jukebox and we were treated to 'Sussudio' followed by 'Easy Lover' and then the same two tracks again. I imagine that this is the kind of thing that they keep on a loop tape in hell, though I am sure Old Nick would throw Phil's rendition of 'You Can't Hurry Love' into the mix as well.

I took the Phil Collins onslaught as a sign to leave before the tracks came on again and, with a beery appetite, headed off for what turned out to be an overpriced yet distinctly average meal in the town's own little Chinatown – an area which consisted of two restaurants adjoining a car park around the back of Marks & Spencer. The menus of each were pretty interchangeable, though one of the restaurants did offer you the chance to see your food being cooked in the kitchen 'in front of your very eyes'. I think I must have chosen the other one, as I couldn't see much at all from my table.

I still don't fully understand the current trend for restaurants that cook the food in front of you. I mean, you don't hear fish and chip shops bragging about your proximity to their deep fat fryer or your local greasy spoon offering 'tea brewed before your very eyes'. Most of us have seen some kind of food prepared in a kitchen, so unless you are the type of person who has hired help to do that kind of thing for you, I really can't see why watching someone stir-frying noodles in a restaurant setting is so exciting.

Likewise, the appeal of those restaurants where you pick out a bowl-full of ingredients and have someone cook them for you is lost on me. Expect a chain of restaurants where you are sent off to bring your own food back from Tesco's and then do the washing up afterwards any time now. Entertainment for the online-shopping, dishwasher-owning generation.

On my way out of the B&B the next morning, I noticed the

visitors' book. I always like to examine visitors' books but can never actually think of anything much to say in them. Or at least anything nice.

My girlfriend, on the other hand, has recently taken to writing lengthy visitors' book screeds about the flora and fauna of the area, the standard of ventilation and the best time to catch bunny rabbits frolicking on the lawn. All of which I find slightly embarrassing, despite the fact that I always want to know exactly what time the bunnies will be frolicking on the lawn when I am staying in the countryside. It's just that feeling that before long she will start leaving our phone number and we will have to field calls from the Frobishers of Farnham enquiring as to the best time to catch the goldfinches feeding.

The guest book at this B&B was notable for its inclusion of many names from Switzerland and Germany. Obviously the Barnstaple tourist board has given up on trying to fool Brits that it is the place to be and has instead taken to duping people for whom English is a second language or complete gibberish. The only explanation I can think of is that they concentrated on the cream tea aspect of the area, as the Swiss and Germans seem keen on only the most calorific of dairy products. Though I suppose there is the possibility that the Swiss and Germans are big fans of *Tarka the Otter*.

I said goodbye to the proprietor who was standing near to the door. She completely ignored me.

The bus ride to Combe Martin at the edge of Exmoor was shaky, but the view it afforded was stunning in places. There is some outstanding coastline in the area around Ilfracombe and the bus passed through the picture-postcard-perfect village of Berrynarbor with its strange flowerpot men scattered throughout the village, climbing ladders and sitting on rooftops.

It was not too hard to spot the gaggle of pilgrims I was due to meet in the car park by the beach. The pilgrimage leader, Ray, had the look of a charismatic man of religion and there were a good few fifty-somethings garbed in Oxfam's shabbiest, which is always a sure-fire signifier that a person is involved with either far too many cats or a kooky religious group. As I couldn't smell cat pee and Whiskas, I rightly assumed that they were the poeple I had come to join up with.

The group were all members of the Aetherius Society, an English-founded religion that practises a kind of wholefood-Christian-Buddhist-Hindu-earth mother-yoga-flying saucer worship. They were in Devon as part of a series of annual pilgrimages to what they consider to be holy mountains. The mountains, it seems, have been charged with energies by a variety of gods and aliens using the religion's founder, Dr George King, as a conduit.

Luckily for me, Holdstone Down, on Exmoor, had been charged by Jesus in 1958, so it is pretty special to the society. The very first of the world's nineteen holy mountains, it was, apparently, zapped with energy after Jesus – who the Aetherius Society claims was actually from Venus – summoned King to the summit. There is even a stone there painted with the inscription 'GK 2371958' to mark the day in July when the energy charging took place. Sadly there is not one emblazoned with the legend 'Jesus woz 'ere', so it is hard to say if he was there in the form of a vision or in person. Shame that. If these god-figures really want belief in them to live on, they should at least leave a bit of graffiti or a best-selling auto-biography behind.

Ray set me up with Aetherius staff members and long-term devotees Tony and Nikki, who gave me a lift from the car park to Exmoor and the mountain where the pilgrimage would culminate. I had envisioned that we would be taking the long walk to the mountain, as George King had done when he lived in Combe Martin, but it seems that the modern pilgrim prefers the comfort of dual airbags and air conditioning to the traditional sore feet or crawling on their knees.

As Tony drove he gave me a run down on the beliefs of the Aetherius Society, which, if anything, left me slightly more confused than I had been before. This was not his fault, he was very eloquent, it is just that the religion is endlessly complicated and even members who have been with them for ten years or more are still confused about exactly what it is that they are being asked to believe in.

The basis of the religion seems to revolve around a gang of higher beings or 'Ascended Masters' who commune with an intergalactic network of beings and help to run an inter-planetary parliament, which is, naturally, based on Saturn. After his death in 1997, George King is said to have joined Ascended Masters such as Jesus and Buddha and the search is now on for another earthly master to replace him. According to a cosmic prophecy from 1958, this man will 'stand tall' and wear shoes that are 'soft-topped, yet not made of the skin of animals' which means they are on the lookout for a man in plimsolls or maybe those Nike aqua socks. I had a good look around at the meeting, but most of the group were wearing walking boots or brogues – definitely not master material. Do let them know if you see someone who fits the bill. It could well be important.

I had initially stumbled across the Aetherius Society several years ago. On a Christmas shopping trip down London's Fulham Road, I was intrigued by the giant neon flying saucer outside their office. They still have the office (as well as another office and a health food shop) on Fulham Road, but the flying saucer has long gone, seemingly as a deterrent to those who came to the religion for UFO-spotting rather than spiritual enlightenment. As we pulled into the car park, just a hundred yards from the peak of the holy mountain, Tony told me that UFO fanatics are often selfish sexual fantasists whose tales of rectal probing and abduction give extra-terrestrials a bad press. He also likened the sky-watchers to trainspotters.

'After all, why would these beings fly a round trip of millions of miles to probe someone?' he said.

This seemed like a fair point. Though I guess if you were a bored teenage alien then a spot of zooming off in your super-fast spaceship to sexually probe some humans or make a weird formation in a field of wheat may be exactly the kind of thing you might want to do for kicks on a boring Thursday, or to piss off your parents.

'Zobgloxxg! How many times have I told you not to impregnate humans and cut their cows in half? And for Bydsqqmoizd's sake will you stop writing swear words and drawing pictures of your genitalia in their crops?'

'So what about crop circles, then?' I asked, as we wandered towards the top of the holy mountain. 'Surely you must think they are some kind of message from alien beings?'

At this both Tony and Nikki looked at me as if I were some kind of idiot and just managed to stop short of tutting at me for my foolishness.

'Pixies,' said Tony. Resisting the temptation to add 'you imbecile'.

'You might call them elves,' chipped in Nikki helpfully, in case I knew the little people by a different name to the one they generally used.

'Oh ... right ... pixies,' I said, mentally switching my suspension of disbelief to the 'on' position. Believe me, it was not that hard after the kind of summer I was having.

'Why would beings bother to make communication through crop circles when they can communicate with us already?' asked Tony, before going off into a rather complicated story concerning Mother Earth making the circles as some kind of celebration of beauty aided by the pixies or elves – call them what you will – which are some kind of manifestation of her powers. I think.

It was about as clear as mud. If this was the kind of theory that underlay the religion's belief system, it was little wonder that many of its members didn't have a clue what was going on half of the time. Still, at least they are upfront about that fact, unlike adherents of most other religions.

Nikki asked me whether I had a mantra, in much the same way as someone might ask 'Have you got a light?' She then told me that Peter would give me a mantra if I needed one and pointed me in the direction of a man with a battered cassette player who was standing just to one side of the peak. I joined up with a bunch of other newbies who were there to get a mantra too.

According to Peter, mantras have to be physically given, it is really not much use just reading one in a book and then going off and chanting it willy-nilly. The one he gave us was a powerful mantra suitable for beginners and to add a bit more power and a touch of extra flavour it came from beyond the grave in the shape of a recording of the Master, George King. Peter told us not to repeat any other mantras that we may hear without them first being given to us officially. That way lies bad karma, apparently. I won't put you at risk of getting a sub-standard, karma-harming mantra by repeating the one I was given, but you can have a good guess at what it was like. You know, the sort of chant you might have expected to come from a cross-legged George Harrison. And there was an Om in there somewhere.

The pilgrimage to Holdstone Down was not just an annual outing and a chance to admire the beautiful scenery and the Bristol Channel. We were there to carry out some serious work. Or, at least, work that I was trying to take seriously.

The day was part of what the Aetherius Society calls a

'spiritual push', in which we were to harness the power of the charged mountain and send it out to the world in an attempt to do all the usual good stuff – bring about world peace, halt Armageddon and find a permanent cure for piles. All in all, it seems a pretty selfless religion – the members were more concerned with saving the earth and balancing out our karma than saving themselves from the eternal damnation that some more orthodox Christian groups might gladly see doled out to them for the whole 'Jesus is from Venus' thing.

The service began with Ray at the front leading the prayers. A new version of the Lord's Prayer was recited, which is far lengthier and seems to contain a lot of references to beings from outer space and somewhere called Satellite Three. There was also quite a lot of 'blessed are the . . .' going on, though they did not get as far as the cheese-makers.

Ray asked us to raise our hands with the palms flat, facing the sea, and we slowly started to recite our mantra under his supervision. He conducted us as if we were an orchestra, bringing the hubbub to a crescendo before instructing the 'prayer teams' at the front to provide the vocals to our ambient backing track. Some of the praying devotees were too quiet to hear, but several of them conjured up the kind of amateur-dramatics incantations that could only have been achieved through repeated viewings of *The Wicker Man* or previous experience of tree worship in some kind of 'wimmin's' group. One of the main players looked like Richard Attenborough and was similarly florid in his delivery.

Just after we had started the proceedings, Ray announced

that someone back at HQ had left the radiator on. 'Oh great,' I thought, 'now they're all going to have to dash back to London to switch it off so that their spider plants don't dry out.' Fortunately, I had misunderstood. Ray was talking about the Spiritual Energy Radiator and it had been turned on deliberately so that the power generated by our prayer would be multiplied by 3,000.

From the way Ray was talking, it seemed we were pretty lucky that the Spiritual Energy Radiator had been turned on, though he didn't make it clear whether this was because it had to be specially switched on by the Ascended Masters or if it was just a bit of a bugger to get going of a morning. It would have been nice to know but, as Tony later explained to me, the Spiritual Energy Radiator is one of the many things that Aetherius devotees don't fully understand until they have been in the church a good few years. Maybe it just costs a lot to run and the society was having trouble with the bills.

As the prayer went on, Ray got more and more enthusiastic about the energy he could feel radiating and the aura he could see above us. I wasn't paying too much attention to our auras as I was becoming more and more curious about the huge African man behind me with the deep baritone voice, who seemed to be turning the mantra into words. 'Old man he take me home,' he repeated over and over until I was actually visualising the old man taking him home and just wishing he would get on with what happened after that.

I was sure that I hadn't spotted an African giant as I reached the peak of the mountain, so I thought that maybe the new

213

master had appeared on the mountain. I turned round to take a look. The 'giant' was, in fact, a short, unremarkable white man who, when I later heard him speak, sounded like he was from Bolton. Perhaps he was channelling an African Ascended Master, or something.

As we moved on to more complex prayers and mantras, us amateur devotees were instructed just to keep our hands raised to continue sending the energy out while our fellow members of the mountain-side congregation got on with the advanced stuff. The new mantra wasn't that much more complicated than our beginner's one, it was perhaps a little catchier and allowed the hardcore to show off with a bit of a flourish at the end of each repetition. At one point I spotted one of my fellow newbies falling under its spell and starting to repeat it with the rest of the crowd. I felt like putting my hand up and telling Ray, but I figured that karma would catch up with him later. He had probably added a good few years to his journey back to what the Aetherius Society calls the One Creative Source through his errant Om-ing.

As the prayer was drawing to a climax and Ray was once again leading us through the Aetherius version of the Lord's Prayer, a small group of teenage girls on horses appeared over the mountain. Being teenagers and blissfully unaware that we were pretty damn busy sorting out the Middle East crisis and averting war in Iraq, the girls started to recite the regular Lord's Prayer loudly in a mocking tone while riding in our direction. I fought the urge to shout out 'I'm not really one of them' in an attempt to curb my embarrassment at being seen as part of the group. I also somehow managed not to launch into a wetting-myself kind of a snigger, especially as I was dying to go to the toilet by that point in the proceedings.

Ray bravely ignored the girls and went on with the prayer. Being defeated in our efforts at the last minute by a gang of horsey teens was not an option, especially as the Spiritual Energy Radiator was cranked up to eleven back at base. You could see that Ray was pissed off, but he made it to the end and no one mentioned the intervention. It was like it had never happened. Maybe they were used to that kind of thing. I guess it's inevitable that you will draw attention to yourself if you stand on mountains in the middle of a tourist area chanting with your arms outstretched.

As the session ended, Ray congratulated us all for the tremendous energy that we had radiated from the mountain and declared the event a success. I couldn't wait to get the next day's newspapers and see the pictures of George W. Bush planting a big smacker on Saddam or Sharon and Arafat embracing.

As we gathered and talked, one man was setting up what looked very much like a 1950s office fan set atop an ageing amplifier. Having seen enough sci-fi B-movies, I recognised this instantly as some kind of detection device that would allow us to be aware of any passing flying saucers. Either that or take them down with some kind of sonic noise ray.

According to Tony, Holdstone Down is famous for saucer sightings and they have often gathered in large numbers around the time of pilgrimages.

'One time I just got bored of counting,' he said of an

occasion in the 1960s when he had camped out overnight on the mountain. He didn't offer an explanation as to why the saucers would travel millions of miles to buzz a hundred or so religious devotees when they could be off probing middle-aged women living in trailer parks in Nevada.

'Yes, but that was the '60s,' said Nikki. Obviously there were just more saucers hanging out of an evening then, hoping to catch sight of some naked hippies or even of some of the free earth love that they had heard so much about.

On the way back down to the car, Tony asked me if I had felt anything during the prayer service. I wanted to say 'stupid', but I had actually come to quite like both him and Nikki in our short time together, so I just said 'no'.

They were very open about their beliefs and didn't once try to cajole me into attending further Aetherius events, just leaving it with a 'look us up if you're interested' as they drove me back to Combe Martin. They did go to great lengths to reassure me that they were not a 'cult' and had been thoroughly investigated by the Home Office to ensure this fact. It seemed a fair assessment – their belief system may be somewhat outlandish by most standards, but there certainly didn't seem to be anything sinister or suicidal about the group. True, they may have been founded by a man with not too great a grip on reality, but then what religion hasn't?

I wanted to stay on and go drinking with the group at one of the pubs in Combe Martin – which I was sure would be a surreal experience – but the buses between the town and Barnstaple were few and far between and I had to get back so that I could catch my train. I didn't want to miss it and be forced to spend another night in Barnstaple. The only part of that town I wanted to spend any more time in was the inside of the pasty shop on my way to catch the dreaded Tarka Line out of there.

As I boarded the bus I silently chanted my mantra to myself one more time, in prayer that Henry Williamson's National Socialist influence on the area had at least extended to ensuring that the trains ran on time.

9. TOP OF
THE CROPS

After discovering that it was actually pixies that make crop circles, I was keen to try to catch some of them in the act. So when I came across a group that claimed to be involved with the making of these mysterious patterns, I jumped at their invitation to go out with them and witness the making of a circle.

You can imagine my disappointment, when I turned up on a warm summer's evening at our pre-arranged rendezvous outside a tube station in West London, at being met by two men in a beaten-up car rather than, say, a gaggle of little people in a motorised wheelbarrow.

'Maybe we're going to meet the pixies there,' I thought, but this was not to be. As it turned out, it seems that my friends in the Aetherius Society had duped me and crop circles are actually made by humans. Or that is what John and Wil told me when I got into the car and asked if perhaps the pixies were in the boot. After they had stopped laughing, that is.

John Lundberg and Wil Russell have been making crop circles to some acclaim and a good deal of notoriety since 1994. The acclaim has been mostly speculative as the Circlemakers, as they call themselves, never actually tell anyone which circles they make, preferring to leave them as anonymous works of art and the crop circle researchers, or 'croppies' as they are referred to by John and Wil, guessing as to their origin. Which is where the notoriety comes in.

The various groups of croppies spend most of the summer photographing crop circles from the air, carrying out tests on the crops and the fields they appear in and waiting in fields for something mysterious to happen. This must be a singularly frustrating pastime, as none of them, as far as I can make out, have ever actually seen a formation magically appear before their eyes. It often seems that they are doing little more than providing a documentation service to the Circlemakers and the other groups around the country that create circles. I imagine that spending the summer nights in a wheat field, sipping tomato soup from a Thermos flask, may actually be quite pleasant on the odd occasion, but to devote your time to chasing what seems to be a hoax must be a far from life-affirming experience. This is why the croppies hate the Circlemakers and their ilk with a vengeance.

'We have actually been chased by croppies,' said John, as Wil drove us to our destination. 'It was like *Starsky and Hutch*. We were on our way to the field and some croppies recognised us. We eventually managed to shake them off.'

He also told me how one individual went as far as hiring

private detectives to follow members of the Circlemakers in an attempt to uncover which circles they were making. John and Wil's faces are fairly well known to the croppies as the pair have, along with other crop circlemakers, appeared on television to explain how they make the formations. They even accept commissions from advertising agencies to make crop circles promoting anything from cars to breakfast cereal. As the croppies know that these are definitely man-made, they are always slated for imperfections in both design and execution. The same groups often unwittingly praise the complex geometry and astounding designs that are created by John and Wil.

As far as the journey to the site where the crop circle was to be made, well, you'll have to make that bit up. To preserve the Circlemakers' code of not claiming authorship of the circles they create, I was sworn to secrecy as to the location or even the area of the country we travelled to, as well as details of the shape and design.

John jokingly said that they had considered putting a bag over my head to hide our destination from me, so maybe it is best that you assume that he did. Or that they locked me in the boot of the car. You can even imagine that they bound me hand and foot and put one of those ball-gags in my mouth, if that does it for you. A version where there was a blinding light somewhere just after we hit the motorway and I woke up naked in the middle of a finished circle is also acceptable, though in that case you should skip straight past the details of how the circle was made.

John seemed to have an expert knowledge of every wheat and barley field in England and exactly which pathways you had to go up to reach them. As we drove past the field that he'd had his eye on for some weeks, he went over the details with Wil of how best to get to it without being seen by farmers, croppies or suspicious local residents. It was at this point that it all got a bit SAS.

John told me that if we were to meet any walkers or farmers as we approached the field, we should act like hippy walkers enjoying being at one with nature, but trying not to make too much of a show of fiddling with the crystals in our front trouser pockets. In the field we were to maintain near silence and speak only in hushed tones, in case someone walking by heard us and forced us to flee the half-completed formation.

If we did see someone in the field once the circlemaking had begun, we were to inform the others by tugging on a rope or trying to catch their eyes, return to the centre of the circle to collect any equipment or coats and then scarper in the opposite direction to that in which the interloper was coming. I was also told to divest myself of any identifying items before entering the field lest I should drop them in the circle or give the game away if we were captured and strip-searched by enemy forces, farmers or aliens.

Despite John and Wil's expertise in pissing off the croppie community, and hence half of the UFO-watching world, with their late-night pranking, they were surprisingly open-minded about the possibility that some circles are not man-made and could both recount seeing odd lights in the sky when they were engaged in making their circles in the middle of the night. However, they did rule out any possibility of pixie involvement, as well as that of sheep.

We left the car to walk cross-country to our target field, the pair's knowledge and experience of the area coming into its own as we climbed fences and located stiles in neighbouring fields in the rapidly dwindling twilight. All was going well until we happened upon the enemy that the Circlemakers fear most – cows. There was only one way to reach the field that John had earmarked for the night's circle, and that was straight through the cow field.

The cows were not fully grown and looked pretty harmless, but John had been chased by one before. He craned his neck to see if there was another cow-free field we could traverse. There wasn't. He gingerly put one foot up on the barbed wire fence and then the other, before throwing a leg over the fence and jumping down into the field. Wil followed nervously, with me close behind.

As we walked towards the cows, they started to disperse.

'Oh good, they're walking away,' said John.

'Ah, but perhaps they are taking a run up,' I told him.

He laughed a very nervous ' I really hope they're not' kind of laugh, before moving a little more briskly to the safety of the far side of the field.

There was one major problem when we reached the field that John had plumped for. There weren't any crops in it. From the roadside the field looked full of wheat, but it had recently been harvested. As luck would have it, however, the next field up contained a bountiful crop of chest-high golden wheat, which would be perfect for our creation.

I say 'our creation' as the agreement with John and Wil was that I would actually have to take part in the circlemaking process if I were to come along with them. They didn't want me standing idly by while they did all the hard work; and if blue flashing lights and sirens were to appear in the middle of the night, then it was only fair that I should take part of the blame. And anyway, they were a man down as the third member of their regular trio, Rod Dickinson, was out of the country.

Obviously John and Wil had long ago made up their minds on the question of the morality of stomping down a farmer's crops overnight and the financial consequences that may have, but I was keen to clear my conscience too.

'Doesn't this piss the farmers off?' I asked. 'It must cost them a fair bit to lose a big chunk of cereal.'

'Well it can damage a small amount of crop,' said John, 'but they can usually lower the blades on the combine enough that they can still cut the formation. Some farmers just cut them out straight away so that they don't have croppies and tourists trampling on the rest of the crop, but some put a bucket by the gate for donations, or sell postcards. Back when they first really took off, one farmer made about £30,000 from about £100 worth of damaged crop. So no, we don't feel guilty because we actually bring tourist money to the areas where circles occur most often.'

In fact, a cottage industry has sprung up around the annual

appearance of dozens of formations in the west of England. Wiltshire can lay claim to both a pub and a roadside diner that serve as meeting points for enthusiasts and gift shops for the thousands of visitors who are drawn to the area by the chance to stand in the middle of a crop circle. When I made a late-summer stop-off at the Silent Circle Café at Cherhill, the proprietor speculated that they had served 10,000 customers since they opened at the beginning of the circle season in June. The café serves as a kind of tourist board for circles and has maps pinpointing the latest findings, access to discussion groups on the Internet and, when I popped by, was doing a roaring trade selling aerial photographs of the summer's finest formations.

The fact that circles can only be appreciated wholly from the sky has been a boon to those offering microlight and helicopter tours of the area to the ever-growing number of enthusiasts. The dissemination of photographs taken from an aerial vantage point also allows the Circlemakers to admire their handiwork after they have had the chance to go home and have a sleep and a bath.

John and Wil established that the new field was fine for the creation of our circle and that we couldn't be seen too easily from the road or the surrounding pathways. Then we returned to the car, again being wary of the possibility of stampeding cows, to eat some crisps and wait a while for the sun to go down, which would allow us to return to the field by a more direct route under the cover of darkness. We also needed to grab our water and the circlemaking apparatus.

Serious cerealologists (as croppies sometimes like to be known) spend a lot of time deriding the main piece of the Circlemakers' kit – the plank of wood with a length of rope attached at each end. It seems that the primitive nature of the crop flattening equipment is the ultimate insult to groups that talk of 'sacred geometry', 'precision harmonics' and 'unknown theorems'. As far as tools go, you don't get much blunter than a yard-long piece of wood with a knotted piece of rope threaded through it. Not exactly the stuff of science fiction, is it?

Once the Doritos had been downed and the sun had sunk out of view, we were once again roused to our status of not-quite crack commando circlemaking unit as John gesticulated, Wil started to issue instructions and I just stared back in confusion. At this point I was getting pretty nervous that I was going to make a complete hash of the circle and our efforts would be laughed at by enthusiasts everywhere. Thankfully, John and Wil seemed far less concerned about their abilities to turn me into a crop circle-creating artist up there with the pixies – which I still had my sneaking suspicions about – and the extra-terrestrials.

'Oh well,' I thought, 'at least they won't be able to blame me publicly as that would mean breaking their own rules about admitting authorship.'

Wil started up the car and drove us rapidly down the main road to a track that would take us close to the field. We quickly unloaded the stomping planks and our bottles of water and then dived into a hedge for cover as Wil sped off again to park up and make his way back to meet us.

225

After a suitable pause to ensure that we had not been spotted, we picked up the three planks and started to walk towards the field and our rendezvous point with Wil.

'If you see anyone just drop the plank and keep walking,' said John. I thought that I might actually be more suspicious of someone walking along oblivious to the lump of wood they had just dropped, but I figured that John knew what he was talking about.

After a little more time hiding behind a different hedge, Wil arrived and we all clambered over the fence and entered the field. Once in the field, we walked quickly in single file along one of the tramlines made by the farmer's crop-spraying equipment until we reached a suitable centre point for our crop circle. These straight lines of crushed crops, which sit sixty-five feet apart, are present in most non-organic cereal fields and are used by crop circle researchers to estimate the size of a formation without the need to measure it. They also provide a route for the Circlemakers and other like-minded groups to get in and out of fields without leaving clues as to the human origin of the formations they create.

At our chosen centre point, Wil grabbed one of the planks and promptly flattened a circle big enough for us to dump our coats and drinks and sit down in. Once we had a space to sit, John produced a computer printout of the design for our circle. This is the point at which I remembered that I had never made one before and once again started to doubt my ability to do so.

'You're joking,' I said. The design looked incredibly

complex and my guess was that this would take days to make rather than the four hours that John and Wil had timetabled.

'No, you'll be fine,' John reassured. 'It looks a lot more complex than it actually is. It might even take less than four hours.' The fact that he explained to me how the design encompassed both three-fold geometry and the use of prime numbers didn't really help the credibility of his guesstimate as far as I was concerned.

My task was, initially, to be a kind of scarecrow, standing at the centre point and holding the end of surveying tape-measures while John and Wil marked out the guidelines that would form the skeleton of our formation. The first job was for Wil to simply walk round me with the tape stretched to the desired length, in order to mark out the perimeter of a more geometrically correct version of the central circle that he had made on first arriving in the field. Once this was marked, he employed a few deft sweeping movements with his stomping board to turn our base camp into a perfect circle.

The basic marking out and measuring probably went on for about forty minutes or so. Then John and Wil decided to stop for a drink and came back to the centre to see how I was enjoying my experience so far.

'I did warn you it was pretty boring, didn't I?' whispered John. 'Do you want to have a go at some marking?'

'Erm, I think I'll pass for now,' I said, hoping that he wouldn't ask again. I have trouble moving around my own flat without walking into doors and walls, so I hated to think what a mess I would make of the basic outline of our formation. Anyway, I was enjoying taking in all the preparatory work that they had to do as well as the experience of being in the middle of a field looking up at the sky on a mild summer's night. At one point the moon had three bold black stripes of cloud all the way across it, making it look as if it had been char-grilled.

Wil went out and made a few more marks around the edge of the layout and was soon back, announcing that he had finished. We then all headed along a tramline to the edge of the shape that the pair had marked out and prepared to get working on the finer detail of John's design. At first this involved all three of us working with the surveyor's tape-measure, but pretty soon Wil announced that he had a feel for the geometrics and was able to estimate the measurements that we had been making just by using his visual judgment. This came as quite a shock to me as I had assumed that if everything wasn't measured accurately, then the whole plan would fall apart. John had no such doubts.

'Confident?' he asked Wil, in that annoying way that Chris Tarrant does on *Who Wants to be a Millionaire?*

'Yep,' said Wil, a man of few words, and went thrashing through the crop with great gusto. I still wasn't convinced and envisioned our creation being mocked on the front page of every enthusiast's newsletter and in every newsgroup on the web. What the hell was Wil thinking?

The next couple of hours proceeded in an orderly mark a bit, stomp a bit, mark a bit, stomp a bit fashion. Of course, I cannot, as an honorary Circlemaker, say much about exactly how we marked and stomped our crop circle, but I can say that it was a lot more physically demanding than I had expected. The rope on the stomping board is pulled up tense with both hands to act as a kind of handle, one foot is placed on the board and the crop is pushed down using a kind of scything motion as you twist your foot across it. I am sure if you stood back and watched it would resemble some kind of lumbering Frankenstein dance step.

But the flattening of crops is not a simple matter of getting it all down as quickly as you can, the crop must be swept aside in such a way as to create neat swirls, which make it look as if it was flattened by some kind of unearthly downward thrust rather than just some blokes jumping up and down on it. This also makes the patterns created in the crop stand out far better when seen from above.

Stomping crops is tough on the legs when you are doing it for hours on end and I imagine it could well catch on as a fashionable new workout routine. I made a mental note to suggest to John and Wil that we collaborate on a crop circle-making exercise video to cash in on the rise in interest in crop circles in the USA, generated by the Mel Gibson film, *Signs*.

One thing I had not really thought about, but is always brought up by those who argue that humans simply could not create such complex patterns in crops, was the light. Obviously, using floodlights or torches would have exposed us to the risk of being spotted, so the circle was created using only the moonlight and our night vision to guide us. This was more than adequate for the job in hand. I could see clearly for at least twenty feet ahead of me. I was also able make out a good deal of the field and the surrounding area as far as the roads that formed its farthest reaches. Even without my fairly impressive weekly carrot consumption, I think that my natural night vision would have been good enough to enable me to carry out the task. When the moon disappeared behind a cloud, I was still able to swipe my plank across the crop in line with the design without any difficulty seeing. John had some trouble adjusting to the darkness at first and did have to ask me if I could see one of the landmarks that led us to the field, but once they got to work both he and Wil raced around the field without stumbling or tripping once.

Halfway through our task, Wil noticed that some of the shapes we had made did not strictly conform to the design and there was a horrible moment when it all seemed to have gone wrong. There did seem to be a slight warning about this at the marking out stage but it had gone all but unnoticed as Wil improvised a solution. The pair pondered, stroking their chins a while, before John had a 'eureka' moment and decided that the problem wouldn't have any visible effect on the formation once it was finished. John told me that it is amazing what you can get away with in terms of plumb-line accuracy, or lack of it, when it comes to making a circle, pointing out that the bigger the formation, the larger the margin of error you can allow for.

We finally finished our crop circle at 2.50 a.m. Exactly four hours after we had started. There had been one moment when we all thought we could hear someone else in the field, but it was probably just foxes, rats or one of those deadly black panthers that seem to roam the fields of rural England with impunity. We took a quick walk around some of the work of land art and tried to guess what it would look like from above, as well as taking the opportunity for a long-overdue piss.

At first I felt slightly guilty peeing out from the edge of our circle onto wheat that you may well have recently consumed as a breakfast cereal. But considering how much John was itching from the pesticide on the crop once we had finished, I figure that my urine is probably the least of your worries. One thing that did faze me was that the instant my pee hit the wheat, I was struck with a waft of pungent odour that smelt exactly like the scent spewed out by the brewery I used to live near to. So I guess the rumours about their beer must have been true.

I asked John if the itching is a regular problem for crop circle architects.

'Sometimes it's worse than others,' he said. 'But the worst thing is the hay fever.'

Here is a man who suffers for his art. While I studiously try to avoid any kind of nature during the summer months, John spends the height of summer leaping around in wheat, barley and oilseed rape fields with only anti-histamine to aid him. I was thankful that my hay fever had mysteriously held off for most of the summer, with only two really bad days of streaming eyes and non-stop sneezing. Maybe my medication really was new and improved, or it could have been the daily dose of vitamin C that someone had recommended. Either way, I'd had the least sniffly summer since records began. Not that I actually keep records of that kind of thing, you understand. That would be akin to some kind of pollen-related anality that even bus-spotters might snigger at.

After our brief look round the circle, John and I headed back along the tramlines and up the path, repeating our various hiding in hedge manoeuvres as we went, while Wil yomped back to fetch the car from its hiding place. John told me that this can be a dangerous time for being spotted, as the croppies will often watch certain areas at night for signs of the Circlemakers.

Thankfully there was no need for us to bury ourselves in the mud or stretch a fishing line across the pathway to take out an inquisitive group of croppies who knew too much. The journey back to London and two hours sleep was blissfully uneventful, bar the moment when Wil woke a dozing John and me by sounding his horn at a large rat that was crossing the road in front of the car.

About three days after our expedition, John e-mailed me a photograph of our formation that he had found on the web. It looked incredible. The aerial photograph from an enthusiast's site was a bit fuzzy, but you could make out that, despite my amateurish stomping, the formation looked perfect. It wasn't long before more pictures appeared online, including shots from inside the circle itself as well as from above. It seemed that people were quite excited about our work. Gratifyingly for me, and no doubt for the Circlemakers, not one person questioned our geometry or suggested that it was a fake.

Devizes is pretty much at ground zero of the crop circle world. If an innovative or amazing circle is going to appear in the cereal fields, then it is odds on that it will do so nearby. Within easy driving, or saucer-flying reach of the ancient sites of Avebury and Stonehenge, it is an ideal base for anyone needing to keep up with the latest in formations. There is even an airfield nearby for those who want to take up a plane or helicopter to get some decent photographs.

One person who regularly does just that is Francine Blake of the Wiltshire Crop Circle Study Group. And that is why I found myself sitting in a café above The Healthy Life health food shop, waiting for her to turn up. My experience of circle-making with John and Wil, and the subsequent failure of anyone to make a call on our hoax circle, had lead me to believe that the whole phenomenon was one great big prank. But I had also read a lot on the Internet about what charlatans the Circlemakers were and how they wouldn't know a piece of sacred geometry if it appeared in their own beard growth. I had also read of their supposed abilities as media manipulators, so I felt that I owed it to myself to find out if The Truth *was* Out There.

Devizes is an attractive, mostly middle-class market town with a pleasant pond, old stone houses and the requisite number of tearooms, coffee shops and well-kept pubs with abundant floral displays. In other words, the kind of town that makes teenagers want to listen to Korn, customise their mum's old Ford Fiesta ridiculously or simply shag like rabbits to relieve the boredom. On the day that I hit town, it seems that option three was the most in vogue, as twenty-five per cent of the thirteen- to twenty-year-old girls on the streets were sporting fresh purple love bites the size and hue of damsons. Perhaps it was the result of the sudden snap of glorious weather that we were having after days of heavy downpours. Though it could have been alien forces, I suppose.

Whatever it was that had the local teens on heat, it seemed to have affected some of the older members of Devizes society as well. As I waited for Francine, the town's fifty-something Women Who Lunch were discussing lingerie over organic cola drinks and salads and giggling in that way that women do in documentaries about Ann Summers' parties. I mean, no one got out a vibrator and tried it out on their nose, but I could tell that they were just gagging to as soon as I had finished my vegetable soup and left.

When Francine finally arrived, she was clutching a copy of the Crop Circle Calendar. The calendar featured shots of circles that she had taken from the air and was one of the main fundraisers for the Wiltshire Crop Circle Study Group. The calendar included an array of crop circle designs, many of which I had seen during my scouring of websites and a few of which seemed possible candidates for creation by the Circlemakers. This was merely guesswork on my part though; even if I asked, they wouldn't tell me which ones in the calendar, if any, were down to them.

Roughly the same age as the ladies-a-lunching at the next table, Francine was fitted out with a regulation loose New-Ager outfit and no makeup, though she did look considerably younger and healthier than the orange-foundationed twin-sets who had by then moved on to ruminating upon the advantages of aluminium-free deodorants. Shortly after she had sat down, her husband, John, appeared behind her. He said he had come to find her as he couldn't locate her at home, but it seemed like a ruse to make sure I didn't look like the type of guy likely to try to sacrifice Francine to some kind of sun god at the crop circle to which she had promised to take me that afternoon.

John Blake is a firm believer in the notion that We Are Not Alone and that crop circles are a sign of this. In his eyes, the formations are messages that we must interpret. According to John, we are not ready for direct communication from other worlds yet and must instead expand our minds by trying to interpret the signs in the circles, in much the same way that retired professors do daily battle with *The Times*' crossword in order to stave off the onset of senility and mental shutdown. Only when we have learned to decipher these word searches in wheat will we be ready to move on and actually earn a personal visit from the sacred geometricians.

Francine first became interested in crop circles in 1987 when she was living in London. She finally gave in to the draw of Wiltshire five years later and moved to the area where she found she was spending most of her time anyway. Within three years she had set up the Wiltshire Crop Circle Study Group and had become a central figure in the crop circle scene, giving lectures internationally and presenting her arguments to the media. Now research is more or less a full-time job for her and, subsidised by John and the sales of the calendar, she is up in a helicopter taking photographs of circles twice a week during the busy summer months. These photo-taking trips over the fields of Wiltshire don't come cheap at £179 an outing, or roughly the total income before costs from the sale of twenty-one Crop Circle Calendars.

As we strolled from the café through the centre of Devizes to where Francine's car was parked, she enthused about the abundance of quality formations that she had seen so far that summer.

'There are very few hoaxes this summer,' she said. 'At the moment I am photographing maybe six circles a week and they are all very good.'

'How can you spot a hoax?' I asked as we drove out of Devizes, hoping for the definitive answer as to how researchers pick out the wheat from the chaff, as it were. Instead I was given a rundown of paid-for circles that the Circlemakers had made for advertisements or television programmes. While I understood that these were 'fakes' by the definition of those who believe that circles are created by non-human forces, I didn't think that they could really be called hoaxes when there had been no attempt to hide their creation or claim that they had been made by anything other than a group that call themselves artists.

'Yes, but everyone knows those were man-made,' I said. 'No one tried to hide that.'

Francine said that she did not like to speculate about circles created anonymously, but did suspect that nearly all of them were not hoaxes and were created by what she termed 'the real circlemakers'. She didn't like to guess as to the actual identity of these either, but made it clear that they were, most likely, forces from another world.

'This Team Satan call themselves artists, but what they do is not art,' she said. 'They are like the people who call up the police during a murder investigation and give them false information. They are hoaxers.'

'Sorry, who are Team Satan?' I asked, confused.

'These are the ones who call themselves Circlemakers,' Francine replied. 'They are not circlemakers, to call themselves that is false. Before they decided to call themselves Circlemakers, they were Team Satan. But once people started to take notice of them and they had their website, they changed their name so that it seemed like they were *the* circlemakers and they made all of the circles. They are just trying to take the responsibility for something they have not done.'

I must have looked sceptical, as she continued.

'I have a videotape of Team Satan trying to make a crop circle in the shape of a car. It took them an hour and a half to mark out and make a straight line in daylight. And they say that they can make a crop circle without being detected in the middle of the countryside at night in just a few hours. It is not possible.'

I decided that particular moment was not the best time to say 'Yes, but I have seen them make a circle in the dark, I even helped,' and instead kept my mouth firmly shut. Francine was just getting warmed up on the Circlemakers and I didn't particularly want to be booted out of the car in the middle of the countryside, especially as I had no idea where exactly we were. From this moment on she referred to the Circlemakers only as Team Satan and I got the impression that a lot of other researchers did the same, not wanting to take the name of the real circlemakers in vain.

The circle that Francine took me to was in East Field near to Alton Barnes. The field was well known as a regular site for the appearance of crop circles and was surrounded by ancient burial sites and hills such as Goldenball Hill, allegedly so named because of the 'golden balls' or UFOs seen in the night sky above it.

As we walked along the brow of a hill above the East Field the formation came into view, a large spiral with circles at the centre in a field of wheat. There was also a smaller formation in the same field. Francine thought that she could make out another circle in a field to the left, but we weren't high enough to make out whether it was wind damage or an actual formation. It certainly hadn't been there when Francine had flown over the field the day before.

We wandered down the hill and over a stile to the field where the formation lay. Francine said that the circle was two or three days old and, using the tramlines in the field as a guide, she estimated that it was 220 feet in diameter. She told me that I was lucky to be visiting it now, when the energy given off by it was still likely to be high.

Just as I had done with the Circlemakers, we walked into the field using the tramlines so as not to disturb the standing wheat. This time it was done so as not to upset the farmer rather than to cover our tracks. Some farmers are on fairly amicable terms with the researchers and even tourists, so long as they don't cause any damage to untouched crops inside and outside the formation.

As we entered the circle, Francine pointed out how the wheat was bent down gently at the base rather than simply crushed. She said that this, coupled with the way that hardly any of the heads of the wheat had been damaged or spilt their seeds, was proof of the fact that this could not be of human construction. On the other hand, I thought, it could be a sign of just the kind of method we had used to make our circle, scything with the plank at the base of the crop in order to bend it into swirls similar to the ones I saw at my feet.

Upon reaching the centre of the formation, Francine called me over to a twist of wheat that was still half standing in the central circle. This was off-centre and was mirrored by another similar twist on the other side of the central circle. This, according to Francine, was another sign that this circle was other-worldly, since this kind of geometrical feat would be beyond all but the very best mathematicians and perhaps even too complex for them.

'Why would anyone go to the bother of making the centre off-centre?' she asked, after I pointed out that perhaps someone had made that central circle and simply left two tufts of wheat standing at a non-central point before doing a bit of amateur macramé on them.

Francine gave me a look. She also rejected my suggestion that perhaps these twisted sheaves were some kind of signature from whichever group it was that had made it.

'This is not a signature,' she said. 'When the hoaxers sign them they put something like their initials or 'I love Sarah'. Formations like these have an awesome energy that can be measured. It is simple to tell the fakes. We have found silicon crystals in formations which are so pure that they can't be from earth and the heat made during formations also has an effect on the plants in the circles and can expand their cellular structure.'

With my expertise in both chemistry and biology being somewhat lacking, this was all pretty much gibberish to me, but Francine told me that various scientists within the crop circle research community were undertaking experiments involving samples of wheat taken from formations. As she gathered a good few handfuls from the centre of the circle, she informed me that the strains of wheat grown after supposed extra-terrestrial intervention seemed to be stronger than normal wheat.

'So is this some kind of bonus for the farmer for the inconvenience of losing crops and having people wandering through their field, then?' I asked, figuring that this may be a sign of some kind of apologetically benevolent life form showing us that they have the power to help us.

'No, it is just a side-effect of their creation, I think,' said Francine, crushing my dreams of farmer-friendly aliens which might even turn out disguised in Barbours and wellies to swell the numbers on the odd Countryside Alliance march through London.

As we took a chance to sit and rest, a black army helicopter flew low over the circle and hovered above it for a few seconds before taking a spin over the surrounding countryside and coming back around again.

'Do you think they are recording data on the circle?' I asked.

Francine looked at me, giving me a 'maybe' kind of a shrug. 'The army doesn't know what is going on,' she said. 'We don't know what is happening so why should the government know what is happening any better than those who spend their time researching them?' She then cited the example of a friend, a high-ranking naval officer, who has called her to ask what is going on.

As we sat in the sun, chatting about circles, Francine rummaged in her bag and pulled out three canisters of film. She unravelled the first roll and held it up to the light and I could see that these were aerial photographs of crop circles.

'I used to use a digital camera,' she said, 'but after taking one set of pictures I actually broke the motherboard on my computer when I downloaded them. I think that it was because of the energy generated. *They* are far more advanced than we are. When I took my G3 for repair, the person said they had never seen anything like that happen before.'

As evidenced by her calendar, Francine takes a mean photograph and the shots on the reel she had out were just as sharp, showing off the intricate formations at their most stunning. She unrolled another film, the sun picking out the patterns' light sections of flattened crops on the brown and gold fields.

She passed me the film for a closer look while she unfurled the final roll. When she had finished examining that she passed it across for me to view. As she handed it to me I almost dropped it. Even without looking closely, I could make out several pictures of the crop circle that I had made with John and Wil.

'That's a real beauty, isn't it?' said Francine, noticing me lingering over her photos of our formation.

'Yes . . . erm, nice photographs,' I stammered.

I had only seen small, blurry Internet images of our circle so far,[13] but Francine had done us proud with these photos. I felt like punching the air, or asking her for a blow-up to take home and show John and Wil, but thought better of it. Instead, I pretended to have a thorough look at the rest of the formations on the film, all the while admiring the wonder of our nocturnal handiwork and trying not to laugh at the irony of Francine photographing it.

I was glad that I had been able to keep schtum when

---

[13] I later saw a lot more photos of our circle as it appeared in several newspapers, even featuring in a piece dubbed 'Crop Idol' in the *Sun*, in which readers were encouraged to ring in and vote for the best circle of that summer. My oath of secrecy to the Circlemakers prevents me from telling you how well it did.

Francine began talking about 'Team Satan' again as we walked along the tramlines and out of the field. She referred to their 'pathetic on the breadline' existence in south London, which seemed wrong both financially and geographically from what I had gathered from my meeting with John and Wil.

'Why don't you just go out with them one night and see what it is they do?' I ventured. 'Surely if it is that important then you should see them at work and then you could be really sure about your theories.'

'Oh, I know them and what they do, but I don't want to waste any of my energies on them,' she said. 'I would rather die than do that. Why can't they just do something with their lives?'

As we walked back to the car, Francine expounded her theory as to why many people refuse to believe that crop circles are a genuine phenomenon and not merely art hoaxes executed by malnourished south Londoners and their ilk.

'People cannot accept crop circles as it directly clashes with their belief system and would ultimately destroy it,' she said, citing how science and religion through the ages have been guilty of the very same mistakes, eventually having to accept that they were wrong. Of course, the selfsame argument could be made against those pushing the 'not possible for humans to create' line in the face of evidence that they can do so very well.

On the way back to Devizes, we spoke mainly about the beautiful countryside we were driving through. I was starting to have to bite my tongue about Francine's beliefs and she, in turn, seemed to have been agitated by having to talk about the Circlemakers.

When we arrived, Francine, as she had promised, invited me in to watch the Team Satan video she had described to me. In the living room, she rummaged in a pile of tapes next to the television, most of which seemed to be crop circle-related. On the walls were a selection of Francine's aerial photographs, some blown up to poster size.

'Ah, I think this is it,' she said, taking a tape out of its case and loading it into the video recorder. As she pressed 'rewind' on the remote control, the phone rang and she went out into the hallway to answer it, leaving me to watch the twenty minutes of footage alone.

The video footage was hilarious for several reasons and I was glad that I got to see it on my own so that Francine couldn't see which bits I was laughing at. Obviously considered something of an underground classic amongst the crop circle research community, the tape featured John, Wil and fellow Circlemaker Rod Dickinson on a hot summer's day, wearing white sun hats and all looking pretty confused. The formation they were working on was for an advert for a Mitsubishi car and, true to Francine's word, they did seem to be having trouble working out how to execute the basics of the design. There had been no such indecision when I had been with John and Wil, but then the film had been shot four years earlier. I imagine they have learned a lot since then.

But far funnier than the Circlemakers' mild incompetence on this paid job was the running commentary that came from those doing the filming. Voices that sounded Dutch and German were making critiques and reminding each other to check on the marks left by pegs used by 'Team Satan' to mark the site. There were also self-congratulatory whispers about how 'they cannot agree how to do it'. Getting a little braver, they even started to heckle the Circlemakers as they worked. It seemed that they were willing to deny any evidence that might suggest that the Circlemakers may be behind a good deal of the formations that crop circle researchers have attributed to other-worldly forces. To do so would be like a trainspotter admitting that they preferred buses, or denying the existence of Class 47 locomotives altogether.

'He is new to the business?' they asked rhetorically, as Wil looked unsure how to flatten a particular part of the design. From that moment on they referred to him as 'the underling', which, I can assure you, sounds much funnier in a Germanic accent than it does in an English one.

Once the film was over, Francine came back into the room. Perhaps she had been spying on me all along, noting which parts I laughed at.

'I really have to get on now,' she said, signalling that our meeting was over and it was time for me to go.

As we were saying our goodbyes, Francine told me that I should try to avoid any mention of 'Team Satan' in anything I wrote about crop circles.

'That would be better,' she said.

'But they are a part of the story,' I said, 'surely you can't deny that.'

But Francine just went back to her line about how they are just hoaxers who detract from the real story, again comparing them to people who make false claims to the police as they investigate murders or child abductions. That is how seriously she views the role of crop circle investigators and I got the feeling that even if she did spend a night out in the field with John and Wil, she would not change her mind.

The train journey back to London was punctuated only by the discovery of the wrong kind of track somewhere outside Reading. A collective groan went up in the carriage as the guard announced that we might have to wait outside the station for some time while an apparent crack in a rail was tested.

I had visions of being there for hours, awaiting the arrival of engineers and track specialists, but thankfully a solution came before I had to contemplate completing my journey on foot. My fellow passengers and I breathed a sigh of relief when the all-clear was signalled by a train rumbling slowly past in the opposite direction with no grinding of brakes, shattering of glass and appearance of bodies on the track. With our magnificent infrastructure up and running again, we were soon on our way.

10. THIRTY BLOODY
MINUTES AND
NO MONKEYS?

Following the various administrative disasters that had befallen my travels with First Great Western trains, I was well prepared for my journey to St Austell. I had booked it far enough ahead to have the ticket posted to me, had quadruple checked that the £43 one-way fare was correct and the ticket valid. I had even gone to the effort of booking a seat on the advice of the telephone booking clerk.

The reason I had bought a single ticket was because I had purchased a single flight back from Newquay airport from Ryanair. Of course Ryanair were denounced in the media as baggage-losing slackers about five minutes after I received a confirmation e-mail stating that the payment for my ticket had been accepted, but I travel light so that wasn't much of a concern for me.

I was heading to Cornwall to witness the annual voyage of a giant Cornish pasty from the town of Polruan to the small port of Fowey, across the Fowey Estuary. I had heard from a friend that the pasty was sailed across to cheers and applause from the locals. It sounded a bit like a cargo cult or some kind of ceremony involving human sacrifice but, as far as I am concerned, pastry products don't get applauded enough, so I was keen to witness the event – especially as I had found out that there was a chance it would be the last time it would happen.

Fowey regatta week had been marked by a giant pasty since 1955 and for the last twenty-five years the savoury favourite had been sailed over from the Polruan bakery. But the bakery had just been sold, meaning that the days of the pasty were numbered, unless another giant-pasty maker could be found. Thankfully neither village had a McDonalds restaurant, so the chances of the oversized meat-and-vegetable-filled pie being replaced by a Triple Big McPasty Special Meal were fairly scant.

About five minutes after taking my seat on the train, I realised that something was horribly wrong. I knew that it was the school holidays and that Cornwall is a popular holiday destination, but there just seemed to be too many children in my carriage. Then I saw the sign by the window. It read 'Family Carriage'. There was a smiling face logo that slightly resembled the man on Pringles boxes and a notice that said:

This carriage has been designed for use by parents and children, please respect their needs, particularly during school holidays. Thank you.

As far as I could work out, the needs of these children consisted of screaming and eating cheesy puffs until their fingers were orange, then farting the smell of cheesy puffs back out into the carriage. The carriage did not seem to have been specially designed for that, or for any other need of parents or children for that matter. But that was not my concern. My concern was that some fuckwit at First Great Western had thought: Oh, one guy, travelling alone, let's put him in the family carriage. The only explanation could be that it was part of a new government scheme to reduce the birth rate and cut back on the welfare state, as anyone who has spent four hours amid that noise and stench is always going to remember to use contraception and may be put off sex altogether.

So what is the family carriage for? I am familiar with the concept of the family stand at football grounds, the clubs' way of saying that no one will piss down the back of your leg, spill your Bovril or shout 'cunt' loudly behind you every five minutes if you sit in that part of the stadium. But is that sort of thing really an issue on trains? I know that every train contains one group of squaddies swinging four-packs of Stella along with their heavy kit bags, but I don't think there is a particular problem with sporadic outbreaks of violence on the rail system. Apart from in the family carriage itself, that is, which, when I travelled, was a frenzy of smacked legs, crayons stuck in siblings' eyes and struggles over the complimentary colouring-in books.

Perhaps the family carriage is some kind of train feng

shui that was brought in to balance out the introduction of the quiet carriage on many services. Ostensibly a mobile phone-and personal hi-fi-free zone, the quiet carriage is the place where you witness the gradual build-up from one man whispering to his wife that he is 'on the train' to a full-on chatting, texting, novelty-ringing and drum and bassing frenzy approximately ten minutes after you leave London. As a nation we hate being told what to do, but will always stick to the rules until someone has the gall to break them, then it's open season.

Riotous, gaseous, stinking children aside, the train ride to St Austell is one of the finest you could wish to experience, with the highlights coming as you hit the south Devon coast, travelling from Devonport to Saltash and across Isambard Kingdom Brunel's jaw-dropping Royal Albert Bridge. The iron suspension bridge across the Tamar, which was completed in 1859, takes you into Cornwall, where the railway line immediately bears left, giving you a great view of the construction as you look back.

As the train continued through the Cornish countryside, I began to see an increasing number of black and white Cornish flags. I had been to Cornwall previously, but had never before witnessed so many houses, cars and pubs displaying these St Piran's flags. They seem to have increased in direct proportion to the re-adoption of the St George's flag in the rest of England and the fact that they are a kind of monochrome inversion of the English flag made them stand out all the more. It's not exactly clear how many were displayed simply in the name of Cornish pride and how many were part of a visual referendum for a devolved Cornish assembly (or total independence), a call for which has built up once again following devolution in Scotland and Wales. Cornwall also still has its own language, the Cornish for Cornwall being Kernow.

At St Austell I waited for my bus to Fowey which, when it eventually arrived, had only standing room left for me, the family of four and the German couple who got on. This, according to the sign at the front of the bus, was pretty much a full house safety-wise, but the driver kept picking people up, a good deal of them wielding either rucksacks or shopping bags. When I eventually got a seat it was next to a radiator, which was on, despite it being the middle of summer. I noticed it was working as it touched the bare flesh between my socks and trousers, leaving a burn that stayed for several days.

As the number twenty-four bus bumbled through the countryside, cooking its cargo, I took the opportunity to listen in on some local conversation to get a feel for the area. My first choice was the two women in their late thirties who sat behind me, slurring about cocaine, nightclubs and the fact that some bloke fancied one of them but she might need some more cocaine if she was going to sleep with him. Once they got off, I was left with a small boy and his family, who I thought would be far less interesting to listen to but actually turned up some deep philosophical debate.

'So what's going to be in the carnival?' asked mum. They

were obviously also on their way to Fowey, where that night's carnival would precede the following night's pasty-related revelry.

'Everything,' he replied.

'What's everything?' she asked, hoping that he might expand his description.

'All the things,' he said, quite rightly.

Once the woman had managed to get her son to open up a little, the six-year-old showed yet more insight as he told her there would be 'people, apples and jugglers' at the event. The bright young thing had already realised that, strictly speaking, jugglers are not people, though I'm not sure where he was going with the bit about the apples.

Once I had been baked thoroughly for approximately forty minutes, we arrived in Fowey. The bus halted just outside the village itself, as preparations for the evening's carnival meant that the main roads in were closed off.

Tripping down the steep hill into the village, my first experience of Cornwall proper was the Safe Harbour Hotel, which was bursting at the seams with men dressed as Elvis and women in Hawaiian-style flower garlands. Inside, one of the Elvises was belting out a version of 'Fools Rush In'. I took this as a hint and kept walking. I went down the hill, through a churchyard full of teenagers drinking vodka from the bottle, and hit the centre of the village just in time to see a group of men dressed as a mariachi band leading a pony into the Lugger pub.

A local saw me staring open-mouthed at the spectacle of

a group of Mexican musical impersonators leading an imitation donkey into the local.

'Oh, they always do that,' he said. 'All the pubs let them take him in.'

Perhaps Cornwall *is* a different country. The rest of England's pubs are concerned with enforcing a 'no dogs, no boots, no soiled work clothes' regime, but in Cornwall it is just fine to bring in the livestock, just so long as they are accompanied by fake-moustachioed men bearing instruments.

After a couple of minutes, the band and the pony emerged from the pub and wandered down the road to the Galleon. The pony was obviously a quick drinker.

The first thing you need to know if you are travelling to Fowey is how to pronounce its name. If you go around pronouncing it 'Fo-wee', as most visitors do, you will find yourself being corrected by irritated shopkeepers and bus drivers. The correct pronunciation is 'Foy', and it sounds even better if you imagine yourself to have a clay pipe in the corner of your mouth and a woollen fisherman's cap on your head as you say it. The second useful fact is that no matter which shop you buy your pasty from, it will always taste delicious. I tried them all in my short stay, subsisting on a pasty-only diet, and could find fault with none.

Taking my first of many pasties, bought from the bakery opposite my B&B on Fore Street, the village's high street, I walked down to the waterfront to look out over the Fowey Estuary. The fact that this ten-by-twelve-yard quayside-cum-village square area was the only open space in the village made it seem very claustrophobic, but I soon got used to it. Sitting on a bench in the sun, reading the local paper and eating my pasty, I felt the most relaxed I had during my whole trip. I would have preferred sea and sand to estuary and concrete quay, but the warmth and the views across to the hills around Polruan made up for that.

Back in Fore Street, I kept seeing children wearing their nightclothes in the street. Anywhere else this might have seemed strange, but after the Elvis clones and the pony it appeared normal.

'So what if they drive their young through the streets in their pyjamas every night before sending them to bed?' my brain ticked over. 'This is Cornwall, they can do what they like.' I think it could have been something to do with the carnival, but I really can't be sure.

I went back to my B&B to freshen up and watch the news on my room's patriotically Cornish black and white television. The small room was a twin, so instead of the usual sink/urinal there was another bed, leaving me about a call box-sized area of floor space to myself. Still, it was comfortable and the capacious shared bathroom made for a luxurious pre-carnival bathe and shave.

Outside, the streets were beginning to fill with those who had come to see the carnival procession wend its way through the village. The warm summer evening meant that every adult in the street had a pint glass in their hand and every teenager in the churchyard had a can of whatever brand of lager was on special offer at their local off-licence or corner shop. It was the event of the year. A realisation that brought a hint of sorrow for the paucity of the locals' social calendar, as the half-arsed fancy dress parade appeared from around the corner and into the view of drinkers outside the Ship Inn, where I had elbowed myself into a small nook.

There was a Harry Potter-themed carnival float, a gaggle of superannuated baton twirlers calling themselves the Major Rejects and a group of men who were blacked up in face paint. It was unclear whether this was something to do with a sinister Cornish custom or casual racism, but the odd dress and the joke hands waved in the air gospel worship-style suggested a combination of the two.

The main point of the carnival was to show off the carnival kings and queens from Fowey and the surrounding villages. I was used to seeing carnival queens in their early teens from summer nights in Margate, but most of those on display in Fowey were hardly out of nursery. Some youngsters were paraded in pairs on trailers, which were covered by giant versions of those plastic domes that upmarket coffee shops use to keep the flies off of their cakes, while others were displayed in the boots of their parents' Volvo or the back of their 4x4s. This gave the parade the appearance of a paedophile car boot sale. The whole thing was incredibly creepy.

As the cavalcade of under-aged, over made-up children came to a halt, everyone broke for a pub, which wasn't too much of an effort as you are never more than ten yards away from one in Fowey. The night then descended into a New Year's Eve's worth of drinking, carousing, snogging and spewing – most of which went on outside my bedroom window at 2 a.m., when I was trying to sleep.

After being woken twice in the night by drunken serenades of 'I Will Always Love You' and 'Like a Virgin', both sung by men, I rose late the next day. Having missed breakfast, I went across the road to the delicatessen, bought myself a posh pasty and walked down to the quay. On my way to the seats on the waterfront, I noticed a sign for cruises on the estuary and a man standing next to it with a clipboard.

'When's the next cruise?' I asked. I had come to Fowey with the intention of ignoring those messing about on the water, as I find anything to do with yachts generally bores me to tears. My reaction to the continuing coverage of Ellen MacArthur's world voyage had been: 'So what? She was in a boat. Come back and tell me when she has circumnavigated the globe without one, then I'll be interested.' But I figured that a tourist river cruise wouldn't be too bad.

'Next one goes in fifteen minutes, mate,' clipboard man said.

I sat down and finished my breakfast pasty, then boarded the small boat, which could carry about ten passengers, when it arrived at the quayside. Ahead of me in the queue to get on were an elderly trio – two women and one man – and a well-spoken young couple with their two sons. On board, our tour guide and driver munched enthusiastically on the vitamin C tablets that one of them had just produced from a bag. The fact that another bottle of the orange tablets was sitting on the boat's dashboard suggested that warding off scurvy was still a major concern for the modern sailor.

Chewing his vitamins was the last thing that our tour guide did with any kind of enthusiasm. He ran through a list of sites that we were passing, clearly wondering what he was going to have for his dinner at the same time. The board advertising the trips had promised a chance to see dolphins and kingfishers, but what we got was the china clay works and some manky seagulls. Maybe it was the dolphins' and kingfishers' day off.

Despite the fact that the guide was standing just two feet away from me, it was often hard to pick up his spiel above the boat's engines, and the elderly threesome had taken to giggling at the stern, like the inattentive kids who sit at the back of the classroom. For their sake I was hoping there wouldn't be a test on what we had learned once the tour was over.

After taking us inland, the skipper turned the boat around and we headed in the direction of the sea, which proved to be a more picturesque route. We got a better look at Daphne Du Maurier's house, the twin blockhouse towers that used to guard the harbour and the sandy beach at Readymoney, which was full of sunbathers.

'I would like to be a fisherman,' declared one of the young boys to his parents as we drew close to the quay. The laid-back, sun-drenched lifestyle of the slacker seamen had obviously appealed to the nine-year-old.

'No, you can't. We really want you to do a science degree,' said his mother in all seriousness, shattering his youthful dreams of a life on the ocean wave. The pensioners at the back sniggered behind their hands at her no-fun attitude.

I followed my boat trip immediately with another, this time taking the ferry over to Polruan, which turned out to be a ten-minute ride to nowhere. It had a couple of pubs, a gift shop and a beach the size of my room back at the B&B, so I had a quick pint and then headed back to Fowey.

From the ferry stop I took a walk along the coast, up past the fancy Fowey Hall Hotel, with its very English tea garden, and then down the cliff to Readymoney beach, where I sat and read while enjoying a cider-flavoured ice lolly. My reading was, however, rudely interrupted by what sounded like a gun battle going on in the estuary.

'Excellent,' I thought, putting down my book and picking up my pencil and notebook, 'the cod war has resumed, and I am right on the spot for exclusive coverage.' I was just about to start calling news desks when I remembered – the regatta. What sounded like gunfire was actually the start of the races that were taking place. Or was it the end? I watched for a while and was still none the wiser.

When I arrived back in the village centre after an hour or so at the beach, I was surprised to see that all the shops were closing. It was not quite 4 p.m. yet many were putting up signs in their doors saying 'closed for Red Arrows'. The RAF stuntmen had been appearing as part of the Fowey regatta for the past twenty-five years, yet the enthusiasm for any kind of entertainment in the village was such that the streets were emptied as residents took to the waterfront and the hills to witness the coloured smoke trails and aerobatics for which the Red Arrows are famous. Still, at least the locals had got used to the shock of horseless carriages now. I imagine that the first of those Red Arrows shows must have instigated some end-of-the-world stories about 'great flying devils' and 'metal birds' from the local soothsayer.

I opted for the crowded quayside and grabbed another pasty from a just-closing sandwich shop to get me in the mood for the coming of the giant pasty later that evening. Was this the best yet? It was so hard to tell. I was not sure that so many pasties in such a short space of time was good for me, but they were so flavoursome and there was a distinct lack of non-pasty food in the village. I am sure that Daphne Du Maurier ate nothing else during her time in Cornwall, but they didn't seem to have anything about her diet in the Fowey gift shop that bore her name.

Before long, the noise of jet engines filled the air as the Red Arrows appeared, as if from nowhere, and powered up the estuary before turning steeply upwards and breaking formation – red, white and blue smoke trailing in their wake.

'Wouldn't it be great if they crashed and landed on someone's head,' piped up a boy behind me to his mother. She tried to explain the ethical and moral reasons why he shouldn't think it so great, but the thrill of the potential for disaster to happen is essentially what the show is about.

Like a bigger, scarier, vicarious roller-coaster ride, we watch them flying straight at each other – only to pull away just in time – for the danger and not to appreciate what a good job RAF pilots do. We were really here to see a plane plough into that hill on Polruan where a good few people had gathered to watch the show. It wasn't anything personal, it was just that it would give us the best view of the fireball if it went off there.

'Why are people clapping?' the same kid asked. His mother had no answer for that one. I had been thinking the same. I imagine that it must be pretty hard for the pilots to hear even the loudest cheer when they are a couple of thousand feet up, travelling at 400 miles per hour and sitting over a noisy engine. Similarly, Hollywood directors can't hear the morons applauding their latest blockbuster at the local Odeon when they are holidaying on their own private island or snorting cocaine off a prostitute's breasts in their trailers.

Once the Red Arrows had safely completed their display, which I have to admit was pretty spectacular, the waiting for the giant pasty began. No one seemed to know what time it was due or which boat would bring it across, so we all just stood and stared at the water, willing the giant pie to come to us. Rumours abounded – someone could smell pastry, someone else had heard that it was still in the oven at Polruan and another said that it might have been dropped – which had actually happened in the past.

When we heard the Tijuana strains of the Fowey Town Band and saw them in their Mexican gear, though, we knew that all was okay. The band escorted the pasty across the estuary on the waterborne equivalent of a flatbed truck and landed with it at a small quay about one hundred yards from where we the crowd and the hungry children of Fowey were waiting. Tradition dictates that the pasty is divided up between the local youngsters, and they had begun to get whiney and restless in their impatience for sustenance.

When the pasty finally arrived in the quayside square, being held aloft by the band as they waded through the crowd, I was a little disappointed. I had been expecting a bloated version of the type of pasty that I had been guzzling since I hit town – plump and crescent shaped, with the crimped crust to one side – but this five-footer was shallow, held together by the baking tin and a full foot shorter than I had been lead to believe. I got the impression that if a giant strode across the hills of Polruan and stepped over the estuary to grab the pasty for his tea, it would flop and crumble in his hands. I think being surrounded by pasty shops, postcards, recipe books and folklore for the last twenty-four hours had pushed my expectations a little too far.

The pasty was cut on the steps of the King of Prussia pub so that the gathered masses could see six-year-old Peter Tucker and his eleven-year-old sister Amy, the king and queen of the carnival (refreshingly free of make-up), take the first bites of the beast. Amy was obviously not born for the role, as she asked for a piece without onion in it, which is probably considered as damaging as government ministers who assure us that beef is safe to eat politely refusing to taste any in public. I imagine that the local paper was full of the scandal later that week.

After the king and queen had swallowed their helping, the tray containing the golden-crusted delicacy was passed down to a shelter beneath the pub, where it was divided up into child-sized portions for greedy little hands to grab. The portions were served up on small polystyrene trays, most of which could later be seen discarded around the square with the pastry gone but the lightly mashed meat-and-veg filling left behind. Proof that you can't get most kids to eat vegetables, even if you sail them across a river with a musical accompaniment.

The casting aside of their culinary heritage didn't seem to bother most of the locals. They repeated the previous night's celebration, filling the village pubs and the pavements outside them. Children washed down their pasty with a bottle of Pepsi served with a straw, while parents soaked up their beer with a pasty from the now re-opened bakeries.

The next morning I settled my bill and left the B&B early to set off for the Eden Project. Being of a hay-fevery disposition, my interest in plant life and gardens is almost nil. I was actually drawn by how much one of England's most successful new tourist attractions resembled the domes of Centerparcs. I had plans to visit Centerparcs at the end of the summer, so I decided to go along so that I would be able to make comparisons.

Eden represents the new face of tourism in a county that, until recently, had been sold to tourists with images of beautiful coastlines, Arthurian legend, mysticism and the promise of waterborne pastries. The area could certainly do with the money, although the vandalism of some of the prominent English Heritage signs for the attraction suggests that local sensibilities weren't always at the forefront of the project planners' minds.

The route by bus from Fowey to Eden was somewhat convoluted, involving going back on myself by taking a forty-minute trip back to St Austell and enduring a further twenty-minute ride to The Eden Project at Bodelva, so I had decided to walk – at least part of the way. The tourist information office had given me a map, which had a rough computer-generated drawing of how to reach the site from St Blazey, a short bus trip away. This was, at least, in the right direction. So, after buying a final pasty for the trip, I set off for the bus stop.

Before the Internet took off, there was another type of information super highway – the village Hopper bus. Actually, it is more of an information rural B-road, but you get the idea. Instead of a virtual chat room, the Hopper is a real-time face-to-face gossip salon, where everyone is welcomed as they enter and everyone knows everyone else's name, diseases and exactly how many of their friends and relatives have died in the last year.

Mostly utilised by widowed women in their seventies and eighties to travel to underground card schools and out-of-the-way shops offering five pence off cat food, tea and gin, these buses spread news of death, divorce and double loyalty card points from village to village far quicker than the post or the local paper can. On my brief journey, the price of cheese was up for debate, we discovered that one of our number's sons had lost his battle with cancer and also that one of the regulars was absent as she had to take her cat to the vet. These buses provide the kind of bang-up-to-date local information with which dotcoms just can't compete.

Stepping off the bus outside the, sadly not yet open, Four Lords pub, I looked at the map in my hand and realised that there was no scale, no landmarks outside of St Blazey and scant instructions on which turnings to take. Considering I was going for the ecologically sound route to the self-styled environmental theme park, you would have thought that I might have been given a little more help.

Having been advised to avoid the first, often boggy footpath by the woman at the tourist information office, I walked up the road that led to Eden, carefully avoiding being flattened by the cars racing to grab the best of the site's 3,000 parking spaces. Only one turning was marked on my map but there were, in fact, two. I initially took a wrong one, which lead me down a dirt track, before returning to the road and finding the correct turning for the final stretch of footpath to my destination. This, of course, was marked with a small sign on the wrong side of an opened gate so that I couldn't actually see it. For such an avowedly environmentally friendly project, they certainly like to throw you into an unfriendly environment on your way there.

As I emerged from the wooded footpath, the sudden sight of the Eden Project's dome-shaped biomes was a breathtaking surprise. I had expected the walk to be a little longer and wasn't quite ready for the vast clear foil greenhouses. They looked as if they were made of giant bubble wrap. I wondered how hard and how satisfying it would be to pop one of the bubbles. I imagine it would only be truly rewarding if you had a thumb and forefinger big enough to burst the hexagon-shaped air pockets by hand.

One reward that I did get for my twenty-minute walk was a £3 discount on the regular £9.80 entrance fee, an offer which also applies to cyclists, and I was allowed to jump the queue for tickets. It was not yet 10 a.m., but the entrance hall had already filled up with family groups taking advantage of the school holidays. There was an occasional touch of rain in the air, but it was still warm, with the sun threatening to emerge from behind the clouds.

There were two main ways down from the entrance of the Eden Project to the biomes. One took you on a slow meander through the outdoor plants and another took you down a zigzag path that allowed your excitable child to drag you past the pasty-shaped lake and straight for the Teletubby-style grass covered mound that contains the entrance to both biomes. Most people with children went straight for the domes. I witnessed one child shouting 'dome, dome, dome' as her parents stood at the top of the hill surveying which route to take. If only the Millennium Dome in Greenwich had elicited such excitement.

With almost two million visitors in its first year, the Eden Project seems to have been a triumph of architecture and good PR rather than a signifier of any particular increased interest in horticulture. The content, though wonderfully displayed, is not a whole lot different from what you could find at Kew Gardens, but by cleverly not mentioning the word 'gardens' and having two space-age domes, Eden manages to bypass children's natural suspicion of anything that doesn't involve television or fast food.

I took the slow route down with the posh kids, whose parents had insisted they look at every single plant, and the grown-up visitors who really wanted to get to the dome too but felt that they had to take the non-philistine route to keep up appearances. I started off by feigning interest in the odd specimen, but the outdoor garden was actually surprisingly rewarding.

On the way down, I learned that betony was used by Anglo-Saxons to combat elf sickness, which I made a note to ask the people at the Aetherius Society about. Perhaps the crop circles that the little people make are actually cries of help that read: 'We're really sick, bring betony'.

In order to please the eco-warriors, old hippies and fourteen-year-old schoolboys among the visitors, a good few yards of the garden had been given over to a healthy crop of hemp and a display of the things that can, and have, been made from it. The New Age hemp industry is actually one of my pet hates. I have no particular problem with people wanting to smoke marijuana, but arguing that you should be able to do so just because you can make very good rope and really awful trousers out of it makes no sense at all to me. It's a bit like saying that we should slash the duty on cigarettes because they ward off mosquitoes, or legalise handguns because some of them look pretty stylish.

I plumped for the Humid Tropics Biome first, which starts off with a pleasant 18°C air temperature and increases to a sweat-inducing 35°C as you reach the depths of its simulated rainforest. Between the palms, the rubber trees and the bamboo, only the sound of whingeing teenagers was audible over the dripping water. They'd been had. They had set out for an exciting day at a futuristic tourist attraction, but had discovered too late that it was – 'boring' – full of plants and – 'so dull' – educational. To add insult to injury, the hemp plants weren't even the kind that you could take the odd leaf from to smoke in the toilets, they were de-marijuanated. One Slipknot T-shirted, baggy-trousered grouch became the voice of a disaffected generation as he fired the existential rhetorical question: 'Thirty bloody minutes and no monkeys?' at his parents upon passing a sign which told him how much farther into the tropics he had to go to before reaching the exit.

Passing on to the Warm Temperate Biome was a relief after the heat of the tropical zones, though obviously not as effective a place to finish off elderly, climate-sensitive parents as some families seemed to be intent on doing between the banana trees and the cashews. 'Come on dad, keep up. You must have been hotter than this in the desert when you were fighting Rommel. Now, where did you say you keep your will?'

With its tomatoes, olives and peppers, the warm zone was more like an Italian deli than an environmental exhibit. One plant, however, was absent, and a notice about a problem that Eden was having with pests stood in its place. I could see what they were talking about, there were pests everywhere – rubbing leaves, telling anyone who would listen the Latin name for things, criticising the upkeep of the tomato plants and refusing to divulge the exact contents of their last will and testament to their middle-aged children. But even these ageing green-fingered nuisances had absolutely no idea what was going on with the olive exhibit – which consisted of one barrel with a model of a heart in and another which contained a model of a David-like athletic figure, waiting to be anointed with olive oil.

After my dash around the biomes and a coffee in one of Eden's many restaurants, it was almost time to go. My flight from Newquay airport was at 5.30 but there were only two buses from the project to Newquay a day. One arrived ten minutes after my flight took off and the other – the one I was forced to catch – got me there four hours early. I've always been one of those dolts who checks in precisely when the airline tells me to, if not before, but four hours was a bit much even for me. I just hoped they had some good video games or some decent shops to browse in.

I exited Eden via the cunningly placed gift shop, avoiding the temptation to go wild in the aisles for hemp soap or lip balm. The bus stop was a short walk uphill from the entrance and was situated next to a coach park. The only problem was that no one seemed to know where exactly it was. Perhaps no one ever used it. I was initially advised by Eden staff to take a cab when I asked about the buses. I know that an environmental project wouldn't want to be seen to be encouraging the use of short-haul flights, but surely acknowledging that they exist and having passengers use a bus rather than travel to the airport in individual taxis would be better.

Eventually, I found a member of staff who did know where the bus stop was and I made my way there to wait in the midday sun, which had decided to show itself just as I was leaving.

The bus arrived on time and thirty minutes later I was ensconced in the lounge at Newquay airport. Actually, it would have been difficult to have been anywhere else at Newquay airport, apart from on the runway, as it consisted of just one small shed the size of the average departure lounge at Heathrow or Gatwick. No arcade games, no gift shops overly laden with Toblerone, just one poorly stocked coffee shop for entertainment. Still, at least they served alcohol.

My decision to fly from Newquay to Stanstead had been based not on any desire to get home fast but rather to see how ridiculous it felt to take a journey in England that really should be made by train. At £8.99, my flight had looked dirt cheap on the Ryanair website, but with the added taxes and Gbp handling fee, whatever that is, the ticket actually cost £22.89. Add to that the £12.40 train fare from Stanstead back into London and it didn't look such a bargain. Especially when the time I had to wait for the flight was the time it would have taken me to get back to London from St Austell by train.

As I sat twiddling my thumbs, I began to wish I had purchased a return train ticket, which would, oddly, only have cost me an extra pound – such are the vagaries of our transport system. And I wouldn't have had to feel so bad about the carbon dioxide emissions and whatever else it was that my plane would be pumping out.

A few beers, a couple of newspapers and one of those frightening dropping-off-then-waking-up-with-a-start moments later, it was time to board my flight. Being an egalitarian, low-cost airline, Ryanair only has one class – idiot – so before actually getting on the plane, I had to wait in a lengthy security clearance queue as my fellow passengers were relieved of their sword sticks, machetes, steak knives and stun grenades. Alarmingly, they let the woman wearing the outsized polyester floral frock through unmolested. Just a quick stumble down the aisle carpet and she could have produced enough static to take out the plane's controls or spark off a major conflagration in the cabin.

Once we had all been cleared by security, the disabled and those with children were allowed to walk across the Tarmac to the plane, followed, and overtaken one minute later, by the rest of us as we sprinted past to get the pick of the unreserved seating for our one-hour flight.

Within minutes we were flying out over the north Cornwall coast, getting a visual sales pitch for its coves and bays as we banked, before heading down and along the south coast. As I looked out over farms, back-garden swimming pools, the soft borders of villages and the jagged edges of towns, the flight began to feel less of a stupid folly and more of a reminder of what England is. On paper we may be one of the most densely populated countries in the world, but from the air you can just make out that we are still a green and not altogether unpleasant land.

II. BEARDS, TRUNKIES AND THE FOREST OF FAUX

The train ride to Rye was, thankfully, not marked by ticketing disasters, seats in the family carriage or the wrong kind of track but, nonetheless, it was still a very English affair. Leaving London Bridge we sped towards the incongruous-sounding Ashford International in a modern, if somewhat uncomfortable, train, only to find that our connecting service was a creaking slam-door antique. The kind of train that still has slide-down windows in the doors for ventilation, and for facilitating decapitation by tunnel for those who ill-advisedly lean out of them. They used to run the same trains in Kent and the schoolboy debate around this subject was always about how much longer the body could feel, think or move once the head was lying on the tracks.

I was travelling with my friend Cathy, who had agreed to be my 'beard' for the short stay at Pontin's Camber Sands holiday camp. I suspected that holidaying parents seeing a lone male hanging around the junior knobbly knees contest might come to the kind of conclusion that could result in broken bones for me and a cursory check of the sex offender's register by the local constabulary, so having a travelling companion would save confusion. If a pretend wife or girlfriend worked for Hollywood leading men and well-loved television presenters at staving off rumours about their propensity for sexual deviancy, then I was convinced that it could at least stop me getting a bloody nose at Pontin's.

Cathy grew up in Ashford, before it added the sobriquet 'International' to its name, so I was sure that we would have a good old Kentish knees up, especially as the main constituent of holidaymakers at Camber Sands are those from our home county. To those stuck in Kent, Sussex is a strange and foreign land, full of the exotic.

From Rye station, Camber Sands was a fifteen-minute bus ride, aboard what Cathy christened the 'trunky' bus. Trunky, one of Cathy's favourite words, is an Ashfordian variation of the accusation of inbreeding and the mental deficiency caused by the fact that your father is also your brother.

'Oh my God, they're all from Kent,' Cathy whispered to me on the bus. In front of us a man in his thirties was holding a conversation with his dog. I think they may have been man and wife, though that didn't stop him trying to chat up the fifteen-year-old girl sitting across the aisle from him. Ancient byelaws mean that polygamy is still legal in parts of Kent and Sussex, so long as you don't marry two of the same species.

Thankfully, dogman stayed on the bus as it dropped us

off outside the holiday camp, but a good deal of trunkies followed us from it, lurching along the road with their suitcases full of shell suits and Reeboks direct from the bargain bins of Bluewater or the pub car parks of Dover. We raced ahead towards the reception desk, fearful of being caught behind any of them as they struggled to make an X on the checking-in forms.

We had been allocated an apartment in the two-storey blocks of Surf City. I don't imagine that the 1950s motel-type construction could possibly have been the inspiration for the Beach Boys hit of the same name, but they were a lot nicer than I had expected. The muted yellow, blue and green of the various blocks recalled Miami on a shoestring budget. It was a far cry from the prison-camp image from which many such holiday parks suffer and altogether more appealing than Stalag Butlins in Bognor.

'If this was in America they would call it the World's Largest Motel,' said Cathy, on taking in the initial stretch of blocks, which were placed in threes around a central garden – where a car park would have been if we were alongside a freeway in the US.

The interior of our middle-of-the-range 'classic' apartment was basic but functional, a bit like a one-bedroom council flat. A home away from home for the low-income families that nowadays make up the majority of Pontin's clientele at their seven holiday camps. Around the time we were staying, the tabloids were full of gossip about *Sex and the City* star Kim Cattrall (she plays the one who seems to get enough sex for a whole country, never mind a city) staying at a camp in Wales with her mother, but I imagine that Pontin's doesn't take a lot of calls from stars of stage and screen. I suspect that the odd faded *Big Brother* contestant may book in, desperate for a member of the public to actually recognise them.

Once we had settled in and decided who was sleeping where, I got on with unpacking my bag as Cathy played mother, making the first of an endless stream of pots of tea that she brewed during our stay. Once the workers' café brew and the biscuits were downed, we went out to explore the camp, stopping off at the Londis convenience store so Cathy could see if they had any postcards of the camp.

Behind the counter, by the cigarettes, a handwritten sign read:

We are not part of the European Currency Union. Therefore we do not accept Euros.

It seems that milk tokens were off limits too, as the young woman trying to pay for her twenty Benson and Hedges with them was turned down flat by the man operating the till. I got the impression that however far Europe encroached upon our country, the fenced-in camps at Pontin's would be a land of pounds and pence forever; a corner of resistance against the United States of Europe, or whatever foolish name they have come up with for the Union this week.

Londis was all out of postcards, so we continued walking to the centre of the camp, past the place that hired everything from hairdryers to tandems to those who had neglected to bring such items, and on to the main building. The ground floor of this giant block housed a café, a restaurant, an amusement arcade and Lunar's Bar – an entertainment-based theme pub. The upstairs of the building was dominated by the cavernous Fun Factory, the traditional holiday camp ballroom with bars at the edge and a proper stage to hold the talent shows, cabaret acts and magicians.

I am not so sure that the juxtaposition of the words 'fun' and 'factory' is entirely appropriate for an audience that includes a healthy number who work in not-fun factories for a living. Perhaps as our manufacturing base dwindles further it will be re-christened the Crazy Call Centre.

Returning to our apartment to eat after our brief exploration of the camp, I switched on the television, which was broadcasting Pontin's own channel, PTV. This kept you up to date with events in the camp, reminded you to not set fire to your apartment and played awful distorted music, the point of which, I suspect, was to soften you up for the caterwauling you might hear later from the Bluecoats and cabaret acts. Just like Butlins' famous Redcoats and *Hi-De-Hi*'s Yellowcoats, the Pontin's Bluecoats are the entertainment staff; always on hand to help a lost child, sing a moving ballad or call the numbers at a bingo session. They are the semi-talented plankton in the cesspool of entertainment who go on to host Saturday night television shows, reach the last hundred on *Popstars*, or impersonate someone you have never heard of on *Stars in their Eyes*.

Anyway, watching the television channel made me realise that each of the Pontin's camps had near-identical, synchronised entertainment. If it was time to line dance in Camber then chances are that they were wearing Stetsons in Hemsby and Southport. Perhaps that was the inspiration for the name Fun Factory – production-line entertainment for the proletariat.

After dinner we decided to warm up for watching the evening's entertainment with a quiet drink in the camp's Queen Victoria pub, which turned out to be a soulless pretend-a-pub serving a huge selection of Bacardi Breezer-style bottles and a small choice of beer. I opted for a Guinness and Cathy for a white wine, which had been nicely warmed by the lights in the cabinet it sat in. We had expected working men's club prices on site, but the bar tariffs were set closer to West End rates. The apartments may be cheap enough for those on benefits, but the bars most definitely were not. Little wonder then that I saw visitors decanting supermarket lager and duty-free vodka into glasses when they thought no one was looking. As we were reasonably close to Dover, it wouldn't be too big a problem to prelude your stay with a booze cruise across the Channel to ensure you had enough beer and fags to keep you going for the whole week.

After fifteen minutes of pondering my lifeless Guinness, and reminding myself to stick to bottled beer for the rest of my stay, our quiet drink was made all the less bearable by some enforced entertainment. Across the other side of the room an accordion player was kicking off a set of sub-Chas'n'Dave mockney singalongs.

'Come on, don't be so miserable,' he chimed, not realising that he was the cause of most of the misery in the bar.

To drag things down further, he dispatched his 'lovely' assistant to distribute wobble boards to the masses. I think his logic must have been that if the audience were responsible for part of the act, then they would be obliged to stay and suffer. I looked around for the most efficient escape route. If there is one thing I hate, it is being forced to enjoy myself. I made the mistake of making up part of the audience for a yoof culture TV show once and have never quite got over the 'we have ways of making you dance' attitude of the floor managers. Hopefully, my piss-poor sense of rhythm dented the next week's and maybe even next month's viewing figures significantly.

'Christ,' said Cathy, making a face and getting up from her seat. 'Let's get out of here before she reaches us. We'll probably get told off for not joining in.'

Abandoning our overpriced drinks, we reached the exit just in time to hear strains of 'Roll Out the Barrel' being shut out by the swing doors as they closed behind us. Those caught by the wobble board scam were in for a long night.

We walked around the front of the main building and climbed the stairs to the Fun Factory, hoping against hope to avoid being press-ganged into any involuntary fun, such as being sawn in half by a magician or having our lives 'hilariously' picked apart by a fourth-rate comic. Thankfully, when we reached the ballroom all was safe. The under-tens dance competition was in full swing, with girls and boys bopping away to Cornershop's 'Brimful of Asha'.

Cathy went to the bar and got the drinks in while I found us a seat in the centre of the room. As she approached me through the crowd, I could see her making one of her squished faces and signalling with her eyes at the man who was walking in front of her.

'Did you see that?' she said, pointing over at the man with the bulbous forehead and lumbering gait who was struggling to find his seat. 'It's trunky city in here. You can't move for them.' She was right. It was as if the Pontin's staff had driven right across Kent emptying every burger bar and pub serving cheap doubles before forcing the customers on to buses and bringing them back to the camp.

The dance contest was followed by a Mum in a Million competition in which a Bluecoat interrogated several young mothers about their childrens' taste in sweets and films.

'My name is Carol and I'm forty-four,' said one, which set Cathy spluttering on her wine.

'More like sixty-four,' said Cathy, loud enough for the neighbouring tables to hear.

'Another drink?' I asked, fleeing to the bar, just in case those nearby tables contained the woman's family.

By the time I had returned from the bar, the winning mum was being awarded her prize. Her daughter was up on the stage with her and neither could contain their lack of excitement as they were presented with a voucher for a short break at another Pontin's camp in mid-November. I am sure that fifty quid and a bottle of Lambrini would have gone down far better.

The main entertainment of the evening came from the resident group, Xcel, which appeared to have been named in tribute to Microsoft's spreadsheet program and was every bit as efficient, though perhaps not quite as captivating. Seemingly schooled with other Xcels from other camps at some kind of Fun Factory boot camp, their inept routines conspired to make their 'something for the dads' PVC leotards look about as sexy as floral winceyette housecoats.

The atmosphere was not helped by the gawky Bluecoats who had been forced to dance by the side of the stage in an attempt to draw the audience onto the dance floor. One of them looked as if she either had never heard any music before or had become possessed by the spirit of MC Hammer and was flailing her limbs and throwing her body around to beats that no one else could hear.

On the dancefloor one fourteen-year-old boy, whom Cathy had marked out as a definite trunky, spent the whole evening trying to persuade one of the Bluecoat girls to dance with him. Eventually she caved in, foolishly cracking just before the band went into a slow, smoochy number. For the duration of the song she held the youth at arm's length, like a particularly stinky refuse sack that she was taking out to the bins.

Whenever the audience seemed to be lacking enthusiasm, the Bluecoats pulled out the same line. Whether it was when the tots' dancing got dull or during natural breaks in the entertainment, the line 'Is there anyone in from Kent?' was guaranteed to be greeted by cheers and applause. Sometimes they would build it up by asking 'Is there anyone in from

Essex/London/Manchester?' to a faint replying murmur, before delivering the killer line and setting off ninety per cent of the room into a whooping, stomping frenzy. The good people of Kent sure do like applauding the name of the place from which they hail. Try it next time you venture across the Queen Elizabeth II bridge, you're virtually certain of a standing ovation.

The sun woke me early next morning and I arose just after dawn to go for a swim in the camp's pool. I wandered through the footbath, pleased to have the whole place to myself, and dived in. 'Aaagh,' I screamed. It was ice cold. And then I woke up.

I was, indeed, surrounded by icy water – my own now-cold sweat. The single bed I had been sleeping in had the same perspiration-inducing plastic coating as the one I had experienced in Blackpool. The sun pouring through the window had sent me into delirious dreams.

When I eventually poured the excess water from the mattress and got up for real, Cathy was in the kitchen brewing what could well have been her fourth pot of the day. The living room curtains were open and the sun was beating down on the rectangle of grass that sat between the apartment blocks.

After some toast and a quick burst of PTV, we headed out of the apartment and through the exit gate next to the Londis, to make for the beach. As we left the camp, a security guard gave us each a pass so that we would be able to get back in again.

The sand of Camber's beach starts just over the road from

Pontin's, where a higgledy-piggledy development of houses has grown into an *ad hoc* village. Some of the houses are old brick cottages, others are wooden holiday homes that have been extended and there is a smattering of mobile homes that have been added to and made permanent fixtures. This gives the area the appearance of a very English shantytown, akin to the nearby cottages at Dungeness or the strange overgrown beach-hut landscape of Jaywick in Essex. It looks like the village that planning regulations forgot, with its sandy avenues criss-crossing the main path down to the sea.

At the end of the path, the sand dunes were just a walk across the road away and once we were up and over them, the huge expanse of Camber's beach spread out before us. A mile of sand broken up by rivulets running back to the sea and trapped pools of brine left stranded by the tide. The sand was warm under foot, there was enough room for everyone to spread out and the dunes drowned out any traffic noise. It was perfect. I can't imagine that being on any other beach in the world that day could have been any better, though I suppose we could have done without the nuclear power station a few miles down the road at Dungeness. Okay, maybe I should say any beach in Europe. The world may be going a bit far when you start thinking about warm, clear-blue waters, iced beer and delicious food served on a palm leaf.

I found a spot on the sand, later moving into the dunes when the sun became too strong, while Cathy took a long walk to the jetty that extended across the beach in the distance. I read and dozed a little as she went off on her nature watch.

Sensing that it was lunchtime, I walked a little further up the beach in search of food and came across a handful of cafés and burger bars situated around a car park, which also housed the public toilets. The peace of the dunes was replaced by the screaming of ketchup-smeared children and tattooed peroxide-blonde mothers, accompanied by the clucking of a gift-laying hen at the amusement arcade on the other side of the car park.

I walked into one of the cafés and straight into a scene from a Martin Parr photograph. Larger-than-life women with muscular forearms poured boiling water over tea bags, unidentifiable slabs of something that was smoking sizzled on a well-greased hotplate and the condiments were chained firmly to the table by the door. Sit-down customers were trusted with unfettered usage of the salt and vinegar, but shifty takeaway customers such as myself were probably just the type to douse our chips and then take home the containers as souvenirs of our meal.

As I was being served, Cathy popped up from behind me with a look of wonderment on her face. Cathy is an artist who spends a good deal of time photographing the roadside food wagons of Britain, and this greasy spoon was right up her alley.

'Cor,' she said. 'Have you seen the salt and vinegar pots?'

She had catalogued the grimiest of truckers' eateries on her travels, but the manacled seasonings represented a culinary depth that she had not yet plumbed. Within moments she had whipped out her Canon and was snapping away, oblivious to the stares from the staff, who probably assumed that she was from the environmental health department of the local council. I tried to pretend that I was not with her, passing the condiments by and making my way to the benches outside, which were occupied by a pair of overweight teenage girls in crop tops, hiding navel piercings beneath rolls of puppy fat. Both were munching on outsized burgers encased in powdery white, sesame-seeded baps, which cascaded excess fried onions and ketchup on to the table and floor with every bite. I wondered whether either of the falling burger additions counted towards the government-recommended five portions of fruit and vegetables per day.

We spent the rest of the afternoon wandering along the shoreline, paddling in the sea and discussing how great it would be to buy a shack in the chaotic village and how you could cook up some of the mass of seaweed that was laying on the sand. Then I remembered the nuclear power station and realised why it was that no one was collecting it to eat. Perhaps the pollution of London wasn't so bad after all.

After a coffee in another café, which had more bluebottles than customers, a lie down in the dunes and a stroll past a derelict crazy golf course and up the coastal road where a 1960s-style motel was hiding, we decided it was time to head for the camp and another night of entertainment. On the walk back, Cathy noticed that the pub we had walked past on our way down was open, so we went in for a pint. It looked slightly unsavoury, but surely the beer couldn't be any worse or any pricier than it was back at Pontin's.

The pub was advertised on the outside by a huge banner

that read, simply, 'PUB' in large print. The design of the building varied from pre-World War II modernism to bodged and abandoned kitchen extension. In other words, it was a misshapen shambles. With a little attention and some landscaping of its grey concrete surround, it could look outstanding, but as it stood it was just Pub – functional in its blandness.

The interior was deceptively cavernous and at its centre was a curved ship-style bar, which must have been built by a boat builder. The barman said that it had been there since the pub was built in the 1930s.

As we sat in the chairs made from old beer barrels, at a table made of the same, a group of three bottle blondes clad in black Lycra and cellulite came in and sat down nearby, flashing friendly smiles as they made their way to the jukebox and the bar. Two of the women were in their late thirties, the third in her fifties, but all were dressed straight out of Topshop. It was hard to work out whether they were mother and daughters, sisters or just mates out on the pull but they had more cleavage on display than you would see in a whole series of *Baywatch* and an entire evening's viewing on the Granada Men & Motors channel combined.

As one of the trio returned to the table with a round of Aftershocks – a foul-tasting and inexplicably medicine-themed shot drink – the jukebox burst into overloud life, making conversation all but impossible. Cathy rolled her eyes, then drained her glass and pointedly plonked it down on the table, a series of moves that represents the international sign language for 'Get it down you and let's get out of here before Freddie fucking Mercury makes our eardrums bleed'.

We made a point of seeing if we could get back into the camp without showing our passes and sure enough the security guard was too busy on the phone to be bothered by us furtively sneaking past him. Once back in our Surf City apartment, I microwaved some pasta sauce and boiled up some spaghetti for our dinner, knocking back one of Cathy's brews as I waited for the ping that would announce that dinner was served. The sound that kept Marks & Spencer afloat when everyone decided that even their pants were, well, erm . . . pants.

That night we ventured into Lunar's Bar to witness the Hunk of the Week competition, in which half-cut men in football shirts and flip-flops had to prove their worth by rescuing a damsel in distress from an imaginary building. The damsel, of course, was one of the male Bluecoats in drag. They had to fight off invisible assailants, clamber up non-existent ladders and, if they reached the next round, take off their shirts to be judged by the audience. For all these displays of manliness, the winner was awarded a less-than-macho bottle of Lambrini sparkling wine. A girl's drink if ever there was one.

The Hunk of the Week show had been preceded by a strange kind of reverse human bingo in which if your number didn't come up you had to stay on the dance floor of the bar and, for some unexplained reason, execute a pelvic thrust. This seemed all very well, though in slightly questionable taste for the pre-teens in the contest, but the amount of energetic thrusting going on among the grandmothers on the floor looked as if it could result in a considerable deficit in the NHS hip-replacement budget. They seemed to be enjoying it though, and I saw one enthusiastic pair in their seventies grinding their groins to 'The Timewarp' and 'Blame It on the Boogie' well into the small hours.

The comic who finished off the evening's entertainment was a predictably third-rate end-of-pier act, with gags that poked fun at the chalets and the Bluecoats to little reaction, though he did score applause with his 'anyone in from Kent?' line. Thankfully, even the trunkies and cleavage-heavy mob we had seen in Pub didn't raise so much as a titter at his 'funny Chinese man who works at the Chinese takeaway' routine. Egg flied lice. Ha, ha. Oh yes, ha.

The next morning, Cathy and I got up in time to spy on the line dancing in Lunar's Bar, which still stank of stale smoke and spilt booze from the night before. Sadly, the advertised Western-style shenanigans had been replaced by a half-hearted exercise session. I recognised one of the Mum in a Million competitors and both of the aged pelvic thrusters sucking in the vile fumes. They could well have been going all night and never left Lunar's at all. What kind of drugs are they giving old people nowadays? Some kind of ecstasy-laced Viagra speedball if appearances were anything to go by. You certainly can't stay that active on HRT, Sanatogen and half a pint of milk stout twice a week.

After sampling some of the coffee in the depressingly

sterile self-service café, we headed back to the apartment to collect our bags and get back on the trunky bus to Rye. We did have another night booked, but Cathy had to be back in London for an appointment and I figured it would be no fun in Camber without my 'beard' and drinking partner. So I abandoned the dunes and the discos in favour of arrival back in the city in the middle of an unexpected, for me at least, tube strike. I had spent so long that summer heading out of London that following news about how to get around it had taken a back seat.

Half a day spent breathing exhaust fumes on the top deck of a bus when I could have been paddling, eating chips or lying in the sun. Typical.

Whenever I told anyone that I was going to visit CenterParcs, their initial reaction was always the same. Each and every one said: 'Oh that's the place under the big dome, isn't it?' No one said 'CenterParcs, what's that?' or 'Ah yes, the outdoor leisure pursuits centre with the indoor swimming pool.'

None of my friends had been there, but all assumed that somewhere in England lay several enormous domes that held a holiday village and surrounding woodland like a souvenir plastic snowstorm encases a miniature Blackpool Tower or Buckingham Palace. Everyone supposed that should they book in, they would be holidaying in a climate-controlled biome akin to a mile-wide version of those at the Eden Project. They had all been duped by the company's advertising campaigns in the 1990s and added the giant indoor environment to their memory without question. Actually, I was the same until I began to look into visiting it.

'Aw,' I whined, after the brochure dropped through the door. 'Look, it's not really all indoors after all, it's only a tiny bit.'

'Let me have a look,' said Christina, assuming that I had the brochure upside down or something.

'Look, these pictures must have been taken outside,' I said, pointing to the scenes of giant redwoods and boating lakes. 'You can see sky.'

As we turned into the entrance for CenterParcs' Longleat holiday village in Wiltshire we were both still holding out a tiny bit of hope that I might be wrong and a giant dome would appear before us. But instead we were faced with acres of forest, lush green foliage and a piddling little dome off to one side.

Sure, it was big enough to house a pool, several shops, bars and restaurants, but it was not the *Logan's Run*-style indoor environment we had been hoping for. It was, as we would discover, just a clone of a Welcome Break motorway service station with an outsized water feature, no porn mags and scant availability of Hallmark country music cassettes.

We were staying in an 'executive apartment' in a block at the centre of the village, which was just a little larger than, though almost twice the price of, the apartment I had stayed at in Camber Sands. The CenterParcs accommodation was, however, far more luxurious, with a large double bed and a balcony with seating overlooking the forest. Most of those staying at Longleat were based in single-storey villas, which were scattered through the forest. Ours seemed to be the accommodation for young urbanites with no kids who were a little wary about being quite so close to nature.

After looking around our apartment, we set off to find the bike hire centre, which was, according to our handy map, located somewhere near where we had left the car. A bicycle is pretty much essential to get around the 400-acre site, from the swimming pool to the Sports Café and from the super-market to your villa.

Almost everyone hires the unisex, gear-free getarounds, though the particularly snooty like to bring their own mountain bikes, proudly displayed atop their Mondeos as they drive in through the gates. After all, CenterParcs is no sunbathing, slouching holiday for the poor, it is middle-income middle England at play. Tattoos, if you have any, are hidden beneath tracksuit tops, beer guts are winched in and if you find out your neighbour has a better tennis racquet than you, you can trump them by popping into the Sportique store on-site and upgrading.

CenterParcs is probably one of the only places in the world where I would feel safe riding a bike. With my lack of road traffic skills, inability to tell left from right without a couple of seconds thinking time and lack of desire to be crushed by a number nineteen bus, cycling in London is not for me. I would be dead within an hour of leaving my flat. But CenterParcs is mostly car free, so you can whizz down spe-cially constructed wooden walkways and zigzag through the village without fear of being maimed.

Just across the road from our block was the Village Square, which housed a number of cafés. We had looked in our *Making the Most of Your Stay* guide (the cover of which featured a Dennis Hopper look-alike about to drown some children) and decided that the Grand Café bar and brasserie would be a good place to round off our first day.

The square seemed silent as we walked in. At first I thought that we had the wrong place, but there was the Grand Café – a glass-sided goldfish bowl with four people inside and a group of waiters hanging around, waiting to go home.

'Grim, grim, grim,' said Christina, who had been put off coming at all when she realised that the whole place wasn't under a giant dome and felt she was being proved right.

Initially she had visions of CenterParcs being like one of those utopian villages on *Star Trek* that the crew always come across and screw up somehow. She came back round to the idea of accompanying me when I showed her a picture of the spa facilities. She'd probably go to a party at Michael Barrymore's if he told her he had a steam room and a fancy multi-directional shower.

'Well, shall we go to the Plaza, then?' I asked, referring to the shops and bars of the dome across the other side of the site.

'Okay,' she said. 'Let's take the bikes.'

The Plaza was pleasantly downhill from our apartment, so gravity took the strain most of the way, with only the occasional bit of effort required to avoid the rabbits that darted across the road now and again. We parked our bikes up, padlocked them to a rack next to about a dozen identical models and wandered down the steps and into the dome.

It was 10.10 p.m. and the place was almost deserted. Only the Lagoon Bar showed any signs of life and this was restricted to two fifteen-year-old girls trying to pretend they were not interested in two sixteen-year-old boys while the world's worst DJ failed to mix anything that so much as resembled a tune. We tried the ten-pin bowling in the bar next door, but it was closing up. There was no option but to go back to the apartment. At Pontin's everyone would chat and drink until 2 a.m., but at CenterParcs there was no such thing as a late night – everyone had to stay in and be the ideal family before rising early to take part in a sporting activity.

I rose early the next morning, as I had planned to take part in a sporting activity myself. To be precise, I had booked to participate in the five-a-side football tournament. Booking is essential for everything at CenterParcs. In order that you can have a carefree time when you get here, you have to spend the two weeks before your stay perusing brochures, checking schedules and ensuring that you book yourself in for anything from archery to windsurfing before all the places are filled. Just as train seats, football match and cinema tickets have, for some reason that I can't fathom, become things that you must book, so have sporting activities on a holiday.

Whatever happened to queuing? We were great at that – world class some might say – and it seemed to work just fine.

I turned up at the tennis court that had been allocated for

our football tournament expecting a motley assortment of men in golf shoes, tennis shoes and plimsolls, but instead was greeted by a shin-padded, special-five-a-side-football boot-wearing group in sweat bands and thigh supports. Something told me that some of these people were the type to take things too seriously.

'Of course, some people take these things too seriously,' the man standing next to me said to his team-mates once we had all been allocated sides. 'We'll play with two in the middle, one front, one back and the keeper can push up as he sees fit. I think if we try to get a couple ahead and then just slow it off and close it down we should be fine.'

Somewhere in the choosing of teams, the CenterParcs coach with the clipboard and whistle had saddled me with two over-fifties, a twelve-year-old boy and a teenager with back problems who was constantly puffing on his asthma inhaler. Now I knew what it was like to be one of those kids who were always picked last when you were choosing teams at school.

By the end of our first game, we were down to three 'men' and had lost four-nil. One of the older men had gone off with a dodgy knee, never to return, and the asthmatic had to go to see the doctor because he had put his back out. I was exhausted and had a hole torn in the mesh part of my running shoe by the studs of one of the opposition's all-surface football boots. It had gone right through my sock as well.

We had to use the referee and someone's ten-year-old son to make up the numbers in our next game. It didn't help much and thankfully our third poor performance saw us eliminated from the tournament. Goals for: none, goals against: ten. In the end I was just grateful that the matches were only five minutes long.

Of course, the tournament was won by the team which had been organising tactics and sticking to set positions from the off. It came as no great surprise to hear that most of the team actually knew each other and came to the same holiday village at the same time each and every year. They had probably been in training for their victory since they arrived home after last year's holiday, meeting at weekends to discuss diet and strategy.

Seeking to sate my thirst after another sporting humiliation, I discovered that the drinks at the Sports Café, in the sophisticated-sounding Jardin des Sports complex, were even more expensive than those at Pontin's, with the Coke coming in at more than the beer. Not great news if you are a family with a load of Coke-thirsty kids in tow. Still, the sophistication did extend to there beings a kids' cocktail menu, with the Posh and Becks – a Coke float – presumably being the money-maker. I have no idea which bit was meant to be Posh, which bit Becks, and why. If it had been a beer float it would have been more apparent, if somewhat less appealing.

The Jardin des Sports housed the Sportique sporting goods shop as well as a mini-cinema, badminton courts, squash courts and a snooker hall. And if you really wanted a laugh you could watch aerobics classes through the glass front of the exercise studio. A tip for any ladies attending such a session in the future: always check that your leotard fits properly before you leave home and always try to have a, you know, tidy up in the obvious areas before you lean backwards over a giant bouncy ball in front of a glass wall that strangers can see through. I mean I don't mind that much, I'm just saying that you might want to think about it. Maybe a quick trim or something.

Of course, every conceivable activity had been booked weeks, or even months in advance by the organisation obsessives with whom we were sharing the holiday village. They were determined to have fun at 10 a.m., 2 p.m. and 6 p.m. each day and those with a more laidback attitude to relaxation would just have to find something else to do.

In our case, that something else was a bike ride around the whole site, taking in some tough, gearless cycling to the vantage points around the forest and careering down the zigzag path by the lake. We passed a Harry Potter-style crazy golf course and a large amount of cycling, bickering couples. I think the saddle-soreness must have been making them tetchy. I know I wasn't exactly feeling all sweetness and light as my backside was shocked out of fifteen years of non-cycling.

After cycling around for a while, I had an uneasy feeling but couldn't quite put my finger on what was up. It was like one of those 'what is wrong with this picture?' scenarios where nothing obvious leaps out at you.

Finally it came to me. Although we were cycling out into the forest, with a light breeze in our faces, it actually felt as if we were not outside at all. As if a giant dome really was covering the whole village but it was an invisible one.

'Doesn't it feel strange to you?' I asked Christina.

'I think it's because it's all so neat and tidy,' she replied. 'These little pathways take you around and it looks like they trim the grass and sweep the leaves away once an hour. It's the sanitised forest of faux.'

Her phraseology summed it up perfectly. Even though it was real, it didn't feel real or look real. The size of some of the trees indicated that the site had been a forest long before CenterParcs moved in, but it had the appearance of having been planted the previous week. Surely garden centres didn't sell mature giant redwoods, did they?

We had, at least, managed to have the foresight to book into a restaurant to experience what evenings at CenterParcs were all about. Perhaps if they weren't about boozing until dawn then they would be about civilised family dinners.

Arriving at the Country Club restaurant in the Jardin des Sports soon disabused me of that notion. One couple was dining in a corner when we arrived at 8 p.m. and just one family of six arrived after us. It was Saturday night and the place was all but empty. CenterParcs was obviously the holiday destination for families that found even the odd evening excursion to their local Beefeater a frightening prospect – the people for whom that 'don't have nightmares' bit at the end of *Crimewatch* is intended.

We had come for the Spice Garden Indian Buffet, which the restaurant served every Wednesday and Saturday. I had just seen the words 'Indian buffet' and signed up for it. I quite often eat buffets at the Indian restaurants in London's Drummond Street and while those kept-warm dishes are not the most subtle, they are almost always delicious.

Sadly the same could not be said for the food at the Country Club, which was the strangest I have ever encountered. Among the tandoori dishes and the poppadoms was a Thai curry and a Chinese salmon dish, which could not conceivably go with anything else on the menu. It was service-station fusion at its most bizarre.

The realisation that some kind of culinary craziness was under way came as soon as I bit into one of the starters. I know that vegetable spring rolls may not be everyone's idea of an Indian starter, but I reasoned that it was not too far removed from a samosa and put two on my plate alongside the chickpea salad. With my first taste, childhood memories came flooding back – it was actually one of those chip shop spring rolls made from some odd casing housing oriental vegetables in a kind of gravy. I used to eat them all the time as a teenager, as I was going out with a girl whose mum worked at the local chippy and she would bring them home with her. Suitable as an accompaniment to a quick fumble and some chips on a cold winter's evening, but not really a restaurant starter.

Things didn't get much better from there on in – 'roasted potatoes dusted with Indian spices' turned out to be oily boiled spuds with some burnt curry powder spread on them, but at least the cardboard-textured naan bread gave people something to hide them under. Every plate I saw being taken away contained a little naan house with a potato family tucked inside.

The banana fritters were a tasty dessert, but what possessed them to offer herbal tea with fudge as a post-dessert treat I really have no idea. By that point Christina was laughing so hard that she gave herself hiccups. She did eat the fudge though.

In the morning, Christina cycled over to the supermarket in the dome to get the Sunday papers and some pancake ingredients, while I fiddled with the radio in the living room. She had been elected to do the shopping as, being a regular cyclist, she has a hardier backside than me. I was having enough trouble just straightening up after the previous day's cycling and football. Anyway, I was attempting to find out what had been happening in the world of football outside our artificial environment. I tried Radio 5 and TalkSport but to no avail, the whole of medium wave just sounded like alien burbling. Perhaps it really was aliens talking. The fact that they were running the place would explain a lot about the previous night's menu.

I considered the alien theory for a while, but dismissed it out of hand. I mean, my backside hurt but that was not, as far as I could tell, from any kind of probing. This was something else – the emphasis on health and exercise over excess, a drive towards organisation rather than chaos. CenterParcs was actually a backdoor attempt to turn England into part of a unified Europe.

The Dutch company's map of occupation across Germany,

Belgium, France and the Netherlands, which was pictured in the brochure, looked very much like a front of attack. A row of CenterParcs all pointing towards our east and south coasts. It was not too dissimilar from the map in the opening credits of *Dad's Army*. All they needed to do was find a charismatic leader and they could seize control of England from their base camps in Suffolk, Nottinghamshire and Wiltshire, backed up from Hamburg, Eindhoven, Normandy and Amsterdam. The pictures on the same page as the map of Europe outlined a future of wine, olives, funny bread and horse rides through the woods. There had already been hints of a totalitarian future that morning when the television had turned itself on to announce that there were still tables available for the jazz brunch in the Plaza.

If Europeanisaton was indeed the plan, there was every chance that Christina and I would be shot as collaborators once any resistance began. We had arranged to spend the afternoon at the CenterParcs spa, and you can't get much more European than saunas, steam rooms and nudity.

When Christina returned with the papers, lemons and flour, I let her get on with the pancake-making, not wanting to worry her with the theory that had come to me while she was out, just in case she began to fret about the firing squad or tried to have me sectioned.

'Delicious pancakes,' I said, tucking into the sugared and lemoned melt-in-the-mouth treats, hoping they wouldn't be our last.

In the changing room at the spa, which was situated in

a phoney Roman-fronted building near the Jardin des Sports, I wondered what to do about my shorts. This was my first time in a proper spa and I really didn't know what to expect when I walked through the door and into the world of steam. *Making the Most of Your Stay* said that the sessions were 'adult only' and 'natural choice' but I had a sneaking suspicion that no English person in their right mind would actually walk out of the changing room in the buff. I had my complimentary robe to protect me but decided to keep the shorts on.

I was glad I had. Everyone was clothed, there was not so much as a saggy bare breast or a chicken's neck scrotum in sight. Most people had dispensed with their robes – using them to claim chairs in a very un-English, towels-on-the-sun loungers manner – but the men wore shorts or trunks and the women swimsuits or bikinis. I waited for Christina to emerge from her changing room, ready to run and disassociate myself from her should she come out naked. Luckily she had donned her swimsuit.

Like me, the majority of those present seemed to be spa virgins, not conversant with the practice of sitting down and taking it easy. Instead we all went in a constant circle from the Greek herbal bath to the Japanese salt bath, round to the Tyrolean sauna and into the laconium.

After all the flitting, ice bathing and showering, the laconium was where I finally got the idea and put my feet up to relax. The warm Roman sauna had just the right mix of heat and humidity. I finally realised why Christina, who had by then gone off to have a massage, raved about spas so much and went to them with her friends whenever the opportunity arose. It was wonderful. Bliss. Or at least it was until they started pumping Enya through the speakers. Up till then they had been playing anonymous relaxation tape musak which my brain had been blocking out, but one chorus of 'Sail away, sail away, sail away' and I was out of there.

Once over the shock delivered by the sudden burst of ambient Celtic rock, I got quite into the spa life, taking in the bubbling outdoor pool and the atmospheric Turkish hamman for lengthy periods, reading by the pool as the sun beat down through the conservatory roof and losing all sense of time. It was only when staff began tidying up around me in preparation for the next three-hour session that I realised it was time to go.

Back at the apartment, I fell asleep almost immediately. I had been relaxed to the point of unconsciousness. My sports-related aches had gone and even my backside was starting to come back to life after all the steaming it had received.

'Shall we go to the pool?' asked Christina, when I finally came round from my slumber.

'Aren't you shrivelled enough already after three hours of steam and sweat?' I replied.

'Yes, but the pool under the dome has slides and stuff, don't you fancy it?'

'Well, considering I have just spent the best part of the day cleaning myself to the cleanest I have ever been, I don't exactly want to go sliding about in what is probably fifty per cent kiddie piss for half an hour,' I said, which seemed to win her over.

We decided to make some food and then go for a late-night bike ride to mark our final night instead.

Setting out at midnight, we felt like the bad kids in a village that was always in bed by eleven. The ratboy and ratgirl of the artificial environment. We did almost a full circuit of the forest, with our whirring dynamo-driven headlights leading the way, but saw only rabbits and other smaller creatures that scattered into the shadows as soon as they heard us coming.

We went up to the car park to see if it was the hub of some seedy after-hours wife-swapping scene, but found nothing. Not even any illicit teenage snogging or smoking. Everyone was either tucked up tight in their villa or packing their cases in preparation for an organised and efficient start to their journey home the next day. We tried the bike equivalent of handbrake turns and wheel spins in a particularly sedate-looking cul-de-sac of villas, but nothing stirred. Only the sound of diligent pre-bed flossing and the occasional 'thunk' of a suitcase lock interrupted the perfect silence. This was Euro-Stepford and they'd got everyone.

By the time we got up the next morning, everyone was leaving. As we rode to the cycle centre to return our bikes, we witnessed a steady and regulated stream of estate cars, seven-seaters and four-wheel drives exiting the site – their occupants conscientiously recycling their rubbish before returning their keys and customer satisfaction forms. I wondered if some had booked their place in the exit queue before leaving home, just to ensure a smooth ride back to middle England – probably via a Welcome Break to allow them to decompress themselves back into normal society.

Once our bikes had been checked in and our deposits returned, we emptied the apartment of our belongings, threw the bags in the car and joined the queue, inching closer to the exit and the real England that lay beyond it with every minute.

While we had been lost in the forest of faux, the summer had left without us. The calendar had moved from August to September, bringing the fall of golden leaves and plump brown conkers ever nearer and my journey to its conclusion. I felt sad that it had to come to an end, but reasoned that the adventure would not really be over until my key was in my hand and I was walking up the path to my home. The coming of that horrid moment when you realise that you now have to unpack, you forgot to cancel the papers and don't have any food in the house.

As we finally reached the wooded driveway that led out of the gate, I felt relieved that I would at least be afforded a couple of hours of added English summer, albeit most of it on the M4. I rolled down my window and breathed in deeply, receiving a blast of petrol fumes combined with the scent of cow dung and cut grass as a summer farewell from Wiltshire and from England.

Acknowledgements

Special thanks go to Christina Lamb (for driving, proof-reading, random acts of unexpected baking and just being around), my agent Susan Smith at MBA, Lindsay 'Pixiesixer' Symons, Juliana Lessa and all at Headline, Chris Butler, Charlotte Cooper, Jenny Madden, Mark Pawson, John Quel, Cathy Ward and Eric Wright. The list could go on, but then it would end up looking like a Missy Elliot CD sleeve, which wouldn't do at all.

I would also like to extend my considerable gratitude to all those I spoke to along the way for their insight, entertainment and occasional serving of palatable beverages. Keep spotting, fighting, circlemaking and re-enacting for all you are worth.

You can find links to the websites of those who aided me and many of those I travelled with or met by visiting my own site at **www.iainaitch.com**.

MARVELLOUS, ISN'T IT?

RON MANAGER

'Manager's almost metempsychotic voyage through life has been an inspiration' David Beckham

As illuminating as the Book of Revelations, as musty as the Dead Sea Scrolls, yet as racy as a Jilly Cooper novel, *Marvellous, Isn't It?* is the definitive football memoir from the definitive football man. Packed with hindsight, untouched by insight, Ron opens a right old can of soccer worms.

From his days as a precociously talented wing half with a cultured left foot, through the years spent thrashing about furiously in the managerial melting-pot, to the heady day he was named the Pundit's Pundit, *Marvellous, Isn't It?* is nothing less than the bible of the beautiful game.

This is the book Fergie wishes he could have written.

NON-FICTION / AUTOBIOGRAPHY / HUMOUR
0 7553 1077 2

PORRIDGE: THE INSIDE STORY

RICHARD WEBBER, DICK CLEMENT and IAN LA FRENAIS

Porridge is regarded by many critics as Britain's best sitcom. Ronnie Barker and Richard Beckinsale were perfectly cast as the experienced lag and the naïve first-time offender and their developing relationship had viewers gripped until Slade Prison closed its doors for the final time in 1977.

This is the first time the real story behind the much-loved series has been told. Illustrated with never-before-seen photographs, this ultimate companion reveals all and includes profiles of and interviews with the actors, directors and other members of the production team. All 21 episodes are detailed in full and *Going Straight*, the sequel to *Porridge*, is also extensively covered.

A must for all the millions of *Porridge* fans who want the inside story of this classic comedy.

NON-FICTION / TV TIE-IN 0 7472 3304 7

DOMINATRIX

MISTRESS CHLOE

'Claire Mansfield's sharp, hard storytelling might have readers of a particular proclivity on their knees, breathless with anticipation' *Express*

'Witty and revealing' *Guardian*

Meet Mistress Chloe, latex-clad humiliator of politicians, spanker of captains of industry, and paddler of pop stars – a vision, atop the best legs in Britain, in gleaming black rubber.

It wasn't ever thus. This is the story of how a shy greengrocer's daughter from suburbia became a punk groupie, a New Romantic 'face', and a pirate radio personality before realising that her true calling was . . . kink.

Read on if you've ever wondered what really goes on in a dominatrix's dungeon, who goes to them, and why – or how to keep mind and soul together when there's a cross-dressing dwarf in the living room. Wry, provocative and truly revelatory, this memoir is guaranteed to give your preconceptions a vigorous flogging.

NON-FICTION / MEMOIR 0 7553 1014 4

Now you can buy any of these other bestselling non-fiction titles from your bookshop or *direct from the publisher*.

FREE P&P AND UK DELIVERY
(Overseas and Ireland £3.50 per book)

Emma Darwin Edna Healey £7.99
A beautifully researched and elegantly written portrayal of the wife of one of science's greatest geniuses.

The Tiger Ladies Sudha Koul £10.99
This remarkable book is an enchanting account of the author's life growing up in a beautiful, remote valley in Kashmir, set against the troubles of the region.

The Celebrated Captain Peter Radford £7.99
  Barclay
This extraordinary and unique story maps one of the greatest sporting challenges ever: 'to walk a thousand miles in a thousand hours for a thousand guineas'.

Cane River Lalita Tademy £6.99
The compelling tale of the lives and relationships of a family of slaves in the American deep south, and of their ultimate emancipation.

Hildegard of Bingen Fiona Maddocks £6.99
A fascinating insight into the life and social times of this incredible medieval abbess and composer who was later made a saint.

TO ORDER SIMPLY CALL THIS NUMBER

01235 400 414

or visit our website: www.madaboutbooks.com

Prices and availability subject to change without notice.